TECHNOLOGY AND INTERNATIONAL TRANSFORMATION

SUNY SERIES IN GLOBAL POLITICS

James N. Rosenau, editor

TECHNOLOGY AND INTERNATIONAL TRANSFORMATION

The Railroad, the Atom Bomb, and the Politics of Technological Change

GEOFFREY L. HERRERA

STATE UNIVERSITY OF NEW YORK PRESS

Published by
STATE UNIVERSITY OF NEW YORK PRESS,
Albany

For information, address State University of New York Press
194 Washington Avenue, Suite 305, Albany, NY 12210-2384

Production, Laurie Searl
Marketing, Fran Keneston

Library of Congress Cataloging-in-Publication Data

Herrera, Geoffrey L., 1965–
    Technology and international transformation : the railroad, the atom bomb, and the politics of technological change / Geoffrey L. Herrera.
        p. cm. — (SUNY series in global politics)
    Includes bibliographical references and index.
    ISBN-13: 978-0-7914-6867-8 (hardcover : alk. paper)
    ISBN-10: 0-7914-6867-4 (hardcover : alk. paper)
    ISBN-13: 978-0-7914-6868-5 (pbk. : alk. paper)
    1. International relations.   2. Technology and international affairs—History.
3. Technology and state—History.   4. Military history.   5. Technological innovations—
Political aspects.   I. Title. II. Series.

JZ1254.H47 2006
303.48'3—dc22

                                                                                    2005031415

10 9 8 7 6 5 4 3 2 1

For Sally

CONTENTS

ACKNOWLEDGMENTS

This book has had a long gestation. Along the way, and in the project's various guises, I have received help and advice from a number of teachers, colleagues, and friends. Beginning at the beginning, my mentor as an undergraduate, James Kurth got me thinking about the interconnections between technology, history and international politics. He remains a treasured source of guidance and has watched over the development of this book from afar. My dissertation advisors, Robert Gilpin and Aaron Friedberg, had to suffer with this project in its original, sprawling incarnation. I am grateful for their inspiration and patience. Emily Goldman has been a tremendous advocate of my work, and this book in particular, and her encouragement is greatly valued. Colleagues and friends James Davis, Richard Deeg, Michael Desch, Michael Doyle, Colin Elman, Christianne Hardy, Jeffrey Legro, Thomas Mahnken, Gary Mucciaroni, Stephen P. Rosen, Joseph Schwartz, Paul Talcott, William Wohlforth and especially Janice Bially Mattern read some or all of the manuscript at various stages. Their input always improved things; I retained the ability to make things worse. A special thanks is due Fred Steffen, who sharpened and polished my language in the final stages. Finally, thanks for encouragement and advice go out to my family, especially my beloved Sally. I received generous support for the research and writing of this book from the Andrew W. Mellon Foundation, the John M. Olin Institute for Strategic Studies at Harvard University, and the Christian R. & Mary F. Lindback Foundation.

CHAPTER ONE

THINKING ABOUT TECHNOLOGY
AND INTERNATIONAL POLITICS

In the late fifteenth century the French king recruited Swiss mercenaries to strengthen his armies. Unlike the horse-dependent French
noblemen the king often coerced into fighting for him, the Swiss were
infantrymen armed with pikes or long spears. The soldiers' battle
technique was especially formidable against a mounted knight, and
their introduction on European battlefields tilted the advantage away
from horsemen and toward massed infantry. Socially and politically,
the Swiss pikemen contributed to the shift from the feudal social
system from which the knight drew his power and position and toward states and other large military–political organizations that were
capable of building and maintaining large armies.[1] The pike did not
end feudalism, but its introduction was necessary for the premodern
to modern transformation.[2]

The Swiss mercenaries were agents of change to the international system. They were carriers of knowledge and skills that for
centuries had served effectively for cantonal defense at home. European states transformed the Swiss practice into an important new
military technology—the modern army of pike and gun. Mastery of
this new technology was essential to Maurice of Nassau in the six-
teenth and seventeenth centuries, who, despite the small resources of
the United Provinces, kept the northern part of the Low Countries
free from French and Spanish rule. It was also critical in King Gustavus
Adolphus of Sweden's spectacular military feats during the Thirty
Years' War. But the successful introduction of the modern army did
more than just enable Holland and Sweden to gain international

1

prominence and power—it transformed the nature of the international system and the states that constituted it.

Yet the pike, the object, is only the beginning of the story of technology and system transformation. More important were the institutions, social practices, and politics surrounding it and giving it political (and military) meaning. The pike was embedded within one set of social institutions (Swiss security practices). It was rethought and reshaped by a different set of social actors (European states). The French king recruited the Swiss because he sought an advantage over his Spanish rivals. He was engaging in balancing behavior, one of the central mechanisms of international political systems.[3] The mercenaries' success led to the spread of their innovations around Europe—to states also in pursuit of security and/or conquest—and to a gradual disintegration of the existing political order. The technology of the pike wasn't just a thing, but a thing embedded in and given meaning by social and political practices. The bundle of practices ("the pike" for short) was transformed and spread by international politics.

The story of the pike symbolizes the objective of this study: to investigate the relationship between technological change and international system change. I make four arguments. First, we have little theoretical understanding of how technology and the international system are related. Second, against those who place technology outside the sphere of social science, I argue that technology is a critical part of the international political system. It is much more than a power resource; it is the medium of interaction for international actors. Third, technology is not just a physical artifact. Technology is part of the structure of international politics; international politics is one of the factors governing technological change. Together they mutually constitute complex sociotechnical systems that are political at their core. Fourth and finally, uncovering this relationship offers insight into the process of international system transformation.

New technologies are not created by exogenous shocks to the international political system. Their transformative properties are not a simple consequence of their material features. Technological systems of communication, transportation, and/or destruction are a permanent, constitutive part of all international systems. Their development and the transformations they engender are conditioned by international politics. Change emerges out of the operations of the international political system itself. I use two case studies—the railroad and the atom bomb—to substantiate these claims. They are both sociotechnical systems that shaped the environment of international politics.

Technology looms across disciplines as a source of social, economic, and/or political change. It is often the master variable that explains everything. In economics, technological change unlocks the mystery of economic growth itself—albeit as a powerful residual variable.[4] In communications theory, in particular that inspired by Harold Innis, communications technology is the central factor shaping the political structure of human societies.[5] Marxism and the various social theories inspired by it explain the structure and change of human society and economy as a consequence of their technological base.[6]

Technology also plays an important role in a range of studies relevant to international politics. Scholars associate most system transformations since the medieval-to-modern transition with technological change. The pike and gun, the sailing ship, and the book have all been linked with the end of feudalism and the emergence of a states system in Western Europe in the seventeenth century. The rise of nationalism and the development of the nation-states system have been explained by the emergence of the newspaper in the late eighteenth and early nineteenth centuries. The geographic expansion of the states system in the nineteenth century is attributed to steamships, railroads, and telegraphs. The development of nuclear weapons in the second half of the twentieth century spawned a large literature on their system-altering effects.[7] The end of the cold war has raised the question of technology and system change again. The spread of digital information technologies has led to speculation on their likely international impact. Some perceive technology to be transforming the nation-state system into something else—a postmodern world order or postinternational politics or a partially globalized world.[8]

In other words, the relationship between technology and international politics is everywhere we look. So it is surprising that there are few attempts in international relations to systematically integrate the two.[9] There is a poor fit between our existing frameworks in international relations and the nature of technology as an object of social and political analysis. Our tools for analyzing political change in international politics, in general, are poorly developed. Static and mechanistic models dominate the discipline of international relations. Factors thought to account for change—technology, the expansion of market economies, developments in military science, or some other force—are placed outside of, exogenous to, international relations models. This approach safeguards rigor and simplicity, but it leaves too much out. The models are mute on the sources of change. Even equilibrium models of change imagine a static system, perturbation by an external shock, adjustment and recovery, and a new equilibrium.[10] These models are apolitical. By placing the sources of change outside the purview of politics (and by giving them autonomous force), static models strongly suggest a deterministic social universe independent of and superordinate to human agents.

I advocate an alternative to these conventional approaches. I conceptualize the sources of international change as endogenous to (inside) the international political system. I argue that international system theory can be adapted to account for change. I do this by redefining the international system to include technology and by theorizing technology as a political phenomenon. The relationship between international politics and technology is fundamental and mutually constitutive. Technology is deeply embedded in international and domestic political practices. What looks to be technologically induced systemic change ("the pike ended feudalism") is instead the evolution of a sociotechnical system that resists separation into the political and the technical. This term, the sociotechnical system, is key to my analysis. Technology is a "special" kind of variable, though. The relationship between international politics and technology does not follow the common logic of actor and role in which mutual constitution means the two are one and the same. The two are not prima facie balanced or equivalent.[11] The evolution of sociotechnical systems follows a path-dependent logic much like institutions. As systems mature, they lock in certain political possibilities and lock others out.[12]

In tracking the development of these sociotechnical systems, I draw on historical sociology and constructivism for theory, and path dependency and process-tracing for method. Historical sociology emphasizes the variability and evolution of political systems and the dual nature of the state constituted by domestic and international forces.[13] When applied to sociotechnical systems, two elements stand out as important: the domestic, international, and transnational institutions that shape their development; and the phases of development and spread of those systems across the international system. Constructivism (of both the international relations and the technology-theory kind) provides the tools to view technology as a political phenomenon. Technical artifacts are constructed by human action and beliefs in the same way social institutions and identities are. In this study, the appropriate methodological question is not *do* technology and system change coincide, but *how* do they? Path-dependency and process-tracing methods for establishing causal relations within cases are well suited to mapping how sociotechnical systems develop.[14] Path-dependent processes are historical sequences in which contingent events establish institutional patterns that become relatively deterministic.[15] I argue that the development and maturation of technological systems follow this logic. Process-tracing allows the investigator to make causal claims when the absence of large numbers of like cases makes covariance methods impractical. Causation is established by temporal succession and contiguity between chains of processes. Technological systems are ill suited for covariance methods. Their development and spread are linked processes. Theories of technology and international politics provide the mechanisms within each case to link stages.

In the next chapter, I develop the argument that new technologies are an important and misunderstood component of system change. Their impact is not a result of simple and unambiguous effects of the material characteristics of the technology. Instead, they interact with the international system as *a part* of that system. I make this argument in three steps. The first step is primarily an analytic exercise familiar to students of international relations theory. I investigate the weaknesses of conventional understandings of international system structure and change and show how, at the level of theory, adding technology to the conception of the system is one solution to their problems. The second step investigates how we should understand technology as a component of political systems. The third step synthesizes the first two and develops a theory of technology, international politics, and international system change.

The first step addresses the nature of the international system and the characterization of international system change. Systemic theorizing in international politics has been important and productive for decades, but the puzzle of conceptualizing and explaining systemic change eludes it. I argue that the dominant theoretical traditions in international politics offer useful conceptions of systemic change, but the causes of change are outside the theories. The realist conception of system change focuses on changes in the distribution of power. Other theoretical traditions broadened the list of sources of significant change, including: changes in the nature of the units in the international system, changes in the level of economic interdependence, changes in unit self-identity, and a shift from subsystem dominance to system dominance.[16] But in all of these conceptions, the sources of change are outside the framework of the theories.

What do I mean by systemic change? The previous examples show that there are a number of available conceptualizations. These conceptualizations are often treated as competitors. Waltz allows for a change in ordering principle, from anarchy to hierarchy, or change in the identity of the important actors and nothing more.[17] Gilpin distinguishes between systems change, systemic change, and interaction change that correspond to change in the nature of the actor, the identities of the great powers, and the rules of the system, respectively.[18] My purposes are better served by combining conceptualizations not choosing among them. Table 1.1 summarizes most of the prevailing understandings in the literature. The kinds of change are arranged in order of descending "importance" or at least relative frequency (changes in the polarity of the system happen frequently; changes to the ordering principle of the system (almost) never happen)—though the order is rough. Neither deductive reasoning nor the historical record are clear on whether, for example, shifts in collective identity are more or less frequent or more or less significant than changes in interaction capacity. Each of these will be discussed in greater detail in the next chapter, but, briefly, the table tells us two things. Each of the changes is to a systemic feature of the system, not to the units (though in some cases the two are the same). There are no good a priori reasons for ruling one or another class of change illegitimate or nonsystemic. Second, the table shows that none of the wide variety of conceptualizations of system change is logically or historically mutually exclusive. A change in the distribution of power can accompany the rise of a new hegemon that may or may not coincide with a shift in the nature of the units. Therefore, my contribution, which focuses on changes to the interaction capacity of the international system, is not intended to supplant other conceptualizations of systemic change, but to deepen and enrich our understanding of the phenomenon.[19]

The second step concerns technology. How should we understand the relationship between technology and politics? The answer to this question is critical to developing an ontology of technology and incorporating it into a conception of the international system. Technology in the political science literature is usually conceptualized as either an independent variable (deterministic) or a dependent variable (instrumental). This dichotomy between determinism (the material characteristics of the technology determine the political results) and instrumentalism (politics governs the development and use

Table 1.1 Typologies of International System Change

Feature of International System	Nature of Change	Dominant Theoretical Tradition	Example
Ordering Principle	Shift from anarchy to hierarchy	Realism, Liberalism	Waltz, Keohane
Nature of Units	Shift in the dominant unit or to/from heteronomy to homonomy	Constructivism	Ruggie, Buzan, Spruyt
Collective Identity	Change in collective identity	Constructivism	Wendt, Adler, and Barnett
Hegemony	Rise of new great power(s)/ hegemonic war	Realism	Gilpin
Interaction Capacity	Technological change	English School, Constructivism	Buzan
Economic Interactions	Increase/decrease in economic interdependence	Liberalism	Keohane and Nye
Distribution of Capabilities	Shift in the identities and/or configuration of the great powers (change in polarity)	Realism	Waltz

of new technologies) is too restrictive. The best studies of the history of technology show how technology and politics are mutually constitutive. Technology is both a social product and an important independent force because it confronts actors as a real resource or impediment. The best way to show this in international relations is by treating technologies as complex sociotechnical systems.[20] Technologies are, in this view, like institutions; they are much more than physical objects. They are bundles of physical artifacts and social practices that together make up a given "technology."

Putting these steps together links the international system and technology. The two cases I investigate involve significant change in what Buzan, Jones, and Little term interaction capacity, which they define as the combination of technological capabilities and shared norms of the international system.[21] Any social system structures interactions among its constituent units. The structuring can be material, in the form of limits on the speed, scope, and character of communication, or normative, where shared understandings define acceptable and unacceptable forms of interactions. I focus on the material half of interaction capacity to bring technology within our theoretical conception of the international political system.

Like the other sources of change in Table 1.1, interaction capacity is a component of the international system, not a characteristic of the system's units; and technology's development is transnational and political. Technological systems are one of the core components of interaction capacity, so technological change can produce change in interaction capacity. Yet these systems are also complex sociopolitical and material entities. Their development and evolution are a transnational sociopolitical process linked by the mechanisms of emulation and diffusion.[22] The evolution of certain complex sociotechnical systems spurs change in interaction capacity; yet the development of these complex sociotechnical systems is simultaneously a complex global political process. Technology and interaction capacity (technology and international politics in essence) are intertwined in a particular set of mutually constituting processes.

The studies of railroad and bomb flesh out these mutually constituting processes. For each case, I need to substantiate four separate claims: first, that each technology is not just a set of material objects, but a complex bundle of artifacts, practices, and institutions. Second, each technology developed in a transnational political setting, not a purely domestic environment. Third, these particular sociotechnical systems became an important part of the international system's interaction capacity. Finally, the change in interaction capacity was systemic change. Each study is divided in two. The first part traces the construction of the sociotechnical system—meeting the first and second claims. The second part discusses the impact of the sociotechnical system on interaction capacity—satisfying the third and fourth.

The first part of the railroad case study begins with its origins in Britain. Britain had advantages over its European competitors in demand for a faster and more efficient inland transportation system, in available capital, in technological resources (the steam engine), and in engineering expertise. So the British were the first to construct a rail network—the combination of ties, tracks, locomotives, rolling stock, lines, firms, schedules, safety regulations, government loan guarantees, and management practices that became the technology of the "railroad."

The industrial revolution was a transnational and competitive process, and the British monopoly did not last long. A home market saturated with railroads and an overabundance of skilled engineers drove large numbers of them out of Britain in the 1820s and 1830s. Many of them were drawn to Germany by new rail projects and re-cruitment by activist states. The railroad was reimagined and recon-structed in Germany as an instrument of national military power. It was here that the sociotechnical system of the railroad began to mature and rigidify, and it was here that the elements of choice and contin-gency are clearest. The use of rail was a contentious issue within the Prussian military in the 1850s and 1860s. The bureaucratic methods, educational attainments, and technical expertise necessary to make and manage an effective military rail system did not sit well with the traditionalists. They made no effort to hide their disdain for the "en-gineers" (who were more likely from a lower social class) on the General Staff who struggled technically to construct a system and politically to win it approval. The success of the system in the Austro-Prussian War consolidated the political position of the modernizers. Only then did the system gain the full support of the Prussian mili-tary, and only after the defeat of France in 1870 did it become a model for the rest of the world.[23]

The railroad entered the international system as a military tool. But its speed and carrying capacity did more than vault Germany near the top of the international hierarchy. It also altered the relationship of time and space to security and diplomacy. Railroads vastly ex-panded the range, speed, and size of armies. Germany was literally made possible by railroads, as their range offered a solution to the two-front problem (France in the west and Austria then Russia in the east) that had hindered unification prior to 1871. Continent-sized states like the United States and Russia were likewise made more feasible by rail transport, as were industrial-era colonial empires that combined political control of large territories with intensive economic exploitation (such as British India). Finally, as a consequence of the state becoming heavily involved with railroad financing, line plan-ning and construction, and civil–military coordination, the railroad also altered state–society relations. States became much more inten-sively involved in their economies, and military planning extended deeper into peacetime. Thus, the railroad's transportation and security characteristics made it a part of the interaction capacity of the industrial-era international system. The railroad's transformations to force, state composition, and state–society relations constituted systemic change.

The atom bomb case study begins in German universities. It originated as pure theoretical knowledge in the German system in the 1920s and 1930s. The Germans had invented the idea of the research university in the 1870s, and in the early twentieth century dominated the sciences generally and the emerging fields of theoretical and nuclear physics in particular. But these physicists were also part of a transnational knowledge community and the German university system was an object of emulation around the world, particularly in the United States where great resources were available for the sciences.

In the 1910s and 1920s, the exchanges were gradual and diffusion to the United States subtle. A few departments managed to lure Germans to the United States and university positions. But, by the early 1930s, the situation had changed dramatically. The Depression and anti-Semitism drove a large number of German scientists— disproportionately specialists in the fields of quantum and atomic physics—from their positions. Many were drawn to the wealthy and underpopulated American university system where new empire-builders in physics departments across the country openly recruited them.

By the advent of World War II, the center of gravity of nuclear physics had shifted to the United States. The United States drew upon the considerable resources of the diaspora physics community for the Manhattan Project. The war was the crucible in which various stands of pure knowledge were welded to industrial production techniques to produce something thought impossible just a few years before. After the war, the United States used nuclear weapons to protect itself and Europe from Soviet aggression, and to obtain and hold a dominant role in world affairs. Like the railroad, the development of the bomb as sociotechnical system hinged upon choice and contingency. As with the rail case, war was a conjuncture, but there was also a second: the rise of Nazism in Germany. The expulsion of many talented nuclear and theoretical physicists made it highly unlikely that those remaining could direct a successful bomb project.[24] The nuclear physics community had made progress in unlocking the operations of the nucleus, but it is doubtful that a nuclear explosive device would have been constructed in peacetime.[25] The crucible of war was needed to concentrate the resources and talent on the problem.

The bomb had profound consequences for the international system. The United States (and the Soviet Union) constructed elaborate sociotechnical "command and control" systems for the use of the weapon. When wedded to long-distance delivery systems, the bomb shrunk time and space even further and faster than had rail. Its destructive power made nuclear states at the very least highly cautious when confronting each other and many argue it made major war impossible. The bomb also deepened the penetration of the state into peacetime societal relations. Armies at borders could no longer provide security through the management of space, so states turned to the management of technology by forging permanent relations with industry and science. Thus, theoretical physics, instantiated as nuclear weapons, defined the interaction capacity of the atomic era. The bomb's destructive power and speed and its effects on diplomacy and state-society relations meant the changes to interaction capacity were systemic.

The case studies support the book's central argument: technology must be considered as an important, transformative element of the international political system. Their effects on force, security, geography, diplomacy, and state-society relations, and the transnational process that constructed them, make the two examples clearly something more than a unit-level factor—part of the international system. Yet the origins of both technologies were at their core sociopolitical events. Neither the military railroad network nor the fission bomb were 'discovered' by humans; neither were stumbled upon. Instead, each was constructed to perform specific human social, economic, political, or security functions. Each was a product of chance, contingency, and conjuncture. Key choices and events (with foreseen and unforeseen consequences) pushed the development of the technologies one direction and not another with critical consequences for international politics. In my conclusion I sum up and speculate on the likely applicability of this analysis to the information technology revolution.

CHAPTER TWO

INTERNATIONAL SYSTEMS THEORY, TECHNOLOGY, AND TRANSFORMATION

THE INTERNATIONAL SYSTEM AND INTERNATIONAL SYSTEM CHANGE

International relations' excessively narrow conception of what is inside and what is outside the international system has hampered efforts to understand change in and to the international system. Since the publication of Kenneth Waltz's *Theory of International Politics* in 1979, the academic study of international politics in the United States has been dominated by systemic analysis—investigations that take as their theoretical starting point the analytic primacy of the international political system in explaining international outcomes. This has been a welcome move from the perspective of theory building, giving rise not only to a robust neorealist research agenda, but the institutionalist (or neoliberal) and constructivist research agendas as well.[1] The debt to neorealism for both alternative traditions is real and obvious. The two most significant challenges to neorealism in the 1990s—constructivism and a kind of reconstructed liberalism—are either grounded in systemic thinking or are conceptualized principally as a response. This is evident in their choice of titles (constructivism offered *Social Theory of International Politics* and neoliberalism gave us "Liberal Theory of International Politics") and their theoretical aspirations.[2] Yet given the importance of the concept of the system, the meaning of system in its primary sense has received surprisingly little attention.[3] Waltz defined the system as being composed of units and their interactions—the interactions forming the structure of the system.

John Ruggie's attempt to bring the concept of system back to first principles via his analysis of Durkheim is admired as an excellent critique of *Theory*, but it has not spurred much follow-up work.[4] Meanwhile, the end of the cold war and the ongoing processes of globalization have increased the importance of the question of system and systemic change. Not only did the end of the cold war upset established understandings of international politics, but the persistence of American hegemony coupled with the continued rise of powerful nonstate actors such as multinational firms and global terrorist organizations has kept the discipline's eye on the ball of change, even if our ability to understand and account for change is limited. Can systemic theorizing help cast light on these and earlier transformations? I think that it can, but to do so requires that we pay greater attention to the question of what is an international political system and how we understand systemic change.

It is useful to begin with first principles as Ruggie suggests. Social systems are made up of actors and their arrangement or configuration. They are open and interact with their environment, and determining what is the environment and what is the system involves difficult choices. Systems experience feedback—both positive and negative—with their environment and within themselves and can display purposive, intentional behavior.[5] Conceptualizing a social system as closed is possible but runs the risk that external factors will so impinge on the operations of the system that theory based on the conceptualization will be useless. In an open social system, on the other hand, the perspective of the system is valuable to the extent that it makes a useful distinction between inside and outside. A particular conception of a system is useful to the extent that its choice of inside and outside (1) captures a coherent set of interrelations and (2) allows meaningful statements about activities within the system and changes to it without depending on ad hoc relations with the environment. The ability to capture change is particularly important because change is the one constant feature of social systems. If our concepts and theories have to depend on external deus ex machina to explain persistent features of their social systems, they are of little use.

Because of the importance of the relationship with the outside, deciding what is system and what is environment in social systems is a critical analytic task—equal in importance to choosing the components of the system and their relations. We can judge our choices by weighing factors such as: density and complexity of interactions, tolerance of analytic division, characteristics and behavioral regularities that can be attributed to neither the environment nor the actors, and the extent to which actors' behavior is caused by the system. Yet in the end the determination of the boundaries of any given system is simultaneously a theoretical and an empirical enterprise. Determining the boundaries of a social system by deduction alone is impossible. In international politics, the theoretical basis of anarchy—the existence of a political system distinguishable from domestic political systems—is premised on an empirical observation—the absence of a centralized global political authority. We speak theoretically of an anarchical international system because (though not only because) we think we observe it.[6]

Existing conceptions of change in and to the international system have been hampered by overly narrow conceptions of what is inside and what is outside the system. Bringing technology within the conception of system is one solution to this problem. This theoretical review proceeds along two distinct tracks. The first track is a conventional discussion of the shortcomings of the three dominant approaches in American international relations—realism, liberalism, and constructivism—when it comes to system change. I also pursue a second track. I show how, in recent years, a number of writers working consciously in one tradition or another have tried to accommodate change—by adding components to their conception of the international system just as I propose to do. These efforts have been for the most part afterthoughts or otherwise unsuccessful. But they show that I am building on a group effort within the discipline, not an isolated enterprise. More and more international relations thinkers are trying to loosen the strictures of theoretical parsimony and elegance in exchange for something more complex yet more useful.

NEOREALISM

Waltz defined the orthodox conception of the international system. His system is quite open to the environment and has a parsimonious list of system components. It is made up of the units in interaction (states), the fundamental nature of their interaction (what Waltz calls the ordering principle, or anarchy in the case of international politics), and the distribution of power between the units. The 'environment' of international politics is everything but the distribution of military power. So when Waltz speaks of systemic causes and effects, he is referring to the distribution of power almost exclusively. He writes that, "differences of national strength and power and of national capability and competence are what the study and practice of international politics are almost entirely about."[7]

When considering change from the neorealist perspective, there are three sets of possibilities: a change in the ordering principle from anarchy to hierarchy, a change in the nature of the units, or a change in the identities of the major powers and/or the distribution of power between them.[8] A change in ordering principle is too unlikely to be theoretically interesting. Because of the constraints of anarchy, a change in the nature of the units is improbable. So, for neorealism, significant shifts in the distribution of power are the substance of systemic change.

Because of the limited list of system components, the causes of change are, logically, all found in the environment outside international politics, not in the system itself. Three factors feature prominently in the realist and neorealist literature as sources of change: uneven economic growth, aggressor states, and uneven technological development.[9] In scenarios featuring the first factor, rapidly growing states attempt to seize power from older, slower-growing great powers. The touchstone example for realism is third-century B.C.E. Athens whose rapid growth, according to Thucydides, brought it inevitably into conflict with Sparta. Aggressor states are geopolitically frustrated, or perhaps in possession of a dysfunctional domestic political system. Such states upset the international status quo through military aggression, and the efforts to stop them effect systemic change. Nazi Germany is the often-used example.[10] In the third scenario, some dramatic change in the technological environment—especially in military technology—gives a state or states a decisive advantage over real or potential competitors. A prominent example, investigated in the Cipolla and Parker books, is the rise of Western Europe (and its settler states) to global dominance.[11] But to the orthodox conception of the system, all three of these sources of change are extrasystemic. Their effects on the distribution of power and the identities of the major powers are systemic, but the causes of systemic change occur outside the theater of international politics.

There are at least two reasons to be dissatisfied with this characterization. First is the causal status of the international system in neorealist theory. In neorealism, the international system is given such explanatory weight in determining international political behavior and outcomes that it seems counterintuitive to eliminate the system from among the causes of international politics' most significant outcomes. The implicit argument, that the system strongly conditions behavior but lacks the ability to constitute itself or condition its transformation, is implausible. The logic of this orthodox view on systemic change demands a generative logic to the international system structure. There should be some theoretical mechanism to explain how international systems generate and change themselves even if the standard version of neorealism fails to provide one, or, as Ruggie puts it, "Waltz's theory of 'society' contains only a reproductive logic, but no transformational logic."[12]

The second reason for dissatisfaction is the severe limits placed on the kinds of change the theory allows. Waltz insists that significant international change can only take two forms: change in the distribution of power (or the polarity of the system) or a shift from anarchy to hierarchy. But this seems inadequate. There are strong intuitive reasons for this. For example, surely the transition from the medieval to modern international systems is a great one, or the difference between Moghul hegemony over India and Soviet hegemony over Eastern Europe exceeds their similarity in distribution of power. Neither of these distinctions is captured by a shift in the distribution of power.

Three efforts to amend neorealist theory have tried to make up for this second shortcoming. Buzan, Jones, and Little argue that the neorealist conception of political systems logically allows for four types of system structure: unlike units under hierarchy, like units under anarchy, but also like units under hierarchy and unlike units under anarchy. The latter two forms may be, as they allow, less common or less stable. Yet the medieval European international system is an example of an unlike-anarchical system and, regardless, they argue, Waltz's insistence that anarchy must lead to sameness is, "an unnecessarily extreme view."[13]

From a similar viewpoint, Spruyt offers a systemic explanation for the emergence of states in early modern Europe.[14] States replaced feudal political structures and defeated their competitors, city-states and city leagues, because of greater evolutionary fitness. States' superior ability to build and sustain a uniform economic and institutional environment made them more adaptable to early capitalism. Yet despite adding unit-type to neorealism's conception of system structure, and despite emphasizing economic structure at the expense of military/security, Spruyt explicitly roots his explanation within the neorealist systemic tradition, "The structure of the system is . . . determined by the particular type of unit that dominates the system in a given historical period. Such structure is not derivative of the interactions between units, nor is an aggregation of unit-level attributes."[15] Others with a deeper attachment to neorealism have also been attracted to an evolutionary mechanism to explain change within a systemic theoretical framework.[16] Yet the source of change remains outside the model itself—for Spruyt in the emergence of new forms of economic activity and organization.

Stuart Kaufman has also tried to expand the analytical possibilities of structural realism.[17] He suggests that instead of a narrow focus on polarity, different types of international systems can be characterized by their position on a spectrum from fragmented (an even distribution of power) to consolidated (an imperial or hegemonic distribution of power). Degree of fragmentation or consolidation is a characteristic of systems (and so an appropriate subject for systemic theory) and not, according to Kaufman, determined by the distribution of power. Instead it is a product of four forces: anarchy itself, the level of economic interdependence, the dominant principle of unit identity (greater concern with self-determination will tend to favor fragmentation), and state administrative capacity (greater capacity favors greater consolidation). Each of these is promising. Yet none has achieved acceptance within the mainstream of international relations theory and neither addresses the first problem—that the sources of change in neorealism are all extrasystemic. In the bid for parsimony, too much has been left out of the conception of the system, leaving the theory with only one thing to say about the sources of systemic change: they come from outside. This is, beginning with Ruggie's essay previously cited, a long-standing criticism of neorealism. The same problem is found in the other dominant theoretical approaches to systemic theorizing as well.

NEOLIBERALISM

Systemic liberal theorizing depends on a conception of the international system largely in accord with that offered by the neorealists, with three interesting exceptions. Liberal international relations theory in the 1960s and 1970s offered a more comprehensive critique of the realist conception of system structure. Integration theorists, interdependence theorists, and more normatively oriented legal and international community scholars conceptualized a system of considerable complexity and dynamism. Systemic liberalism retreated from this more complex vision in the 1980s and remade itself as neoliberal institutionalism. Still, elements of this more fruitful and daring era of liberal theorizing leak into systemic liberal thought. For neoliberalism, the components of the international system are anarchy, states and their interests, and the distribution of power—the same as for neorealism. Yet neoliberals disagree with realists about how the system operates—about the relationship among the system's components. Specifically, systemic liberals (though not always the same ones) argue that changes in the level of interdependence, changes in the quantity and kind of nonstate actors, and the prevalence of cooperation and institutions in the international system each or all affect the operation of the system. In the end, the latter two are subsumed by the first—more interdependence means more nonstate actors, more cooperation, and more international institutions; less means less. All three of these represent significant efforts to expand what counts as part of the international system—though they are not always understood as such. Yet each of the three is in the end explained by forces outside of systemic liberal theory.

Liberals have long argued that greater interdependence between states—or ever greater and faster connections between states via trade, information, capital, and culture—changes international politics. Norman Angell famously argued, before World War I, that increased trade made war between the great powers too costly to rationally contemplate, so great power war could only be the result of irrational forces.[18] Greater interdependence means more transactions and greater complexity, which means a greater need to coordinate activities and policies. Actors then gain a material interest in maintaining smooth flows and are more inclined to cooperate and support international institutions to manage the increased complexity of intersocietal flows. Interdependence also affects the character of power. More interdependence means the bonds linking societies are costlier to break, and force is less and less useful. Because of increased complexity, power will tend to vary by issue area. Nye has argued that what he calls soft power (cultural influence and moral authority) is more effective the higher the level of interdependence.[19]

Interdependence in this sense cannot be understood as a property of the units, but instead as a property of the international system. The density and flow of commercial, cultural, and political bonds between social actors may be hard to quantify precisely, but it is not reducible to individual states. Thus, for systemic liberals, a change in a component of international system structure changes the fundamental nature of interactions between units. This implies a theory of systemic change on a profound scale. But what causes an increase in interdependence? By the standards established earlier, for interdependence-liberalism to truly constitute a theory of system change, it should account for the source of change. Unfortunately, liberal thought on the issue is disappointing. Higher or lower levels of interdependence are explained by reference to economic conditions and technological changes in the communication and transportation realms exogenous to the international political system that is the object of their analysis.[20]

For example, in *Power and Interdependence* Keohane and Nye write, "A model of regime change based on economic process [the complex interdependence model] would begin with this century's many technological and economic changes. Particularly during the last thirty years, economic growth in the industrialized world has proceeded at an unprecedented pace. . . . Behind these changes lie remarkable advances in transportation and communications technology, which have reduced the costs of distance."[21] The book sketches a continuum from absolute, realist-style independence on one end to complex interdependence on the other. The debate with realism is where on the continuum any particular international system is. As the previous quote suggests, however, no effort is made to explain *why* a particular international system is at one point or another on the continuum. This is because the core features of the theory are rational actors, their interests, and their choices in a given environment. Neorealists and neoliberals differ on the question of interdependence, over the nature of the environment, but not over why we have the "environment" we do; neither have the theoretical resources to bring the problem of system change within their theoretical apparatus.

The second addition systemic liberals make to system structure involves the prevalence and significance of nonstate actors in world politics. Systemic liberals have argued at various times over recent decades that the rise of significant transnational organizations represented a transformation of the international system, that increases in the activities of multinational corporations were changing international politics, that the aftermath of World War II and the postwar boom had created a totally new type of state no longer committed to traditional interstate competition, and that the emergence of large global networks of nongovernmental organizations (NGOs) was transforming international politics.[22] What these works all have in common is a theory of system transformation. The new, or newly important, actors are components of system structure. Waltz's second tier (the unit) does not drop out, but is instead filled by a variety of international actors other than the state. This matters for systemic theory because it promises the erosion of the power and authority of the state in the international system and either the sharing or replacement of that authority by other actors who may operate by different logics (e.g., NGOs who operate on a nonterritorial, issue-oriented logic). The more modest of these theorists argue for a conception of the international system that merely includes transnational political institutions and actors. More aggressive analysts foresee the demise of the nation-state system and its replacement by some sort of transnational political institution or institutions.[23] In either case, change to the nature of the units is system change.

Do liberal systemic theorists who wish to add new actors to the international system offer a compelling explanation for why and how new actors emerge? Does the greater systemic complexity pay off in a theoretical account of change? Explicit explanations are hard to find, but two underlying causes are clearly implied: first, new actors emerge as the international arena becomes more crowded with transactions, communications, and movement. As the international system grows more complex and interdependent, it is better able to support a greater diversity of actor types. This throws the explanation back to interdependence liberalism, and from there to the same vague notions of technological change. Second, as cooperation and institution-building grow at the international level, it becomes easier, and more likely, that new actors will emerge free from the security concerns that states evince. More cooperation between states is likely to generate more and more significant nonstate actors. These explanations rely on mechanisms for change—the same ones as interdependence liberalism—that lie outside the theory.

Third, systemic liberals claim that cooperation between states, and the robustness of international institutions built to facilitate cooperation, can be greater than neorealists allow. In the standard neorealist view, anarchy forces states to focus first on security, making cooperation less likely than a neutral observer might guess.[24] Liberal institutionalists reject this pessimism.[25] They imply that the relationship between anarchy and state behavior is not tight but actually fairly loosely linked. The level of cooperation and degree of institutionalization in a system

can only exist *between* units, so they are systemic features not characteristics of the units. If the competitiveness of anarchy varies with
cooperation and institutions, then we have a theory of system change:
change in these variables changes the logic of the system's operation.
When the logic of this principle is pressed to its limit, the effect on
the system is clear. The security communities literature argues that
cooperation can actually generate community between states.[26] When
levels of security cooperation between states reach a certain point, the
logic of their relationship shifts from competitor to ally to joint member of a community.[27]

Systemic liberalism offers two sorts of explanations for an increase in cooperation and institutions. The first is interdependence
itself. When interdependence increases, relations between states and
between firms in different states become denser and more complex,
which in turn leads to greater desire for formal cooperative arrangements. This is what Keohane implies when he speaks of the demand
for international regimes.[28] Microeconomic motives—such as transaction costs, and market and informational failures—dominate his
explanation, but they in turn mean an increased density and velocity
of transactions. So this explanation offers no advantages over those
provided for nonstate actors and interdependence itself—the motive
force is found outside the conception of the international system.

The second explanation given for an increase in cooperation
and institutions is more interesting. Systemic liberals argued in
the past that cooperation and institutions themselves can be self-
reinforcing—the two lead to more cooperation and more robust institutions.[29] These same arguments are repeated in recent liberal
scholarship. Keohane and his co-authors argue that as transnational
dispute resolution spreads, the transaction costs associated with international exchange will fall and that in turn will lead to an increase
in cooperative behavior and compliance with the rules promulgated
by international institutions.[30] A game-theoretic treatment of international conflict stresses the importance of reassurance through costly
signaling in order to establish the trust necessary to avoid conflict.[31]
In other words, cooperative behavior that rises to the level of costly
signaling is the necessary basis for cooperation over even greater issues (avoiding war, in this case). Implied here is some kind of learning
mechanism, or what Adler, Crawford, and Donnelly have called cognitive evolution—a tendency for cooperation and institutionalization
in the international system to naturally increase as humans come to

understand the benefits of cooperative behavior and the best strategies for ensuring it.[32]

These are intriguing arguments, and they do at first glance meet the criteria of placing the motive force for systemic change within the theoretical conception of the international system. However, it is unlikely that, by themselves, these very general propositions can lead to a theory of international system change. As has been noted elsewhere, the cognitive demands of liberal theory might be unrealistically high to generate steady increases in cooperative behavior.[33] More important, while a liberal learning model can give an internal account of increases in cooperation, it can offer no guidance for periods of stasis or even decreases in cooperation. Explanations for the variance would have to come from outside the model: an increase or decrease in interdependence (i.e., the structural incentives to cooperate or not) independent of actor learning, or particularly intelligent or irrational actors.

These three exceptions from systemic liberal theory—interdependence, new actors, and degree of cooperation—are worth serious consideration. They provide insight into the mechanisms of change in the international system, but they are only suggestive. Why and under what conditions they become transformation mechanisms is not theorized by liberalism, except briefly and ahistorically via vague references to the tendency of things to grow increasingly complex or to underdeveloped notions of actor learning. As with neorealism, useful sources of systemic change are still outside the model of the system, and a theory of system change still depends on exogenous and ad hoc forces.

CONSTRUCTIVISM

Orthodox constructivist theory is more explicit than neoliberalism about amending neorealist system structure.[34] Rather than treat the identities and interests of social actors as pretheoretic givens and proceed from there, as neorealism and neoliberalism do, constructivism argues instead that identities and interests are social constructs perpetually in the process of creation, maintenance, and reproduction. While intriguing as a starting-point, this is at root an ontological and epistemological stance and not a theory of international politics, a point acknowledged by constructivists. As such, it is necessary to add theoretical content.[35]

To anarchy, the interaction of units and the distribution of power, constructivism adds collective identity—the actors in the international social system would, through their interactions, come to share a conception of what it is to be a member of the international system and the rules and norms that govern membership. Anarchy has no intrinsic logic or effect on the states that compose the system. Instead, the understandings states arrive at through the process of interaction is the logic of the international system. Wendt, in the most comprehensive statement of mainstream constructivism, defines the three cultures of anarchy as Hobbesian (states understand other states as "enemy"), Lockean ("rival") and Kantian ("friend").[36]

Wendt's formulation has built into it a conception of systemic change. If the logic of the system can be described as Hobbesian, Lockean, or Kantian, then at some point the system must undergo a transformation from one collective identity to another. Wendt defines this process as cultural change—a shift in the culture of anarchy—and devotes an entire chapter to the subject. He narrows his focus to four different (he calls them master) variables that can cause underlying shifts in collective identity: interdependence, common fate, homogenization, and self-restraint.[37] Each operates via the underlying mechanism of social learning to alter states' understandings of themselves and others, and each is necessary, but not sufficient, for cultural change. The greater the interdependence between states, the more likely they are to view their identities and interests merged with other states. The more states share a common fate, the more likely they are to see themselves as sharing a common identity. The more states converge on regime type, internal economic structure, and so on, the more likely they are to construct a prosocial (i.e., Lockean at least, Kantian at best) collective identity. Underlying all of these as a permissive cause is self-restraint. For states to trust that the objective conditions of interdependence, common fate, and homogeneity lead to cooperation and not exploitation (to a subjective understanding of shared interests), there must be enough states in the system practicing self-restraint. This means that some states will pass up the opportunity to exploit others and thereby embed a sense of safety or trust in the normative framework of the international system. When all four of these variables are in operation, the likelihood of systemic change is high.

The version of constructivism popularized by Wendt and other like-minded scholars suffers from the same shortcomings as neorealism and neoliberalism when it comes to system change—conceptual narrowness and ad hoc exogenous explanations for change.[38] Like Waltz, before even beginning theory construction, Wendt truncates his definition of the international system to include just relations between states. Also like Waltz, he admits that the states system is only one of the things under the broader heading of international relations.[39] This rules out by definitional fiat the possibility of including technology in our conception of international system, or even some of the neoliberal systemic components such as interdependence and nonstate actors. Interdependence and technology may play a role, via the master variables, in systemic cultural change, but from a position clearly exogenous to the theory.

Wendt goes so far as to term structural components like interdependence as part of the "objective" environment of states to distinguish them from state's subjective needs based on their understandings of the degree of interdependence in the system, and so on.[40] The objective conditions in this conception of the system function just as the material environment does for neorealist theory: as a background condition that constrains but does not force states to adapt. So if shifts in the underlying technologies of communication, for example, should increase the objective amount of interdependence in the system, then technology would be a deus ex machina driving systemic change and not one that can be accounted for by the theory. This is a curiously anticonstructivist conclusion to arrive at for a supposedly constructivist theory of international politics. Yet Wendt admits this shortcoming, too, declaring that he has no (theoretical) idea what might make the master variables change their (objective) values.[41]

Mainstream constructivism looks at first blush like a promising departure for international theory: it emphasizes the constructed character of human social relations, the importance of actor identity, and offers an explicit account of systemic transformation. But it, too, suffers from an overly narrow conception of the international system and pushes all change mechanisms outside the theory's purview. Despite appearances, constructivism cannot offer a theoretical account of systemic change without relying on exogenous factors.

LEARNING FROM REALISM, LIBERALISM, AND CONSTRUCTIVISM

All three of the principal theoretical schools in American international relations have trouble accounting for systemic change. Even when they have expanded the conception of the international system beyond neorealism's bare bones, the expansion is incomplete and the mechanisms of change remain outside the theories' reach. Yet they lay the groundwork for the fuller conception I wish to advance here. Each of them, including neorealism, has demonstrated despite themselves the narrowness of conventional definitions of the international system—in particular when it comes to the question of system change. Each of them has suggested ways of expanding the definition of the international system while staying within the constraints of systemic theory. Works inspired by both realism and constructivism suggest expanding system structure to include unit-type.[42] Interdependence gets votes from all three schools. My particular focus, technology, fits well conceptually within the study of interdependence. It even has implications for unit-type.[43] But adding to these theoretical traditions is not my objective. The problems with their conceptualizations of change have been noted earlier. A different approach is called for: a distinct theoretical role for technology, not an ad hoc afterthought.

I advocate moving technology inside our theoretical conception of the international system. This is meant in two senses: first, that (certain kinds of) technologies are systemic in international politics because they are properties of the system not of the system's constituent units; and, second, that technologies are political. Both senses are necessary, and the reason why takes the argument back to the discussion of what is inside our conception of the system and what outside.

What might systemic technologies be like? Given the diversity of technology, it is hopeless to try to draw general conclusions about the affect of a singular 'technology' on international politics. Some narrowing or classifying is required. Deductive reasoning brings us back to the conception of the system. Social systems structure interactions among their constituent units. Technology is the material underpinning of this structuring. So operationalizing interaction capacity implies two things: purpose and scope. A focus on those technologies that affect the ability of international actors to reach each other—either via communication, or physically via technologies of transportation and/or violence—addresses the question of purpose. Systemic technologies are those that shape the time and space environment of international politics. They address questions such as how quickly can actors reach locations on the globe or each other; how much matter, or how many people, can be moved by what means, at what cost, at what speed, and how far; how viable is the governance of what size political space, by what kind of political entity? Such technologies are systemic, not unit characteristics, even though they may be possessed by individual actors, because they shape the interaction environment in which international actors find themselves. They are irreducible to characteristics of the actors alone.

The question of scope raises the issue of sociotechnical systems. Systemic technologies are big. They are global in scope. Systemic technologies are systems themselves: not the internal combustion engine, but the car, the roads, the traffic laws, border crossings, multinational networks of production, and so on. Interaction capacity is operationalized in sociotechnical systems that span the globe (in whole or in part) so that international actors can materially interact. Combining purpose and scope allows for a precise definition of systemic technologies: those sociotechnical systems—typically communication, transportation, or violence systems—that structure interactions among international actors and are global in scope. Transportation technologies satisfy the purpose half of the definition, though not all transportation technologies are systemic in scope. The definition also rules out technologies that result only in an increase in state power because that is a unit-level, not systemic technology.[44]

If technologies are systemic but not political, we would have no need to think about them as inside the international system. The oceans and landmasses of the globe are more or less environmental characteristics of this sort—notwithstanding the human ability to alter their shape and meaning via the construction of canals and the like. The relationship between technology and the international system is irrelevant to a *theory* of international politics; in other words, if technologies confront social actors as material/physical facts—if there is nothing inherently *political* about technology. If the latter is true, we can easily rule technology out from theoretical consideration. I make the case that this is not so in the next section.

TWO VIEWS OF TECHNOLOGY AND POLITICS

TECHNOLOGICAL DETERMINISM

Technologies can be systemic in the sense previously outlined. But how is technology political? Technology can have an effect on politics (all the theories discussed earlier acknowledge this), but we do not need a political theory of technology unless somehow the affect technology has on politics depends on politics. If technology is an invariable, natural thing, it is apolitical. In the literature on the history and philosophy of technology, there are two answers—determinism and constructivism—and a middle ground. While there are no precise analogs in international relations theory, determinism can be aligned with materialist theories such as neorealism (and economistic forms of liberalism) and constructivism (or social constructionism) aligned with international relations constructivism.[45]

Determinist logic argues that technology is a variable exogenous to political and social analysis but that nonetheless has some substantial, and definable, influence on politics.[46] It has political effects but is apolitical in the sense defined above. It is a natural thing unalterable by human design, so no political analysis is needed to understand it. For determinists, technology is the (or a) key independent variable in explaining social change. Few scholars of technology take the determinist position seriously now, but determinist attitudes pervade the analysis of technology and politics by nonspecialists.

An important collection of essays from the 1990s revisited the issue of technological determinism. The reprinting of Robert Heilbroner's influential 1967 essay, along with a reconsideration of his original argument, is the focal point of the volume.[47] The title of the Heilbroner essay, "Do Machines Make History?," makes a clear statement of the determinist position. In that essay, Heilbroner argued that the broad forms technology takes in a given society will determine the overall pattern of social and economic relations in that society. He notes that technological advance tends to happen in several places at once (simultaneous invention), that technological advance is not rapid but steady and incremental, and that technological development has a definite trajectory and is therefore predictable. He concludes, "I think we can indeed state that the technology of a society imposes a determinate pattern of social relations on that society."[48] There are some qualifications to Heilbroner's argument. He is referring only to capitalist societies and industrial technology (societies that do not innovate cannot be determined by technological change). Nor is he referring to some specific technology, or even a particular country or even region, but to industrial technology development generally. Nevertheless, his position is a determinist one: technology is exogenous to the social system, it enters the system, and generates a specific social outcome.[49]

The central works of neorealism and neoliberal institutionalism—Waltz's *Theory of International Politics* and Keohane's *After Hegemony*—both have a deterministic understanding of technology's role at the level of theory.[50] Technology is important, but it is not political. It requires no political analysis to understand its emergence and its effects. For Waltz, new military technologies can increase the military capabilities of actors.[51] The socialization pressures of the anarchical international system generate adaptive responses—typically emulation—from other actors. What is important here is the nature of the role in Waltz's theory for technology. It can alter the distribution of power in the system (a central variable in the theory), but it operates in an exogenous fashion. There is no possibility of a political conception of technology in neorealism.[52] For Keohane, the benefits of cooperation (reduced transaction costs) can be enhanced and the costs of enforcement (monitoring) can be reduced by the application of technology—particularly surveillance and communications technologies.[53] Technology has only a marginal role and is an external force. Neoliberal institutionalism provides only a little room, in theory, for a deterministic conception of technology in international politics.

While neorealism and neoliberalism do not explicitly acknowledge technology, Deudney does theorize technology from a determinist stance.[54] Updating the work of John Herz and the older geopolitical tradition to a kind of liberal (or republican) geopolitics,[55] Deudney argues that the underlying technological environment determines the nature of political authority or, more precisely, the institutions of security provision. The environment created by gunpowder, firearms, and other conventional explosives has generated the system of states. The environment created by nuclear weapons, because they promise destruction of the state, will eventually create a poststate international system. This shift is "driven by very basic alterations in the material forces of destruction that largely lie outside the control of humans." It is hard to find a better statement of the determinist argument.[56]

James Rosenau's work provides another self-consciously determinist argument.[57] Turbulence in World Politics gives technological change a significant role in the emergence of "postinternational" politics. Yet despite a dizzying array of crosscutting parameters, overlapping levels, and causal complexity, technology itself is an exogenous force. Rosenau's core argument is that the international system is undergoing profound, or "parametric," change—change at the level of the individual, at the level of the system, and in the relations between the levels. The sources of this change are the shift from an industrial to postindustrial social order, the emergence of new global issues such as the environment, drug trafficking, and so on, a decline in state efficacy, devolution of large institutions, and feedback between them. Technological change underlies each of these changes, and Rosenau is careful to draw the connections. He refers to information technologies that collapse time and shrink distance, change the scale of human interactions, and increase the competence of political skills and interests of individuals. Yet technological change itself is outside his analysis, "Except for the dynamics unleashed by technological innovations . . . those noted so far are embraced by the three parameters of the global political system" (elsewhere he refers to "technology-driven exogenous dynamics").[58]

A group of popular writers—among them George Gilder and Nicholas Negroponte, head of MIT's Media Lab, as well as a countless number of management consultants—make the determinist argument for new information technologies even more emphatically.[59] Of and by themselves, digital technologies are/will change the way we live, work, play, even conduct international relations. A tidal wave of technological change will crash over economic and social life and bring great benefits. Those who fail to adapt—whether individuals, organizations, firms, communities, cultures, states, and so on—will be crushed. Negroponte writes, "Like a force of nature, the digital age cannot be denied or stopped."[60] Digital organizations and institutions are decentralized yet global and tilt the balance of power in favor of individuals and their creative energies and against the bureaucratic operations of large organizations. Gilder writes that "with microchips and fiber optics eroding the logic of centralized institutions, networks of personal computers are indeed overthrowing IBM and CBS, NTT [Nippon Telephone and Telegraph] and EEC [European Economic Commission]."[61]

We can call this position the ideology of technology's particularity—whether implicit in international relations theory as in the case of Waltz and Keohane, or explicit in the writings of information-age enthusiasts. It is an ideology, not a statement of fact, or a scientific assessment of technology's role and carries with it all the distortions and simplifications that accompany ideologies. This ideological system believes that the human-fashioned material world impacts the social world in a distinctive, autonomous manner. It asserts that technology stands outside the social world and enters it only to disrupt and alter. This is a view that, after even a cursory survey of the history of technology, cannot be sustained.

THE SOCIAL CONSTRUCTION OF TECHNOLOGY

The alternative pole to technological determinism is social constructionism. It is the philosophical (and political) opposite of technological determinism and the dominant approach in sociological and historical studies of science and technology.[62] The social constructionist approach argues that technology is 'social through and through.' Rather than entering the social world as an exogenous agent of change, technology and its "effects" are instead created and shaped by human interest and creativity, as well as by political and economic power.

Technologies are developed by human beings. They are not, or at least not very often, discovered like a seashell on a beach. Technologists make choices about how and what to innovate. They pursue particular interests and particular curiosities. They have adequate resources to pursue their interests and curiosities (or they don't). They have adequate institutional support (or they don't). The result of this framework of interest and choice is that what technologies get developed—and which don't—is not (just) a function of the technically feasible, not the product of some inevitable technological trajectory. It is instead a function of human choice, interest, ideas, institutions, power, and resources.

There are no obvious examples of this perspective in use in international relations theory, though its analogs with constructivism are clear. Like constructivism, social constructionism argues that the social world and its rules are not natural objects but the creations of human agents and their interactions.[63] MacKenzie's study of the development of gyroscopic navigational systems for ballistic missiles offers a good demonstration of the power of the social constructionist position on a subject of interest to international politics.[64] It is odd, he argues, that the U.S. nuclear arsenal contains ballistic missiles capable of hitting their intercontinental targets accurately to within 100 meters. American ICBMs can do this, he argues, not because developing such accuracy was the natural product of missile development or because urgent strategic need mandated highly accurate missiles. Instead, black-box gyroscopic navigation became a reality because Charles Stark Draper was obsessed with the idea and, despite the presence of serious technical difficulties and the absence of any serious strategic rationale, he was able to convince the air force and the navy to continue to support his research even after persistent failures to meet performance targets. The strategy that made use of the system's accuracy (counterforce) was developed after Draper had already convinced the military to support his project.

The broader claim of MacKenzie's argument is quite far-reaching. It is foolish to speak glibly of nuclear weapons' affect on politics, as nuclear weapons—in the particular form they have come to embody—

are themselves the product of a complex social and political process. Nuclear weapons are, quite literally, social constructs. This does not mean that they do not exist in some corporeal sense. They are clearly quite real. But it does mean that, for the social constructionist, nuclear weapons are not some natural artifact that, once introduced to the human social environment, will have an unambiguous and singular effect on that environment. Instead, nuclear weapons are a human invention, and the particular form nuclear weapons have taken is only one of a presumed multitude of possible "nuclear weapons." Even these same nuclear weapons (the ones we have) are subject to differing interpretations as to their meaning and "effects." As another study puts it, "[Social construction of technology] emphasizes the 'interpretive flexibility' of an artifact. Different social groups associate different meanings with artifacts leading to interpretive flexibility appearing over the artifact. The same artifact can mean different things to different social groups of users."[65] The technologies we have (and don't have) are not inevitable. They are not separate from social, economic, or political forces.

LIMITATIONS OF DETERMINISM AND SOCIAL CONSTRUCTIONISM

Both views of the relationship between technology and politics, in their simplest form, are of limited use. The technological determinists are clearly wrong; technologies don't cause anything—humans do. It is absurd to claim that a certain technology will have a certain, singular, political effect. At the same time, social constructionism is also misdirected. Social constructionists are too concerned with explaining the emergence of technologies and not concerned enough with the political implications of technologies once they have moved out of the workshop or lab and into common use.[66] On the other hand, something like the technological determinist argument seems, intuitively, to be partly right. Some technologies do seem to have certain definitive political effects—they close off certain kinds of social and political action and make other kinds possible.

This is the argument made in different ways by Headrick and Winner.[67] Like the determinists, they argue that technology can have specific political effects. But they argue that the effects are filtered through actor interest and behavior, and institutional constraints and opportunities. They are not inherent in the nature of the material thing, the bare "technology." Headrick argues that just like any other component of social structure, formal or informal institution, codified or implicit norm, technologies can place constraints on human action—roads, buildings, and sidewalks structure our paths of travel; nuclear weapons certainly seem to have made war between nuclear powers impossible. They can also open up two kinds of opportunities. They can either help social actors obtain preexisting goals that the prior material environment had made impossible or nearly impossible. Or they can inspire social actors to imagine new goals that had not occurred to them before the change in the material environment.[68] Headrick provides an example of the former: prior to the development of quinine, Europeans were unable to penetrate to the interior of Africa. As a consequence, all but coastal settlements remained impervious to European conquest. The introduction of quinine removed that impediment and made colonization of the African interior possible.[69] MacKenzie's example of the strategy of counterforce (see above) is an example of the latter.[70]

Winner extends Headrick's observation on constraints.[71] He argues that artifacts can have politics (by which he means political effects) in two ways. They can resolve a particular political argument in favor of one side by creating 'facts on the ground.' His famous example is the bridges over Long Island parkways. They were built on the direction of the New York City planner Robert Moses with intentionally low overpasses in order, Winner claims, to prevent their use (and with it the suburban Long Island communities and recreational beaches) by buses. By building bridge overpasses down to a certain height, Moses was in effect creating a class- and race-exclusive suburban development. Technology choice shaped the social and political structure of the New York metropolitan region.[72] In Winner's second class of political effects, some technologies are inherently political and (may) require a certain kind of social and political organization. So the 'choice' of a particular technological system may also bring with it (intentionally or not) certain social and political effects. Winner points to Chandler's contention that the family firm, in the face of industrial technology, was fated to be replaced by the modern corporation as an example of this effect.[73] A similar example in the international relations literature is Waltz's claim that the characteristics of nuclear weapons will automatically lead countries that deploy them to build centralized command and control systems.[74]

These arguments suggest that determinism and social constructionism are incomplete alone. No technology is truly autonomous;

they are all partly social. Yet neither are the political meanings of technologies infinitely malleable. The two do, however, complement each other nicely. Technology as used here is simultaneously a social and technical product. What this means is quite straightforward and suggested nicely by Harvey Brooks's well-known definition of technology: "knowledge of how to fulfill certain human purposes in a specifiable and reproducible way . . . not of artifacts . . . but of the . . . knowledge that underlies the artifacts and the way they can be used in society."[75] In other words, technology is obviously an artifact: a physical thing.[76] As such, it confronts its user as a material fact— a natural part of the physical world, but technology is also the creation of humans and thus social in character. Thus, while technology may appear to the individual user as unalterable and as natural physical fact, it is also importantly social. It is chosen by some (perhaps) opaque social process and thus in principle alterable by means of those same processes. There is a tendency to treat technology as a found object: outside the world of the social much like the mountains or the oceans. In turn, this tendency views the discovery of new technologies as the revelation or literal discovery of some part of nature that has heretofore been hidden from man but is now unveiled. But while technologies are certainly limited by what is physically possible, and then limited further by the extent of technical knowledge at a particular historical time, beyond that (and the 'beyond' is quite expansive) particular technologies are developed for particular social, economic, political, or personal reasons all of which are amenable to analysis by the social scientist.[77]

Thus, technologies have both social origins (constructionism) and social effects (determinism); are shaped by human intent and interest (constructionism) and resist such intentions (determinism). Determinism and social constructionism are both ideal types and many reasonable historians of technology are found somewhere in the middle (though not necessarily political scientists, journalists, or other commentators on contemporary affairs). The middle is where we should head to resolve the technology and international politics puzzle, but the middle can too easily become vague and insubstantial. Placing oneself there should be done with care.

SYSTEMS AND TIME

The solution to the technology-politics dilemma I want to explore in this book focuses on two elements: defining technologies more precisely as sociotechnical systems, and time. There is a tendency is to think of technology as a single entity or phenomenon for analysis; hard positivism and the search for general explanations for general phenomenon demand it. We seek an answer to the puzzle of technology and international politics that somehow accounts for all technologies and expect that all technologies will be found to have similar effects. This is an error comparable to assuming that all institutions function in the same way and with similar effects. The family and international political organizations such as the United Nations are both institutions in the broadest sense, but we have wisely divided up their study between academic disciplines and do not expect that they are identical simply because they are institutions. Yet when the object of analysis turns to technology, one of two things tends to happen: either individual technologies are analyzed but discussed in the abstract as if they represent all technologies, or "Technology" is evoked as an explanatory variable with little thought given to what exactly "Technology" is. This is a confusing strategy. All technologies are not alike and should not be expected to be alike in their relationship with politics.

This returns the discussion to the taxonomy of international technologies, a subject raised in the first chapter. There is no readily available category of such technologies to parallel what we know to be international institutions. Something like that kind of differentiation and categorization needs to take place, however, in order to speak meaningfully about the relationship between international politics and technology. Earlier, I conjectured that internationally relevant technologies are those that shape the time and space environment of international politics. To make that supposition more concrete, the literature on the history of technology provides a useful unit of analysis—the complex sociological-technological system (or sociotechnical system for short). Most associated with Hughes's work, analysts of these systems argue that certain kinds of large-scale technologies—such as railroads, electrical power generation and distribution, automobiles, even certain kinds of weapons systems—are best seen not as distinct pieces of matter but as a complex of machines, operators, procedures and rules, and social institutions for governing them.[78]

So the railroad as a technology includes not just the wooden ties, steel track, locomotive, and rolling stock, but also the legislation that creates the funding, the timetables and schedules, the market and logistics for the procurement of supplies, coordination between state and civilian authorities, and so on. Likewise, nuclear weapons are the explosive device and the delivery vehicle, and also the command

and control system, early-warning detection systems, arms control efforts, nuclear strategy, and so on. In political terms, all these elements—material and social alike—are part of the "technology" of nuclear weapons, or railroads, or cannon and muskets, or the Internet. The only way for technologies (as simple physical matter) to be socially meaningful—to have any relevance from the perspective of social or political analysis—is when they become embedded in social systems, that is, when they are used. The concept of the sociotechnical system—the mix of material and social institutions that cohere around artifacts—is a useful way to establish an appropriate unit of analysis for the study of technology and international politics. It draws our attention to large technological systems with a complex of associated social institutions.

The second useful insight from the historians of sociotechnical systems is the importance of time—the life cycle of these systems. Complex sociotechnical systems are likely to have differing political impacts at different points in their life cycle. In the beginning, the system does not exist at all. If successfully imagined and built, the sociotechnical system evolves and spreads slowly at first before reaching a "take-off" phase after which it spreads rapidly and widely. Finally, in its mature phase, the system is widely diffused and its further spread slows and possibly even stops. This process follows the famous "S" curve long used by economists, sociologists, and cultural historians to map the spread of new products, technologies, and social and cultural trends and behaviors.[79]

The temporal element implied by the cycle of development and diffusion is the best way to tease out the political implications of sociotechnical systems. It allows us to ask important questions at each stage of the maturation process: by whose inspiration and in whose interest is a system developed and deployed; are the political effects intended or unintended, does the system satisfy existing goals of social actors and/or do they create new ones? Borrowing a page from institutional analysis, Hughes argues that complex sociotechnical systems are more flexible and amenable to social shaping when they are immature, not fully formed. As they mature, and as they diffuse more widely, they are much harder to change—just like institutions.[80] This period of rapid growth and spread is also likely to coincide with the time of greatest political impact. Eventually, the systems fall into comfortable maturity, decline, or even disuse.[81]

This framework captures the explanatory complexity of technology. In the developmental stages of a sociotechnical system's life cycle, the system is the *explanandum* and the socialpolitical world the *explanans*. Buffeted by social forces, technologies struggle to mature and are pushed first one way then another. Gradually, out of this process of social shaping, "successful" sociotechnical systems emerge. As systems mature and spread, the situation shifts and a mature sociotechnical system stands, as far as social actors are concerned, as an independent causal force. The spread of the technology has created facts on the ground: groups with an interest in the perpetuation of a particular sociotechnical system, and "sunk costs"—investments that make switching to an alternative system unpalatably expensive.[82] As systems move into decline, they become more amenable to social shaping once again. Often they are pushed out by a "superior" alternative. The automobile and the airplane have diminished the civilian and military importance of railroads. Other times the system breaks down from within, but rather than be replaced, its use is reimagined and another system coheres around it.

Joining Sociotechnical Systems and IR

The theoretical analysis of technology and politics has clear implications for how we should go about investigating actual instances of their interaction in the international arena. The lessons from the historians of complex sociotechnical systems direct our attention to the life cycles of these systems. They need to be explained and understood as a causal factor as well, which makes two different methodological demands. First, institutional and diffusion analysis is necessary to explain the emergence of new technologies. This requires that we pay attention to the institutions of innovation (scientific and technical organizations, educational systems, the state, markets, and individual entrepreneurs); to the mechanisms of transfer (emulation, theft, movement of ideas, physical transfer, etc.); and to the agents that stand at the intersection of institutions and make the transfer of technologies possible.[83] All these factors are part of the social origins and development of complex sociotechnical systems.

Second, historical specificity is necessary to explain the effects of complex sociotechnical systems. Each technological system needs to be evaluated on its own terms as each will vary in the nature of its effects.

This requires that we pay attention to the characteristics of each sociotechnical system and link those characteristics to specific social and political effects. The next section expands on these two concepts.

TECHNOLOGICAL CHANGE AND THE INTERNATIONAL SYSTEM

The examples that began this chapter—gunpowder, the newspaper, the railroad, nuclear weapons, and digital information technologies— make the case for technology as a great shaping force of international politics. But they are still just a list. They need to be brought under some more systematic rubric to sustain the argument that they are internationally important technologies in a theoretical, not just an empirical, sense. The previous discussion focused on balancing social constructionism and technological determinism by tracing the development and maturation of sociotechnical systems through their life cycle. The key to the development of a theoretically informed perspective on technology and international relations builds on this insight. Plugging sociotechnical systems and time into international relations theory suggests two ways of viewing technology from an international theoretical perspective. The first relates to technological development, the second to technology's effects.

INTERNATIONAL DEVELOPMENT OF SOCIOTECHNICAL SYSTEMS: DIFFUSION AND EMULATION

New technologies develop in an international context. It is rare for especially significant technologies[84] to develop and spread entirely within a single national context. The development and spread of ideas and technologies have never carried only as far as an international border. The diffusion process that economists and sociologists use to trace the spread of innovations in a single-society context exists in international and transnational arenas as well. Diffusion of technologies and emulation of successful practices by states and by actors in different states are permanent features of the international system.[85]

International relations theory has recognized this. Diffusion is an international systemic process, crucial to the way states develop and defend themselves, and identified as critical to theory by the dominant approaches in international politics.[86] Diffusion is also an area that is seeing substantial recent theoretical and empirical interest—and considerable new research.[87] Academic disciplines, epistemic communities, international industries, and simple copying across borders will play a role in shaping new sociotechnical systems, not just domestic interests, actors, and institutions. We have deductive reasons for thinking, in other words, that new technologies are part-international creations. The same social and political forces that shape the international institutions of technology development (science, industry, governments, etc.) will shape the technologies themselves.

This means that diffusion and emulation are more than just the mechanisms of state socialization by the international system, as neorealism would have it. Waltz is right to point to the two as fundamentally international political processes. But they are also the mechanisms of changes to the interaction capacity of international systems. They are the mechanisms by which new technologies of interaction capacity develop internationally and spread.

EFFECTS OF SOCIOTECHNICAL SYSTEMS: INTERACTION CAPACITY

There is still the problem of what counts as an internationally significant technology, or, to put the question another way, is there some characteristic shared by these technologies that can be expressed conceptually? One potential answer offers only a partial solution. Some might argue that we direct our attention to any technology—especially of a military nature—that leads to a significant increase in national power or national military advantage.[88] This approach only gives us purchase on a portion of the list of technological transformations discussed in the first chapter and fails to consider the potential international scope of others. A more satisfactory answer can be found in the concept of interaction capacity. I introduced the concept at the beginning of this chapter. I will place it in its proper theoretical context here.

The idea has its roots in Durkheim's sociology.[89] It assumes that all social systems share a characteristic: the capacity of actors in the system to interact with each other will have a profound shaping effect on the nature of that system. Technology is a very important determinant of the overall capability for interaction in any social system—including the international.[90] We can theorize a class of internationally significant technologies by investigating those that affect the interaction capacity of the international system. Technologies of communications, transportation, and violence feature prominently in this class. This is not a surprising result, but the concept gives us analytic traction on grouping them together.

Our theoretical conception of the international system can and should be modified to include a technological component. As Buzan, Jones, and Little have argued, this is a development well within the standard practice of systemic international relations theory.[91] Interaction is not a characteristic of the units but a feature of the system. Imagine two international systems identical in every important feature—both anarchical and both with an identical distribution of capabilities—but, in the first, horses and sailing vessels are the transport/communications technology matrix, and global computer networks in the second. The whole quality, scale, and intensity of international relations in the two systems will be radically different. That difference cannot be attributed to the characteristics of any given state or even group of states, but is instead a feature of the international system itself. Thus, technology—conceptualized as interaction capacity—is an important feature of the international political system and an appropriate object of study for theory of international politics.

TECHNOLOGICAL DEVELOPMENT AND THE SYSTEMIC DIMENSIONS OF TECHNOLOGY

The combination of these two factors gives insight into two important features of international politics. First, the process of diffusion and emulation gives insight into the international dimension of technological change. Second, interaction capacity gives insight into the scope and scale of the international system and the constraints of system structure. Different interaction capacities can mean that the international system will have different boundaries, will mean that the reach of international actors—to communicate, trade, conquer or be conquered—varies from one technological environment to another. Expansions in the size and scope of the international system and the size of modal units should vary with technological change. Rule of noncontiguous polities should wax and wane with enabling technologies. We should expect that changes in the destructive power of war (and with it war's frequency and/or effects) will also vary with technological change. Technological change will also likely have a "second image reversed" effect on state institutions.[92] We should expect that an increase in interaction capacity will coincide with an increase in societal penetration—in the abilities of states to extract resources from their societies.

How should we investigate the relationship between changes in interaction capacity and system transformation? This is where the above discussion on technology and politics pays off. Turning that discussion to the international sphere focuses our attention on the construction of complex sociotechnical systems with potential effects on interaction capacity, their maturation, and their (international) political effects. This in turn implies a two-step process of investigation. The first step explains the emergence of internationally relevant technologies and shows how they depend on the presence of various domestic and international factors. Technological development depends on adequate resources, appropriate institutions, and intent at the domestic level; and interstate competition and cooperation, and the diffusion mechanism at the international level. Technological development is also a political process that is indeterminate in its outcome: the nature of the technology does not mandate that a particular system develop around it. Much depends on human agency and choice, and on unintended consequences.

The second step explores the effects of technological development on interaction capacity and so on new constraints and possibilities placed on the behavior of international actors. Though there is a strong tendency to focus too much on the second, both steps are necessary. It is not just that technological developments are not predetermined. The political implications of new technologies depend on developmental paths taken and not taken. Thus, accounting for the effects of new technologies means tracing how the social (institutional, political, economic and otherwise) supports build up around them—making them technologies in a socially meaningful sense, pushing them one way and the next, and finally making them resistant to change.

CASE SELECTION AND THE PLAN OF THE BOOK

Two case studies of the railroad and the atom bomb illustrate how these two steps have combined in history. My approach to each follows the suggestions previously developed: I use path-dependent causal arguments and process-tracing methods to account for the development and diffusion of the two technologies and use the concept of interaction capacity to make sense of their international impacts. The objective of this study is to investigate the nature of the relationship between technology and system change. It is not my purpose to demonstrate that there *is* a relationship between system change and technological change. As the list of transformations that began the book shows, this is self-evident. The question is not *if* technology and system change coincide; the question is when they do, *how* do they? Does technology affect international politics as a fully formed, autonomous independent variable; or are the two mutually constituted via path-dependent processes in which technological system emerge, develop, and mature in a transnational context, and with international effects. The nature of technology makes searching for regularities and comparability between technologies foolish. A research project designed to discover why technology A (e.g., nuclear weapons) but not technology B (e.g., indoor plumbing) had substantial international impact is uninteresting. Rather, technologies must be chosen precisely because of their significance.

This intuitive understanding of the value of case selection on the dependent variable is substantiated by recent work on social science research design. When a proposed causal relationship is argued to be necessary, but not sufficient, for a given outcome, selection of cases on the independent variable accomplishes nothing. This is because no claim is being made that a given independent variable cannot be involved in other causal relationships. So in the case of my project, selecting cases on the independent variable[93] would merely show that technological change is associated with all sorts of other causal processes—say, altering patterns of suburban development. This is an interesting finding, but irrelevant to the question at hand. Even qualitative methodologists who advocate sensitivity to the problem of selection bias acknowledge that depending on the nature of the variables, the research question, and the nature of the case, selection on the dependent variable may be both unavoidable and desirable. Another scholar whose work has combined formal methods with large-N quantitative analysis has argued that some of the most interesting and valuable small-N work has come when researchers sampled on the dependent variable. This is because their focus on theoretical or empirical anomalies and carefully constructing 'most likely case' designs has produced work that is both methodologically valid and fruitful.[94]

Thus, there is no need to hew to the methodological rules imported into qualitative research from large-N quantitative studies that were designed to uncover correlative relationships between cases chosen independent of time and place. Instead, the important thing is to ask similar questions of each case to consistently apply the theoretical framework developed, and to explore the possibilities of variance within each case—process-tracing—to establish the strength of the claims being made.[95]

Case selection and research design are governed by historical-institutionalist concerns. These include periodization, locating historical conjunctures to expose the relationship between contingent events and institutionalized patterns, and the investigation of significant cases to illuminate the relationship between theory and history.[96] The railroad and the atom bomb were selected because they are the most recent examples, before the end of the cold war, of a major shift in the balance of power in the international system. The rise of Germany and the United States are the two most significant shifts in the distribution of power in the past two centuries. This is standard reasoning, familiar to any student of international relations theory. The railroad is also an important historical marker of the industrial age, and the atomic bomb of the nuclear era—common periodizations of world history since 1800. If the link between change in interaction capacity and technological change can be made for these two cases, it reinforces our understanding of these eras as distinct international systems.[97] By placing technological change at the heart of international system change for the industrial and nuclear eras, it also reinforces the value of this approach to technology and international relations.[98]

Table 2.1 above summarizes the research design and objectives for each of the two cases. They must establish two things: their respective technologies developed into complex systems in a transnational setting, and the resulting sociotechnical systems significantly altered the interaction capacity of the international system. These are analytically distinct processes. Many technologies develop in a

Table 2.1 Outline of Case Study Research Design

(Step 1) Complex sociotechnical systems are the product of transnational process	*(Step 2) Mature complex sociotechnical systems significantly alter interaction capacity of the international system*
• Process politically contested	• Change the character of power
• Outcome uncertain	• Change the feasible size of political units
• Process contingent and path-dependent (choices close off alternatives)	• Change the relative ease of noncontiguous rule
• Alternatives meaningful	• Change state–society relations

transnational setting, but not all affect interaction capacity. To equate the two is to construct a tautology in which technological change is defined as international system change. The two criteria imply several corollaries for each claim. For the development of the mature sociotechnical systems, I must show that the transnational process of technology development is characterized by contingency and the sequential closing off of alternative paths. I must show that there was political (not merely technical) contestation over the final shape and use of the technologies, that there was considerable uncertainty at the time over the eventual character of the system, that chance and contingency played a role in pushing the trajectory of the system one way and not another, and that the alternatives were meaningful.

For my argument about the interaction capacity of the international system to hold, I must show that the mature technological systems altered the interaction capacity of the international system—by substantially increasing the speed, volume, and/or intensity of the communications, transportation, and/or destructive capacities of the system—and that the change in interaction capacity effected systemic change. To satisfy the first requirement, I need to only show evidence for an increase in speed, carrying capacity, or violence potential. The second requirement is more difficult. I can show a change in the balance of power in favor of the first adopter (this is not a necessary condition, but it is present in both cases). But I also need to show a change in the nature, size, and scale of political authority and that change in interaction capacity enabled (or required—in Winner's sense)[99] international actors to organize themselves differently. This can mean one or more of several possibilities: change in interaction capacity can mean an alteration in the character of power; it can make larger political units more or less feasible; it can make intensive rule of distant, noncontiguous polities more or less likely; and it can require more or less penetration by political authorities into their own populations for resource extraction. The following chapters will fill out these claims.

CHAPTER THREE

EARLY INDUSTRIALIZATION

AND THE INDUSTRIALIZATION OF WAR

No great power wars were fought on the European subcontinent from the end of the Napoleonic Wars in 1815 to the 1860s. But during those years, significant alterations to the nature of economic production—the Industrial Revolution—transformed European economy and society, the international system, and the conduct of war.

Two centuries of expansion of the capitalist mode of production resulted in urbanization, the decline of agricultural labor, the growth of manufacturing labor, and the expansion of a market- and money-based economy. Industrialization, despite important differences, complemented the expansion of market capitalism. At the heart of the Industrial Revolution were a set of technical developments that replaced human and animate sources of power with machine and inanimate motive power.[1] This transformation took root in two, closely linked technologies: the steam engine and advanced iron (later steel) processing techniques. Iron and steam were merged in the quintessential industrial-era technology: the steam locomotive. Locomotives and iron tracks—railroads—became the transportation backbone of the Industrial Revolution. This chapter begins with a brief overview of the development of the railroad and international security. This is followed by detailed examination of the phases of technological innovation, diffusion, and maturation and the settled technology's relationship with the international system.

OVERVIEW

On the European subcontinent, the railroad enabled Germany to successfully challenge first Austria-Hungary and then France for land-based military supremacy and upset a delicate balance. Eventually Great Britain and even the United States were drawn into the conflict that righted it. Outside of Europe, the railroad enabled the European powers to extend effective colonial control over territories in Africa, the Middle East, and Asia that had previously escaped their reach. In this sense, Germany was the primary beneficiary of the railroad. Using the railroad, Germany was able to rise in power and status from a lower to top-tier European power—second, perhaps, only to Great Britain.

The railroad did more than alter the distribution of power. Because of its carrying capacity and speed, the railroad enabled an increase in the size of armies, their speed, and their geographic reach. In so doing, the railroad became not just a feature of the units, but of the international political system itself. This produced a fundamental change in what was possible in international politics. It enabled and strengthened motivation for European expansion to the rest of the world. Consequently, the interaction capacity of the system was changed, and with it the nature of security and the nature of the system itself.

Told like this, the railroad is some kind of independent autonomous force—bursting unexpectedly onto the international scene. This is an inaccurate account. Instead, the railroad emerged from a complex array of international, transnational, and domestic, economic, and political forces. This intermingling complicates the evaluation of the effects of technology on the international system. But ignoring the complexity ensures misunderstanding its relationship to political change. The development of the railroad, and its impact on international politics, is a path-dependent process. From the beginning, it was international in scope, open-ended and fluid. Later, after two conjunctures, the sociotechnical system of the railroad hardened and became more difficult to change.

The process occurred in five stages: development, diffusion, adaptation, interaction capacity change, and, finally, system change. At each stage, development was mediated by a number of domestic, international, and transnational institutions, by political conflict, and by conjunctural moments. Each institution *and* conflict and conjuncture was a necessary factor in the development of the railroad. At each stage, the railroad became more like the railroad that would help transform the international system.

The developmental path of the German railroad, as all industrial-era railroads, began in England in the 1820s. A group of English engineers, most notably Richard Trevithick, George Stephenson, James

Nasmyth, and Isambard Brunel, developed the technological bits and pieces of the railroad, including engines, locomotives, and rail and line design. By the 1820s, engineering in England was already a well-defined profession. Through professional associations, journals, and 'continuing' education in the form of technical bulletins new knowledge rapidly diffused within a carefully structured institution.

Three institutions—the engineering profession, the private business sector, and the state—form the English domestic structural context for the railroad's development. The vast sums of capital necessary to construct all but the shortest of rail lines spurred interested merchants and industrialists to create novel financing methods such as joint-stock companies that came into widespread use in the 1830s and 1840s. Right-of-way issues and disruption created by the installation of rail lines led the Parliament to impose an approval process on proposals.

At the turn of the nineteenth century, the German states were poised to make effective use of railroad technology for several reasons. The states had a growing population, a slow but steady increase in economic activity, and, most important, the example of England. Growth in manufacturing increased the need for raw materials, fuel, and a rapid, efficient and stable transportation system. The railroad was the best among several alternatives (namely, roads and canals). While not as capital rich as England, there was adequate capital available in Germany for the financing of railroads. Once demand for rail lines was present, neither a shortage of capital nor pressure to import it impeded their financing.

The states had considerable enterprise management experience as well. Unlike in England, German states invariably owned at least one armory and several coal or iron mines. While the military—the most important state actor in this story—was minimally prepared to embrace the railroad, it transformed itself, along with the railroad, as the century wore on. The Prussian General Staff had a growing tradition of highly organized staff work and involvement with technological issues. Consequently, it made the fastest and most effective embrace of rail's potential. Lastly, there were strong political incentives for certain, powerful German states to push for the establishment of a German rail network. By closely linking the territory both economically and ultimately militarily, the railroad was critical to the political unification of Germany. Unification was the avowed goal of the Prussian state (few others were at all enthusiastic) and their state managers recognized early on the importance of the railroad.

The diffusion stage—the spread of railroad technology to the Continent in general and the German states[2] in particular—was characterized by push and pull. The technological achievements of English engineers, and the tremendous economic growth they helped generate, attracted considerable attention on the Continent. Almost from the moment in 1769 when James Watt made his successful modifications to Newcomen's steam engine, he had suspicious encounters with European observers at his Birmingham workshop. Many were representatives from German states. The English overcapacity and economic slump in the 1830s and 1840s—two push factors—"transnationalized" the railroad industry further.

In the 1830s and 1840s, railroad technology was transferred to the readied recipient environment. Spying was one way the railroad technology was transferred from England to the Continent. Several legal methods of technology transfer also occurred. For example, continental representatives—of states, principalities, firms, or private individuals—traveled to England as invited observers, obtained license agreements, and imported English materials. A final method involved the recruitment—sometimes legal, sometimes not—of English workers and engineers to help in the planning and construction of continental railroads.[3]

These methods led to the successful and rapid transfer of English railroad technology to the Continent. Only a decade after the first English rail line, substantial German lines were in service. But this German railroad was not the same the Prussian army used to great effect in the latter part of the century. From the railroad's introduction in Germany to the 1866 war with Austria, paralleling the construction of a rail network was the development of a vast and complex set of plans for its wartime use. This transformation was the adaptation phase, and the form the rail network took was shaped by the politics of the German situation not any abstract. technical features or requirements of railroads.

The transformation of the English railroad to the German occurred in two phases. The first was a private-sector-led push to establish a rudimentary rail network for the German states. Largely economic forces drove this development. With little state interference, railroad entrepreneurs decided where to put the rail lines, arranged for the financing, attracted foreign and domestic engineering talent and labor, imported materials, and managed the lines once they were up and running. The state was not completely silent in this first phase. Capital did not flow as easily from the German economy into railroads as it had for the English, and private investors were unwilling to risk an investment without some guarantee of a return. In response, states guaranteed returns of between 2.5 and 3 percent in exchange for cooperation from the private lines in occasional matters of national security. The states also offered some managerial expertise. Their civil service tradition and experience running state-owned mines and munitions factories meant that states had much to offer private firms in the way of large-scale management expertise. Several Ministers of Commerce and Finance served as official or unofficial advisors to various rail lines.

State activity increased in the 1840s—the second phase of adaptation. The Prussian push for a low-tariff economic area—the *Zollverein*—had begun in 1819, but only at mid-century did the number of members expand beyond Prussia and a handful of neighboring states. Prussia saw the *Zollverein* as a preliminary step to full political unification. Mindful of the potential, and concerned about defaults on state-guaranteed rail line loans, the Prussian state began to expropriate the private rail lines in its territory and made plans to build its own lines. The state intended to gain more control over economic development, but it also had a military element. The Prussian army was beginning to take an interest in the railroads. Other states followed suit, if only to avoid falling behind the Prussian behemoth.

By the time of political unification in 1871, the desired level of railroad nationalization had been achieved and military involvement with planning and construction was in full swing. Throughout the 1850s and 1860s, close coordination with civilian ministries and the private sector helped the military to build a tightly integrated rail system that could instantly be transferred to military control in the event of war. In 1864, the Prussian General Staff established an independent section whose sole task was the coordination of men, supplies, and rail cars and lines.[4] All lines, whether private or state owned, and all locomotives and rolling stock were subject to military requisition. Line managers—state civilian and private—were expected to consult with the military on day-to-day operations to ensure an acceptable level of readiness.

Such extensive military intrusion did not meet with enthusiastic cooperation in all cases and command over the rail lines met political battles at every turn. And despite the vast amounts of military manpower and time devoted to preplanning, the actual wartime experiences with rail were far from perfect. Nonetheless, the military persisted. With each war, the system was further refined and, with each use, the interaction capacity of the international system was enhanced.

The railroad, as shaped by Germany, had a profound international impact. The railroad provided a solution to a fundamental political and security problem. Despite being one of the 'winners' of the Napoleonic Wars, Germany was divided into separate states and principalities. The Congress of Vienna created a German Confederation composed of thirty-eight separate sovereign powers, but it was a chaotic and anarchic federation. This fragmentation prevented Germany from posing a legitimate deterrent to Europe's other great, unified powers: Russia, France, Great Britain, and Austria-Hungary. But even a unified Germany would have been vulnerable, owing to geographic bad luck. Long, open, and hard-to-defend borders in both the east and west made Germany permanently vulnerable to threats from two directions and three historically hostile powers: Russia and Austria-Hungary in the east, and France in the west. The railroad made simultaneous defense of two fronts feasible. Troops could be maintained at the center and then mobilized rapidly in either direction. And, in the case of a coordinated attack on both fronts, the railroad allowed rapid redeployment from front to front—or at least rapid enough to make a potential defense on two fronts a legitimate concern for potential attackers.

The defensive value of the rail network built during the 1840s and 1850s proved to be effective for the strategic offensive as well. Prussia was drawn—or drew itself—into one war on each front in the late nineteenth century. First, in 1866, against the Austrian Empire and again in 1870 against France, the railroad network—under the careful direction of the Prussian Chief of the General Staff Helmuth von Moltke and his subordinates—quickly moved Prussian troops to the fronts. The railroads' role was critical. Moltke devised a strategy of movement and concentration on the battlefield that depended on the rail's ability to concentrate soldiers coming rapidly from many directions. The results of the two wars were unassailable. The success of the Prussian armies and their coordination with the other German states paved the road to political unification. Moreover, the military successes against what were thought to be the two strongest armies in Europe instantly transformed Germany into a great power.

Rail's impact was not confined to Germany and spread to every corner of the international system. The other continental nations devised plans for using their rail networks for military purposes. An influential interpretation of the World War I blames the outbreak of the war in part on the rigid mobilization plans of the powers involved.[5] Technical features of railroads (tracks, once laid, cannot be moved), along with the rigid timetables the antagonists developed, made it all but impossible to stop mobilization once it began. There can be no doubt that by the turn of the century, the railroad was a central feature of European security.

The railroad's effects were not confined to the European continent. They were an important factor in economic integration throughout the developing world. They played an important role in the extension of European colonialism. Railroads opened up the interiors of India, China, and Africa to economic exploitation. By providing rapid and relatively safe access to the interior, they offered an effective tool for military subjugation. By bringing new areas under European domination or influence, the railroad expanded the international system.

THE CREATION OF A COMPLEX SOCIOTECHNICAL SYSTEM: THE RAILROAD

DEVELOPER INSTITUTIONAL ENVIRONMENT: ENGLAND AND EARLY INDUSTRIALIZATION

The emergence of the modern railroad must be understood within the context of English industrialization. Industrialization provided both the impetus for cheaper and bigger transportation systems and the capital and expertise to build them. Political and economic conflict accompanied the development of the English rail network at every step, and the actions of the state were critical to shaping the final English system.

Demand

Demand for railroads in England came in two phases. The first was generated by frustration with existing transport systems that produced a willingness to innovate. The second was created by railways themselves. Once in operation in the 1830s, the railways produced cost savings that generated demand, setting in motion a virtuous circle of capacity and demand increases. A few decades earlier, a series of inventions in the textile sector mechanized the production of wool and cotton cloth. The cost savings realized by the cumulative effect of these innovations (estimates for some manufacturing procedures place the savings at several hundred times over that when done by hand) led to substantial increases in productivity. Demand for the produce of the reconstituted industry drove a spectacular economic expansion and additional technical innovation in what quickly became a self-perpetuating cycle.[6]

Textile mills were small, as was the capital necessary to absorb the new innovations.[7] But the success of the textile industry drove demand for machinery, which helped drive the second phase of industrialization—iron and steel. The substitution of coal for wood in the late eighteenth century helped drop the price of inputs needed in the production of iron. A series of technical innovations in the industry—most important Henry Cort's puddling and rolling technique developed in 1783 and 1784—sped production and reduced costs.[8] The availability of cheaper iron spurred mechanization in industries, such as textiles, which only increased the demand for coal—the most important input after ore in the manufacture of iron.[9]

Moving coal from the mines to manufacturing centers, however, severely taxed the existing transport systems. Demand spurred a canal-building boom in the last quarter of the century, but it was insufficient.[10] While coal was by far the largest freight on canals, neither canal nor road contractors built ahead of demand. They remained strictly regional and small-scale, and Parliament-granted monopolies allowed canal operators to ignore demands for increased capacity and charge what they liked for their services.[11] Despite demand, Parliament approved only three new canals between 1795 and 1825.[12] This provided an economic and political opening for a transport alternative.

The steam engine was the missing ingredient for railroads to challenge canals. Newcomen engines had been used in mines to pump water since the early eighteenth century, but when James Watt introduced the separate condenser in 1776—and increased the efficiency of the engine by a factor of four—it became practical to use the steam engine in a variety of applications.[13] Frustration with the canal service led investors in the first railway, the Stockton & Darlington, to experiment with a steam-powered railroad in 1821, even though George Stephenson's early designs were still slower (12.5 miles per hour under load) than horses.[14]

The most dramatic moment in English rail history came in October 1829 and resolved the design issues, though not entirely on technical merit. Over the course of a week, in a contest overseen by the directors of the (as yet unbuilt) Liverpool & Manchester railroad,[15] various locomotive designs competed for a prize of £500. The winner, George Stephenson's *Rocket* was a steam-powered locomotive and its victory was pivotal in the development of rail transportation. It was as much a triumph of public relations as it was evidence of the *Rocket's* technical superiority to stationary steam engines (the motive technology for San Francisco's cable cars). The locomotive's performance was still inadequate for rail-line use. Nevertheless, various competing technologies for propelling rail cars fell by the wayside.[16]

The canal operators moved to counter the threat. They worked on two fronts. Some made long-needed improvements to their existing stock of canals—such as the 1824–1827 construction of a new tunnel by the Trent & Mersey.[17] They also waged a preemptive attack on the railways in anticipation of their success. One example, a pamphlet entitled *Observations on Railways with Locomotive High-pressure Steam Engines*, which appeared in March 1825, attacked railways from multiple sides: the demand for iron would drive up the price of coal, iron rails would crack in frost, need for water would cause the locomotives to stop frequently, the rails would trap horses at crossings where they would be run over by the locomotives, and engine explosions would be frequent.[18]

Parliament allowed turnpike operators to kill the steam carriage through a system of punitive tolls in 1832, but their more important efforts against rail were ineffective.[19] The Stockton & Darlington was an immediate success, turning a profit in its first year. Share dividends paid 2.5 percent in 1825 and crossed the 10 percent barrier in 1835. Others quickly followed.[20] Railway line mileage jumped dramatically in the first years. Growth rates averaged more than 20 percent per year for the first twenty years. By 1845, there were nearly 4,000 miles of track in England and Wales.[21] Railroads generated cost savings that greatly exceeded other forms of transportation. One recent estimate puts the overall savings at between 15 and 20 percent of national income for the years 1830 to 1870.[22] Thus, the shortcomings of existing transport systems created powerful incentives for coal mining and other commercial interests to experiment aggressively with an unproven and risky new technology.

Capital

The textile factories, and even the iron foundries of the early Industrial Revolution, had a relatively low demand for capital. The inventions and new methods that revolutionized their production did not require huge investments. Small shop owners with little access to investment capital beyond their own savings undertook the improvements. Railroads were another matter. The capital requirements to build a railway easily surpassed other large infrastructure projects such as canals and roads. In fact, the steam locomotive had been invented and shown to be practical as early as 1804, but its large capital cost delayed construction until later in the century.[23] Figure 3.1 gives a graphic picture of capital expenditures on railways and other forms of transport. It shows that the English economy had no trouble raising the capital necessary to fund the railroads.

Railroad financing did not pull capital away from other transport systems. Investment in turnpikes, roads, and canals held steady throughout the most intense periods of railway building, and, for canals between 1825 and 1833, even managed a slight boom in investment. Once the Stockton & Darlington demonstrated that they could be managed profitably, the flood of capital into railroad investments was enormous. From the 1830s through 1843, with the exception of a slight boom in the years 1836 through 1841, there was a steady but unspectacular increase in railroad investment. The constraint was not the availability of capital, but the slow pace of Parliament's approval of railway sanctions and shortages of surveyors and other skilled workers.[24] The period from 1844 to 1854 was another matter. Investment and speculation were so intense it earned the label "railway mania." Between 1845 and 1847, Parliament considered 909 bills for proposed railway lines. They approved 330 of them, sanctioning 5,700 miles of proposed track at a total capital cost of £167.6 million (that amount

Figure 3.1
Capital Expenditures on British Transport Systems: 1800–1850.

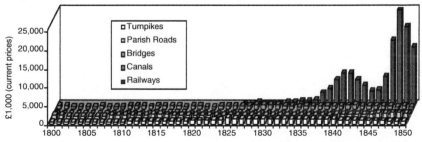

Information source: Gary Hawke and Jim Higgins (1983), "Britain," in Patrick O'Brien, ed., *Railways and the Economic Development of Western Europe, 1830–1914* (New York: St. Martin's), 174–75.

would grow to £230 million by 1849).[25] In historical perspective, the amount of capital raised for the construction of English railways was staggering. The German experience was not as swift or smooth.

Engineers

The railroads were a rich combination of engineering innovations. They brought together steam engine technology, iron rail manufacture, surveying, bridge building, and machine parts and tools. The railroad embodied the accumulated knowledge of the Industrial Revolution. Since the beginning of the eighteenth century, British engineers had been world leaders in the development of these technologies and skills. They put the parts together to form the railway system— in some cases the same ones who had pioneered the development of the inputs in the first place. What explains their achievement? The answer is a combination of two processes: invention and innovation, and diffusion within the national market. Engineering shops were at the center of both, linked by an apprentice system and professional engineering associations.

The technological achievements of the early Industrial Revolution owed little to scientific discovery. Innovations resulted from practical solutions to existing problems rather than the application of abstract principles.[26] These innovations and new knowledge were efficiently disseminated throughout the engineering profession—a profession that was highly structured, trained its practitioners carefully, and policed its members' behavior.

Engineering was not a large profession. One estimate places the number of practicing engineers in 1850 at less than 1,000.[27] But every major city and important industrial area (such as coal mining and iron deposits) had at least one and usually several competing shops. Engineers generated the Industrial Revolution from the ground level. Revolutionary new machinery was made to order—the antithesis of mass production.

A handful of prestigious shops dominated the profession. They were differentiated by region or area of specialization and functioned like universities. A single dominant figure, a father-and-son team, or a small number of partners controlled the sorts of projects pursued and the course of technological innovation. In apprentice programs, they also trained the best of the next generation of engineers who would found their own shops.

A few prominent figures trained entire cohorts. For example, the Manchester shop of Henry Maudslay, founded in 1797, made several important contributions to machine tools and steam engines.[28] The shop, a "nursery" for talent, had as apprentices three men who were among the most renowned engineers of the mid-nineteenth century: James Nasmyth, Richard Roberts, and Joseph Whitworth.[29] Samuel Smiles, the biographer of many British engineers, used a university analogy to describe their role, "Indeed it may be said that what Oxford and Cambridge are in letters, workshops such as Maudslay's and Penn's are in mechanics. Nor can Oxford and Cambridge men be prouder of their connection with their respective colleges than mechanics such as Whitworth, Nasmyth, Roberts, Muir, and Lewis are of their connection with the school of Maudslay."[30] A constant stream of apprentices and visitors through Watt's Birmingham shop sought to learn, buy, or steal the secrets of his steam engine.[31] He and his partner Matthew Boulton trained their sons to succeed them, as did George Stephenson who is often credited with inventing the steam locomotive. As the business grew in the late 1800s, "an ever-increasing number of men passed through the Soho works and went out skilled engineers."[32]

Many other shops trained apprentices. Biographies of engineers show them holding posts in London, then migrating to the industrial north (Richard Roberts is an example), or migrating from one industrial area to another in the north and Midlands. Newcastle, Birmingham, Manchester, and small towns in the surrounding areas (as well as coal fields) were all important engineering centers and attracted aspiring engineers. The apprenticeship system enabled engineers and innovations to circulate with fluidity and speed.[33] Given the local, pragmatic, and ad hoc quality of innovation in the early industrial era, the institution of the shop was crucial to their dissemination and standardization.[34]

Engineering associations provided a more organized method of technology circulation. The oldest, the Society of Civil Engineers (SCE), held its first meeting in 1771. The SCE reflected founder John Smeaton's experience as a Fellow of the Royal Society, but extended the Society's mission by focusing on professional instruction and collaboration. A group of young engineers founded a breakaway organization, the Institution of Civil Engineers (ICE) in 1818.[35] At about the same time, engineering journalism emerged with the founding of the *Mechanics Magazine* in 1823—a publication of London publisher Knight & Lacey.[36] The ICE was very successful, and, by 1828, almost all senior engineers belonged. Yet another revolt, this time by railroad engineers, led to the founding in 1847 of the Institution of Mechanical Engineers with George Stephenson as its first president.[37] As the engineering profession grew and specialized, the number of associations proliferated until there were seventeen in 1914.[38]

Even when sharp disagreements broke out between rival specializations, the institutions remained devoted to the discussion of technical and educational issues. From its inception, the ICE banned the discussion of politics and even wage or salary issues. Other associations followed suit. Institution activities were dominated by the publication of periodicals and administration of educational programs for both younger and well-established engineers.[39] In this way, the association contributed to the development of the railroad. For example, in the early 1830s, Richard Roberts, a man with almost no formal education but extensive practical engineering knowledge, presented a paper to the Manchester Mechanics' Institute that solved a locomotive friction problem that had been under discussion in scientific journals.[40] Similarly, Joseph Whitworth used the ICE and IME in his successful campaign to have uniform standards of accuracy and interchangeability in machine tools accepted by the profession.[41]

The twin mechanisms—circulation of young engineers through apprenticeship programs and dissemination of new knowledge through association activities—gave engineers rapid access to current information on new techniques and inventions.[42] Putting together the sociotechnical system of the railroad required the efficient coordination of many engineering specializations and communication of innovations. The institutions of the engineering profession—apprenticeships, labor circulation, and knowledge diffusion—served this purpose.

Most of the major technological developments for the railroad were in place by 1840; only the process of assembling the system and steady improvements to existing technology remained.[43] Thus, railroad materials began making their way to Germany in the mid- to late 1830s in a relatively finished state. The basic technological form of the railroad had been set: high-pressure steam engine, locomotive, iron (later steel) rails, flanged wheels, and tentative agreement on the proper gauge.

The Role of the State

Engineer–builders such as George Stephenson and large contractors such as Isambard Brunel and Thomas Brassey did most of the work of system construction. They chose engine, locomotive, and rail and track design; they selected routes, tunnel and bridge design; and they chose contractors and subcontractors for the manufacture of engines, parts, rolling stock, and the host of other components that went into laying a railroad. However, they played only a technical role in the consideration of routes. Railroad entrepreneurs, investors, and, to a lesser degree, the state carried out the geographic knitting together of England and Wales by railways.

The state's primary involvement in railways was limited to three areas: safety regulation, rate regulation for the poor, and the mediation of property disputes. In the safety realm, the state investigated accidents and certified new lines.[44] It recommended brakes on all passenger trains and publicized railway company misconduct when it was the cause of accidents. The companies were self-regulated in other safety matters. Through the Railway Clearing House—which was a kind of private regulatory board—uniform signaling standards and collision prevention measures were established in the 1840s.[45]

The most significant role for government was in the resolution of property rights disputes. In 1822, Parliament was called on to approve the concession for the first line linking Manchester and Liverpool and to resolve disputes between the railroad promoters and landowners along the proposed route. The concession gave the railroad company the right to acquire needed land, and limited liability for accident or business failure.[46] A Parliament decision in 1840 that railroads were almost always in the public interest gave the railways virtually free rein to build as they wished (Parliament had used a similar tactic to encourage road and canal construction in the eighteenth century). State action forced the sale of land to railway interests and guaranteed the companies a monopoly of transport in their particular region. The state's methods were indirect, but there is no question that the policies amounted to aggressive promotion of the construction of a national railway network.[47]

The history of English state activity supports two general observations about the political nature of the technological development of the railroad. First, it provides a contrast with the German case. The German states were far more activist in their promotion of the railways and had a much more significant role shaping the development of the network. Once it had decided on its priorities, the English state played an important role in encouraging railroad investment, but its indirect methods and general attitude to the private sector gave it little or no influence in shaping the development of the network. The German rail network had a different form and purpose than that of the English. The movement of the railroad from England to Germany resulted in the construction of a railroad system on German terms to meet German needs.

Second, examination of the state's role reveals the political and institutional aspects of technology. The railroad in England, as in Germany, was a technological system that emerged from a technical-political process. In this section three main factors were identified to explain the emergence of the technical side of the steam-powered railroad—adequate demand, adequate capital, and an adequately institutionalized engineering profession. Various political factors that shaped the system's evolution were also identified: fights between canal owners and railroad promoters, state promotion, and arguments within the engineering community over the appropriate technical path to follow. Together, these provide an institutional explanation for the emergence of the railroad in England in the early nineteenth century.

RECIPIENT ENVIRONMENT: GERMANY AND INDUSTRIALIZATION

The first modern English railway opened in 1825. The first German railway, traveling the 6-kilometer distance from Nuremberg to Fürth, began service in 1835. Various plans for public railway lines were proposed to the Prussian, Bavarian, and Westphalian state economic ministries and diets beginning in 1828.[48] England—a small, island country with plenty of capital and a large head start in the industrialization process—was the home of the railway and its presence there seemed almost natural. But Germany, the prototypical late industrializer, was considerably poorer, politically fragmented, and had barely begun to industrialize.[49] How can we accout for its ability to achieve such rapid diffusion of this large and complex technology?

Germany, Prussia especially, was a ready recipient environment for railway technology for four reasons. First, though far behind England, Germany had begun to industrialize. Industrialization was a strategic (and economic) necessity for the European powers because of the massive wealth it generated for England. The gap between England and the later European industrializers was not great—paling in comparison to that which exists between Western industrialized economies and most of the underdeveloped world today. But because of the competitive nature of the international system, falling behind was not an option.

Second, the railroad answered Germany's special geostrategic and geoeconomic needs. Germany was fragmented both economically and politically. The states, kingdoms, grand duchies, duchies, principalities, and free cities that made up greater Germany each had their own tariff and customs barriers, guild and workshop laws, and economic development plans. Unlike England, great distances and several international borders often separated centers of raw materials, production, and consumption. The railroad could forge a larger economic market by bringing these locales closer together and by imposing a uniform system of transport. It could catalyze political unification. The creation of a larger market and unified polity would allow Germany to compete more effectively in European international affairs. These potential effects were not lost on astute observers in Germany in the 1830s, least of all the Prussians.[50]

Third, the various German states, not just Prussia, had considerable administrative capacity and economic management experience. In England, Parliament was asked to do little beyond granting extraordinary property rights-of-way and monopoly guarantees to the railway companies. In Germany, the earliest lines were built by private entrepreneurs, but the states were involved from the beginning in guaranteeing investment returns, chartering lines, and enforcing coordination and other equally aggressive activities. This state expertise was the result of German geopolitics. Early in the eighteenth century, most of the larger states had taken over their advanced manufacturing bases—coal and iron-ore mining, iron forging, and armaments manufacture—for military and security purposes. With potential enemies all around, and the perpetual threat of the French and the Austrians, autarky, or mercantilism, was thought the best policy. As the nineteenth century began, the larger German states owned most of the region's mining, metallurgical, and munitions interests and had been running them for nearly a century.

Fourth, the Germans had long experience obtaining industrial technology from England. There were well-worn paths connecting English workshops to German mines, forges, and manufactories. When Watt's steam engine first appeared in the 1770s, German observers arrived in numbers. Most were state employees, such as the manager of a state-owned coal mine, but some were private individuals traveling on state grants. The foreign visitors roamed the entire country in search of the latest in steam engine, iron-forging, and machine tool technology. Sometimes plans were obtained legally (the export of machinery from England was illegal until 1842), but many were stolen with the help of local workers.[51] A final and much used strategy of German industrial spies was "to entice into their employ skilled English artisans."[52] The thefts, copies, licensing, and purchases of the components of railroad construction and operation—especially steam engines, engineering and machine tools, and iron production techniques—were used to build an indigenous railroad industry. After an initial period of dependence on British imports for rail and locomotives, domestically produced components replaced foreign purchases.

In sum, these four factors gave Germany the capacity, need, experience, and opportunity to acquire the railroad from England. A final element was the work of railway advocates including Friedrich List, Ludolf Camphausen, Friedrich Harkort, David Hansemann, and August van der Heydt. While List's interest in railroads began during an 1824 visit to England, all these men were strong railway advocates in the late 1820s and early 1830s.[53] Part business opportunists and part visionaries, their contributions were vital to the railroad enterprise in Germany.

Early Industrialization

Germany was not an industrial powerhouse in the 1820s. It had a few infant industries and a market large enough to support the second, heavy industrial, phase of industrialization. But in the mid- to late eighteenth century, severe political fragmentation and small, disconnected markets severely constrained economic growth.[54] Small and disconnected concentrations of early industrial activity—primarily mining and other state-run enterprises—were surrounded by a rural landscape substantially poorer than its English counterpart.[55]

By 1815, the Napoleonic Wars and the Continental System had split the economies of the Lower Rhine, Saxony, and Westphalia from the rest of Germany behind a wall of tariffs, and the strains of the war weakened economic health. The manufactories inside the Continental System were protected from British imports, but those outside struggled unsuccessfully to keep their wartime economies vibrant. Deflationary policies and huge public debt resulted.[56] After the wars ended, a massive dumping of British manufactures on the continent erased whatever advantage the protected principalities had gained and deindustrialized the region.[57]

The gap between the continent and British industrialization increased because the Continental System had delayed the diffusion of British machines and techniques.[58] But the wars had generated powerful reform impulses. During the wars, government and economic practices, territorial boundaries, and noble privileges came under scrutiny because it was believed they hindered the war effort.[59] With Prussia leading the way, urban guilds and rural production were reformed, industry liberalized, the serfs emancipated, and the military and education reformed. These last two were especially important. All together, these changes set the region on the path to steady and sustained economic growth.[60]

Opinions on the exact moment of German 'takeoff' vary. Some claim the 1830s, others the 1850s, and still others argue a marked increase in industrial growth rates did not appear until the 1880s or 1890s.[61] A strong argument has been made for a qualitative takeoff in the 1830s. The establishment of the Zollverein customs union and the beginnings of the railroad network laid the groundwork for a national market and generated strong demand for heavy industrial products.[62] But there is no obvious quantitative takeoff. Instead, the German economy enjoyed slow, steady industrial growth from the late eighteenth century, with a pause for the Napoleonic wars, until the strong growth of the electrical and chemical industries in the late nineteenth century.[63] This suggests that industrialization was driven more by institutional changes such as the post-Jena reforms than by the creation of strong demand for industrial products.

With the wars over and reform under way, finance and technology from abroad (especially from England) triggered a transformation of the German economy.[64] New techniques such as the application of steam technology to coal and iron production gradually fed demand in adjacent sectors. Both industries had been in existence for more than a century, but it was the application of new technologies that transformed them.[65]

In Germany, the steam engine was much more closely linked with heavy industry than in England, where it was used more frequently in textile mills.[66] Geheimrat Gansauge, a Prussian official, imported the first engine from England in 1770s for the coal mine at Altenweddingen near Magdeburg. The Germans lacked the skills to build the engines themselves until the 1820s when a plan for import-substitution was implemented. Friedrich Harkort established a manufactory in Westphalia in this decade based on Watt's designs. He had studied with James Cockerill in Liège and, before opening his shop, traveled to England where he recruited a handful of workers, two English engineers, and purchased a steam engine and other machinery. The Department of Commerce and Industry of the Prussian Finance Ministry sent the young engineer F. A. J. Egells to England as a preliminary to the state-subsidized founding of his Berlin foundry and machine shop in 1821.[67]

The steam engine was critical to productivity gains in mining and metallurgy, but those industries did not generate much demand. Coal output increased slowly from 1815 to 1850. Growth in iron production needed railroads.[68] In 1843, only 10.2 percent of the iron stock on Prussian railroads was domestically produced and 88.1 percent was imported from Britain. In 1853, the numbers were 48.4 percent and 51.0 percent, respectively.[69] In other words, the railroad was crucial to German industrialization.

Geographic Need

The geography of industrial production and the division of greater Germany into multiple sovereign territories and economic regions caused enormous difficulties. Economically, the separation of raw materials, production, and consumption centers by large distances, the proliferation of tariffs, systems of weights and measures, and regional transport systems all hampered economic growth and the creation of a large, uniform German market.[70] The fragmentation of Germany was a direct result of geopolitical failure. To the Prussians, the peace at Jena imposed a humiliating collaborative governance scheme with the Austrians. Divided Germany was a symbol of Prussian defeat and a source of weakness.

Both political and economic problems were apparent to rail advocates. They were composed of visionary journalists like List, budding industrialists such as Harkort and van der Heydt, and civil servants such as Prussian Finance Minister Friedrich von Motz. These men believed rail could provide political and economic unification. In proposals to state diets and ministries, they stressed the importance of a national German network to obtain the full benefits from rail, and to unify Germany. Those most engaged in bringing the railroad to Germany were conscious supporters of its likely political and economic implications.[71]

Even before the railroad, there were some attempts to create a larger domestic market. After 1815, Prussia established a customs union that emulated Napoleon's Continental System. The *Zollverein*, founded in 1834 by Hesse, East and West Prussia, Bavaria, Württenberg, Thuringia, Leipzig, Dresden, Breslau, and much of the Rhineland, was a low-tariff zone. Baden and Hannover joined in 1835 and Frankfurt-am-Main in 1836, completing a market unbroken by intervening nonmember states. It was the only nineteenth-century customs union in Europe that required its members to relinquish some sovereignty.[72]

Overall, the *Zollverein* failed to adequately encourage economic integration. Markets remained largely local until the rail network spread. The first railroads in the most developed areas encouraged exports at first. There was not a truly national domestic market until the 1850s.[73] The railroad's achievement at (political and economic) unification was not an unintended consequence of its development but an integral part of the vision and design of those most active in the creation of the system.

State Administrative Capacity

Germany suffered from a limited supply of capital, few large investments reliable enough to attract private funds, and a tiny entrepreneurial class.[74] The states spent much of the seventeenth and eighteenth centuries engaged in "extensive and costly programmes of industrial development,"[75] which, while mostly money-losers, gave them unmatched experience and resources. They owned land, mines, production facilities, central banks, post offices, nationalized industries, and technical and mining colleges.[76] Despite state involvement being frequently on its own terms wasteful and misdirected, it was an important resource to German industrialization in general and to the building of a railroad network in particular.[77]

Prussia was the most active. The state encouraged businessmen, noblemen, and local governments to set up enterprises in textiles, glass, chemicals, and metals. The Prussian program was, given its narrow political goals, a success. By the end of Frederick I's reign in 1786, Prussia was nearly self-sufficient in four targeted industries. State activity continued unabated into the nineteenth century.[78] The state nationalized a series of mineral deposits in Silesia and created several large, state-run mining concerns. The Prussian Overseas Trading Corporation (or *Seehandlung*) was an important program of state management and subsidies for private industry that operated throughout the eighteenth and early nineteenth centuries.[79]

The German states were not drawn to these enterprises out of strong interest in industrial progress. In Prussia, the Junkers, the powerful noble-agricultural class, opposed industry. The states' interests were political. Their geopolitical position was precarious and the perceived need to pursue advances in military hardware led them to munitions manufacture, foundries, and mines. Geopolitical motivations drew the German states to industrial activity.[80]

The balance between public and private shifted away from the states by the 1840s, but in the 1820s and 1830s state enterprises were still an important presence in the economy. Finding adequate capital was still difficult, and private entrepreneurs themselves argued that public investment was necessary to spur industrial development. Organizational skills and technological expertise made the civil service as valuable as any financial guarantees.[81] The next section will show how useful state expertise was in the planning and construction of the railways. The management and technical training of German civil servants facilitated the transfer of rail technology from England, technical expertise in iron production aided the substitution of domestic for British iron, and the machine-tool skills accumulated in state armaments factories helped overcome numerous engineering problems in the construction of rails, locomotives, and rolling stock.[82] State officials intervened, successfully, in the management of new railroads. Joseph Schumpeter gives credit to the private builders of the railroads, but claims, with slight hyperbole, that civil servants, "supremely efficient, quite above temptation, entirely independent of politics, did much, in many ways besides exerting discretion in charting, to prune promotion, to sober finance, and to steady advance."[83] State officials at the time expressed similar views. Prussian Finance Minister and Director of the *Seehandlung* von Rother wrote in one of his reports from the 1840s that "I have shown how false is the familiar cry that a civil servant cannot compare with the private citizen when it comes to running an industrial enterprise successfully."[84]

Espionage

The German states were used to stealing technology from England. Beginning in the 1750s, German states actively promoted both industrial espionage and legal methods of technology transfer. Some private entrepreneurs and engineers undertook the transfer tasks themselves, but the expense of lengthy and repeated trips was state-subsidized. The Prussian state even had an administrative branch, the Technical Industrial Committee, to coordinate such trips.[85] There were hundreds of trips made between 1780 and 1830. According to one source, top officers and deputies of the Prussian Department of Mines and Ironworks took eight separate trips (sometimes lasting many months). German visitors were seemingly everywhere.[86]

From the moment word of marvelous new English technologies reached Germany, the states made a concerted effort to acquire them.[87] The Prussian mining official Friedrich Wilhelm Graf von Reden, whose official role was special industrial commissar for Silesia, visited England in 1786–1787 and carefully observed Henry Cort's puddling and rolling technique for processing iron. The patents for Cort's invention were issued in 1783 and 1784, and, shortly after Reden's return, the technique was successfully introduced into the Silesian foundries. On a later trip in 1789, Reden obtained one of the first steam engines for Germany from the engineer John Wilkinson—a machine built in violation of Watt's patents.[88]

English attempts to prevent industrial espionage failed. A 1750 law forbade the export of machinery and the emigration of skilled workers, and imposed penalties on any who sought to induce or help them leave the country. The laws against emigration remained in force until 1825 and those governing the export of manufacturing machinery until 1842.[89] Yet those Englishmen who did venture abroad played a very important role in Germany's industrialization and trained the next generation of German workmen and engineers. Sometimes the visiting English were simply sources of technology. In 1786, Samuel Homfray of the Penydarran Ironworks in Glamorgan visited von Reden in Silesia and gave him a steam pumping engine. Three years later, at Reden's request, William Wilkinson helped introduce lead-smelting with coke to the Silesian Tarnowitz foundry.[90]

Other visitors fulfilled a pedagogical role. Friedrich Harkort, the great Westphalian industrialist and locomotive manufacturer, found the Englishmen he imported foul-tempered, ill behaved, and unreliable, but necessary.[91] He awaited the day when all their lessons had been learned and "the Englishmen might all be kicked out."[92] The Germans were at first slow to absorb the new techniques, but after the Napoleonic Wars, when the level of education and technical sophistication had improved in Germany, the substitution of local expertise was rapid.

Their hard-won experience in obtaining English technology in the eighteenth century was repeated in the nineteenth when interest in railways gained momentum. In 1826 and 1827, two Prussian mining engineers, Carl von Oeynhausen and Heinrich von Dechen, visited England to inspect the railways for possible use in Prussian mines. They observed the Stockton & Darlington Railway and paid a visit to George Stephenson's locomotive works in Newcastle and a steam-engine shop in Leeds.[93] Peter Beuth, then Director of the Department for Commerce and Industry in the Prussian Finance Ministry, visited England in 1826 to observe the railways and bring back recommendations for Prussian plans.[94]

Summary

These four factors—early industrialization, the incentives generated by German political and economic geography, state technical expertise, and state-aided technology transfer—prepared the ground for the arrival of railroad technology. They explain the desire of German entrepreneurs, state officials, and engineers to acquire English railways and their successful and rapid adaptation of the technology. Early industrialization gave Germany the general capacity to build railways, its economic and political geography provided need and incentive, state management expertise supplied the technique and experience to acquire and adapt, and the technology transfer from England provided source and opportunity. The four factors also show the political underpinnings of technological development and the importance of the institutional framework (a political factor as well). Geopolitical dynamics in particular were critical to the reception of the railroad in Germany, yet the success of that reception cannot be explained without reference to the institutional expertise built up in the German states. The next section completes the cycle of invention, development, diffusion, and adaptation by detailing the transfer and adaptation of rail technology to Germany.

DIFFUSION AND CHANGE

The railroad was the single most important factor in German industrialization.[95] Politically, the railroads were vital to the two late-century wars and to unification. Railroad-led industrialization and nation-building were the same process.[96] Diffusion and adaptation are the final phases of the development of the sociotechnical system. The diffusion phase moves the English rail system to a new institutional setting with new political and economic imperatives. The adaptation phase transforms the English system into the German system and begins the maturation process of the railroad into a component of the interaction capacity of the international system. My analysis of these phases has four sections. The first section discusses the causes of technology transfer from England. Two sets of factors—one pushing English machinery, iron, and engineers to Germany and another generating demand for rail in Germany—are identified. Both were driven by geopolitical imperatives as well as narrow economic interest. The second section details the mechanisms of diffusion. They include observation and theft; imports of iron rail, locomotives, wagons, and machine tools; and English visitors. The third section covers civilian adaptation of rail technology and spans two periods of railway building. The first, from the 1820s to 1848, was characterized by private-sector construction and public-private and public-public wrangling over the direction and method of that construction. The second, from 1848 to roughly 1866, is characterized by increased state intervention—beginning just after the failed 1848 revolution with intensified public-private cooperation and ending with nationalization of the rail network in the 1850s and 1860s. The fourth section covers the same time period as the third, but from the military's perspective. It details the strategic considerations that went into the network's planning and construction and the military's involvement with railroads up through the 1848 revolution.

Diffusion was a geopolitical process as much as it was an economic one. Britain was creating a new global political economy dominated by the British economy and knitting together much of the world in supply, production, and consumption of industrial manufactures. For the later industrializers, especially France, Germany, and Russia, the pursuit of British technology had an explicit strategic element. Falling behind in the race to industrialize meant risking military defeat or loss of influence.

The process of adaptation in Germany was also deeply political. There were three principal actors: private railroad entrepreneurs, state managers, and the military. Each had debates within their own circles and with the others about the wisdom and form of the rail network. The military was interested in the geostrategic dimensions of rail. Private entrepreneurs wanted the freedom to build wherever and whenever they wished. Civilian state officials battled with themselves and the private sector over rationalization, nationalization, and centralization. For all three actors, institutional histories and their attitudes and capabilities are critical to understanding how the actors behaved and the shape of the network that emerged.[97]

The Causes of Technology Transfer

The causes of the diffusion of railroad technology can be divided into 'push' reasons that explain the exit of technology, plans, and technicians from Britain, and 'pull' reasons that explain their movement into Germany.

Several factors contributed to pushing rail technology from Britain to the Continent. The oversupply of engineers in Britain grew as the century wore on. But even in the 1830s and 1840s, when the big burst of railway building in Germany took place, the opportunities abroad frequently outshone those at home, and emigration was common.[98] A second, more significant push factor was productive overcapacity both in railway construction and locomotive manufacture. The two biggest railway construction firms in Britain, Brassey and Peto & Betts, accumulated substantial idle capacity and began to look abroad even in the 1830s for railway projects.[99] Likewise, the biggest British locomotive manufacturers, Robert Stephenson & Co. and Sharp Roberts, welcomed the overseas business that emerged in the late 1830s.

British push factors explain the supply of rail technology, but local interests in Germany in the 1830s were more decisive in determining the pace and nature of railway development. Private entrepreneurs and a handful of interested state managers played central roles. They were driven by simple economic need. As early as 1825, Friedrich Harkort, a Rhineland industrialist, proposed railways along the right bank of the Rhine in western Prussia. He wanted to reduce the cost of moving coal from the Ruhr to the industrial areas in the Rhineland and avoid burdensome Dutch river tolls at the mouth of the Rhine. In 1833, Ludolf Camphausen, a Köln-based corn merchant, proposed a railway from Köln to Antwerp for similar reasons.[100]

State actors, as stewards of the national economy, were motivated to ensure long-term economic growth. The Prussian Finance Minister, Friedrich von Motz, was convinced of the importance of rail for Germany's future after hearing the reports of Peter Beuth and Oeynhausen and Dechen (see earlier). He suggested to the King in

1827 that a railway be built between Minden and Lippstadt in Westphalia. Beuth, director of the Department of Commerce and Industry within the Ministry of Finance and otherwise a rail skeptic, enthusiastically encouraged development of a railroad connecting Ruhr coalfields with textile mills in the Barmen–Elberfeld area to create a regional textile center strong enough to fend off the British.[101]

Rail's perceived political and strategic possibilities were a final factor pulling it from Britain. Its advocates were the military, industrialists such as Harkort and Camphausen (who would always slip a strategic rationale into any proposal), and crusading intellectuals and journalists such as Friedrich List. List was a businessman, government official, and investor, but his greatest success came as a journalist and pamphleteer. From the 1820s to his death in 1846, he was a relentless rail advocate who submitted plan after plan to any German government that would accept them. He correctly foresaw that railroads would help cement German unification, and also would be a greater strategic benefit to Germany than any other European power. For entrepreneurial railway advocates such as Harkort and Camphausen, strategic considerations were central to their vision of railroad's future. There was a natural affinity between grand plans for economic growth and political unification, and the strongest proponents of railroads also tended to be passionate about German unity.[102]

The military itself was not blind to the railroad's promise, though in the 1830s they feared more its exploitation by the French. Although they were not opposed to railway development in western Germany, when presented with a proposal in 1829, they demanded the right to destroy the railway without compensation in time of war and restricted the width of the bed to five feet to prevent it being used to move enemy cavalry and artillery.[103]

The three interests—civilian, state, and military—together exerted a powerful pull on British rail technology. Although there was plenty of skepticism (the state approved of railroads in the late 1820s and early 1830s but had no interest in funding them), in the end opponents to rail were not effective. The first ten years of railway construction in Germany, from 1835 to 1845, saw faster growth than the analogous period in England. The German network measured 2,143 kilometers after the first ten years versus only 544 kilometers in Britain.[104] Thus, there was no doubt in the 1830s that railroads were going to be built in the German states. What the network would look like, and what ends it could serve, were still open questions.

Diffusion Mechanisms

The diffusion of rail technology from Britain took three forms: licensing, borrowing, learning, or theft of industrial techniques from Britain; importation of iron rails, locomotives, and rail wagons into Germany; and emigration of British contractors, engineers, and skilled construction workers to Germany. While quantitative measures of the impact of British rail technology are scarce, the anecdotal evidence is persuasive. The lines built in the earliest years are few in number (approximately eight in the first five years, near double that by 1845), so individual stories of British involvement on a handful of lines constitutes a large share of this evidence. The secondary literature also firmly supports the view that British materials, machines, and expertise were vital.[105]

The previous one hundred years of industrial espionage were a useful prologue to the acquisition of rail technology. The iron, machine-tools engineering, and steam-engine industries that the German states had 'imported' in the late eighteenth and early nineteenth centuries had never been economically competitive, but at the beginning of Germany's railway age they were there.[106] German engineering was largely dependent on English industry. All the important engineers and businessmen in the sector, including two future locomotive manufacturers in Harkort and Egells, had either visited England or had extensive experience in some other way with British techniques.[107] Harkort's shop was, "a revolutionary enterprise, a machine shop operating in accordance with English models."[108] The coming of the railroad meant sudden, massive demand for the produce of German heavy industry and it created them as industries in the modern sense.[109] The importance of the earlier borrowings should not be overlooked.

Another, more immediate form of borrowing also took place. In the 1830s, German railway concerns would often submit their plans to British experts for their analysis before proceeding. At least three German civil engineers traveled to England to observe railway construction in the 1830s and 1840s. Karl von Etzel visited England in the winter of 1836–1837 to study railway construction before undertaking several projects, including the Plochingen–Stuttgart–Heilbronn railway, in his native Württemberg. Baron Christian von Weber, a student at Borsig's engineering shop in Berlin, spent the year 1844–1845 in England studying under Robert Stephenson and Isambard Brunel. The very first German railway, the Nuremberg & Fürth, was built by the German Camille von Denis in 1835 after careful study of English railways. The line also used an English gauge, required by the English locomotive to run on it, and an Englishman to drive the train once it was completed.[110]

The second form diffusion took was imports: "without the existence of locomotive and rail manufacturing industries elsewhere the German railways could not have been so quickly built."[111] Initially, dependence on British locomotives, wagons, and iron rails was almost total. The locomotive on the Nuremberg & Fürth was English, as were the six locomotives on Prussia's first railway, the Berlin–Potsdam (completed in 1837), and the fifteen on the Berlin–Anhalt (completed in 1841). The first German-built locomotive on a German railroad was the *Saxonia* that ran on the Dresden–Leipzig railway in 1839. By 1846, Germany had purchased 237 locomotives from England, 168 of which were from the two firms Stephenson's and Sharp & Roberts. Only 102 of the 237 were operating in Prussia, an indication of the evenness of German locomotive development in the earliest years.[112]

But railway inputs were eventually replaced through import-substituting industrialization. Demand stimulated the growth of engineering and iron industries and created the locomotive, wagon, and coach industries. Dependence on Britain for the iron rails took longer to shake than for locomotives, but by the late 1850s, local industry had overcome reliance on imports for all the basic inputs to railway enterprise.[113] Figures 3.2 and 3.3 below show the substitution of local

Figure 3.2
Origin of Locomotives on Prussian Railways by Country, 1838–1853.

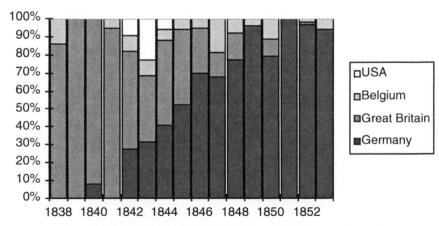

Information source: Rainer Fremdling (1975), *Eisenbahnen und deutsches Wirtschaftswachstum 1840–1879* (Dortmund: Gesellschaft für Westfälische Wirtschaftgeschichte E.V.), 76.

Figure 3.3
Origin of the Stock of Rails on Prussian Railways, 1843–1863.

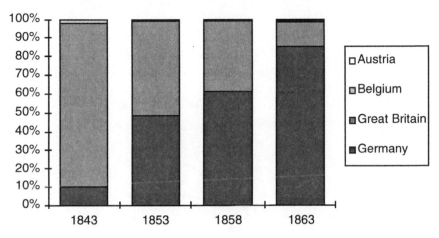

Information source: Rainer Fremdling (1983), "Germany," in Patrick O'Brien, ed., *Railways and the Economic Development of Western Europe, 1830–1914* (New York: St. Martin's), 128.

German product for British, and the dominance of British goods in the first years is striking.

English emigrant engineers and skilled laborers were the third form of diffusion. Large-scale contractors were one group of emigrants— successful entrepreneurs or civil engineers in their employ who added foreign construction contracts to their lists of projects. Thomas Brassey was the most important of these. In 1840, after a successful but brief career in England, excess capacity turned his interests abroad. Brassey built railways all over the world, including in France, Italy, Germany, Canada, Austria, Norway, Sweden, Spain, Turkey, India, Australia, and Peru. His firm was among the first to build technological systems of great size, scope, and complexity and was widely emulated.[114]

Charles Vignoles, another important English engineer in Germany, was closely involved with the first German railways. In 1835, he consulted with the cities of Hamburg and Hannover on the choice of route to connect them with Brunswick. In 1843, he advised the states of Saxony and Württemberg where "his various tours and journeys of inspection in Southern Germany, together with his able and comprehensive reports, were no inconsiderable factors in the origin and development of the railway system in that country."[115] Other English civil engineers and contractors who built railways in Germany include John Hawkshaw and James Walker, contractors for the Leipzig–Dresden Railway in Saxony (completed in 1839 and the fifth line built in Germany);[116] Stephen Ballard, an associate of Brassey's, the engineer on the Arnheim–Prussian Frontier railway; and George Buck and James Kitson, chief engineer and locomotive engineer, respectively, for the Altona–Kiel Railway in 1840.[117]

Skilled workers and common laborers were a second category of emigrants. They were anonymous (the large contractors and engineers such as Stephenson and Brunel were industrial celebrities), but were more numerous and equally important. The nameless Englishman who built and then drove the steam-locomotive on the Nuremberg & Fürth line has already been mentioned. English workers invariably came with their countrymen-contractors to supply the skilled labor, instruct the local workers, and afterwards maintain and drive the locomotives.[118] They were relied on because of their superior skills and because the low skill levels, poor work habits, and lower standards of living of the local labor made it necessary to employ a permanent English staff to instruct them in the advanced techniques of railway construction.[119]

In sum, railway technology was transferred from Britain to the German states through three processes of diffusion: technology licensing, importation, and immigration. Antecedent political and economic conditions (a history of technology transfer, state administrative capacity, and a concern for international competitiveness) facilitated and even created diffusion. Contemporaneous state policies assisted. When linked with the causes of diffusion discussed earlier, the case for the political nature of the diffusion process is clear. Political and economic forces pushed contractors and workmen abroad, led to the policy of import substitution, and helped create the engineering expertise needed to adopt English techniques.

Railway Adaptation in the Civilian Sector: 1830–1850

The economic and political impact of a mature network was dramatic. Dependence on overseas trade for industrial expansion was reduced and cost savings made coal cheaper and more plentiful. Railways helped create an integrated market in Germany and directly spurred economic growth in the 1840 and 1850s.[120] They also made the young Zollverein effective. The absence of political barriers to trade within the union pleased railway developers, but was not an important cause of railroad construction. Railways did, however, make the 'national' market of the Zollverein a reality and paved the way to eventual political unification. Thanks to its place at the political center of railway development, Berlin became an important industrial center as well. The network in eastern and central Prussia was centered around Berlin, as were early engineering and locomotive and rolling stock manufacture. Without the railways, this concentration would not have occurred.[121]

These effects were the product of a relatively mature rail network that connected all corners of Germany. That development, while envisioned in the 1820s and 1830s, was not a reality until the 1850s. Early railway construction was localized. A network of lines stretching in four directions from Berlin took shape in the 1830s and 1840s, but a connection to the industrial areas of the Rhineland was not made until the late 1840s. A smaller complex of lines grew up around the Rhineland in the first decade. Although Harkort first proposed connecting the 150 miles between Minden on the Weser and Köln on the Rhine in 1833, they were not linked until 1847.[122] Figure 3.4 shows the growth of the network in absolute length and its rate of growth from year to year. The remarkable rates in the earliest years obscure the tiny size of the network. An increase from 6 kilometers to 21 kilometers accounts for the near trebling of the network in 1837 and one from 21 to 140 for the 566 percent growth in 1838.[123]

To illustrate the adaptation of rail in the civilian sector, I trace the evolution of the German railway network from its origins to 1870

Figure 3.4
The German Railroad Network 1835–1914.

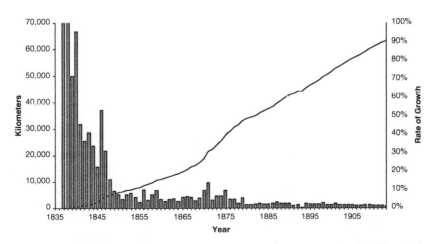

Information source: B. R. Mitchell (1975), *European Historical Statistics, 1750–1970* (New York: Columbia University Press), 581, 583.

using examples primarily from Prussian history. It is by far the most important, and Prussian railway policy became by default German railway policy.[124] There are three phases to the evolution: (1) the 1830s when debates within the Prussian state were on whether and how to support railway construction; (2) the early, private-sector period of rail construction from the mid-1830s to 1848; and (3) from 1848 on, when integration and nationalization dominated developments.

Several themes carry throughout all three phases. From the beginning, political interest and process intruded in the construction of railway lines. In the 1830s, disputes between railway advocates and skeptics within the government delayed progress on four important lines in Prussia for several years. Disagreements between private carriers and governments over the rules and regulations of operation shaped the integration and rationalization of the network. Over time, the regional, economic rationale behind the early railways was replaced by the ideal of the national network—the goal of bringing rail transportation to all of Germany regardless of profitability.[125] This was a turning point in the maturation of the railway as a sociotechnical system and in its development as a tool of military policy.

Pervading every phase is the state. Whether hindering progress, guaranteeing returns, providing capital, or building strategic railways, the state had a profound shaping influence on the direction of railway development. State activity imposed a level of governance on railway operations that proved useful during the military campaigns of the second half of the century. State interests also built lines where private interests would not and, through guarantees or outright ownership, were the financial prop for the entire network.[126]

There was a flurry of railway activity in the early 1830s, some but not all of it emanating from private interests. The Prussian Minister of Finance, Friedrich von Motz, had in the late 1820s favored construction of a line from Minden to Lippstadt. King Frederick William had rejected the proposal as premature, convinced by a 1828 Interior Ministry report that the costs of construction could never be recouped.[127] Pressure on the king to provide state aid mounted as proposals from southern Prussia joined those from the Rhineland. Once again, skeptical state officials passed judgment: the state should not go into debt to finance projects whose present costs were great and future profitability questionable. After Motz died in 1830, two of the most powerful Prussian bureaucrats, Peter Beuth and Christian Rother, firmly opposed state-sponsored railway development because they feared it would draw capital away from their more favored industries (textiles, iron, and coal) and generate uncontrollable economic growth. The king accepted Rother's recommendations. The resulting 1835 legislation denied public support for railways and placed draconian financial and regulatory responsibilities on private construction.[128]

The tide began to turn in 1837 with the assistance of Crown Prince Frederick William and several younger Anglophilic ministers who were his allies. They were instrumental in the passage of a railway law that allowed firms a three-year carrier monopoly on lines they built. Skepticism within the army was also beginning to wane. While still doubtful of the long-term utility of railways, an army report produced prior to the 1837 legislation recommended lifting some of the harsher impediments to railway construction. The legislation, and the approval by the king in that year of four important concessions—Aachen–Köln, Köln–Minden, Magdeburg–Leipzig, and Berlin–Potsdam—marked the beginning of the railway age in Prussia.[129]

Short lines in the east and west were finished quickly and easily. Four spurs radiating out from Berlin were completed by 1842 (one via a government loan) and three small lines in the Rhineland. At the same time, developers for some of the longer lines were having trouble raising additional capital and feared imminent collapse. In response to the crisis, the government established the Railway Fund in 1842 with an initial capitalization of six million Thaler. The fund invested 3.8 million Thaler in the shares of five troubled lines either stalled in construction or yet to begin—the Minden–Köln, the Halle–Weimar–Cassel along the Prussian–Thuringian border, a line from Breslau to the Austrian frontier, the Berlin–Königsberg (or *Ostbahn*), and a spur joining Breslau line with the Berlin–Königsberg at Posen. The fund also guaranteed a return to all investors of at least 3.5 percent.[130] By 1845, three of the five lines were in operation or nearing completion. The government's entry into railway financing also bolstered the perceived safety of the investment, and private capital poured into all lines even if they lacked the government-guaranteed return. The two eastern railways, supported by the state more for security and political reasons than economic need, failed to find adequate capital and eventually the state would undertake their construction alone.[131]

Government help did not come free of restrictions, and, in the eyes of railroad firms, the regulatory burden was oppressive. A unified *German* rail network was created through opposition to government regulation. A ten-year debate between the finance minister and the private lines over the regulatory framework led in 1848 to the creation of a German railway federation (despite the name): the Union of Prussian Railroad Administrations.[132]

In the late 1840s, overspeculation led to crisis. By 1848, many railroads were debt-ridden and poorly run and their stock valuations were sinking. Government policy was also responsible—the revenge of the anti-railroad faction. Beuth and Rother managed to convince the king and the new minister of finance, Ernst von Bodelschwingh, to limit railway growth to stave off financial collapse. A series of 1844 ordinances forbade the licensing of railways that were not in the "overwhelming common interest." The government also slowed approval pace for new concessions—there were fifty-six concession requests in 1844 and only seventeen received licenses—and the stock value of the affected companies plunged.[133]

In this financial climate, the military, which had been interested in state-built lines since the late 1830s, worried that gaps in the national network would remain and existing lines would lack adequate capacity, speed, and strength to suit military needs. Two lines in particular, the Saar Railway and the Berlin–Königsberg, or Ostbahn, led the government to conclude that some lines must be built and run without private enterprise. The Ostbahn in particular was vital to the military defense of East Prussia. But because there was little in East Prussia to interest private rail consumers, the company building the line had failed to raise the necessary capital. In March 1847, the government proposed that the state build the line.[134]

Once political stability returned after the 1848 Revolution, the state began to build and nationalize in earnest. One man, August Von der Heydt, was most responsible for the nationalizations. A former entrepreneur and railway builder, Von Der Heydt was appointed Prussian Minister of Commerce, Industry, and Public Works in December 1848 and held the post until 1861. He believed that only the state could run the railway system in the public interest and proceeded accordingly. He proposed the building of state lines, took advantage of financial or operational mismanagement to acquire existing lines, imposed additional rate and operations regulations, and denied concessions to private railway companies.[135] He obtained approval and funding for the Ostbahn and the Westphalia Railway in the Rhineland. The two were completed, except for two bridges on the Ostbahn, in 1853. His ministry used a variety of ingenious methods for seizing control of private lines. Private railway companies who came to the government for financial assistance were told that aid was conditional on their ceding administration of the line to the state. In 1853, von der Heydt had legislation passed that allowed him to tax the profits of healthy lines to pay for nationalization of troubled lines. By 1857, about half of all Prussian railways were either nationalized or under government administration.[136]

After 1850, innovations in the physical technology of railways were largely incremental; development of railway technology was in the hands of men like Von der Heydt.[137] Using their tools—capital, maps, management expertise, political persuasion, and the authority of the Prussian state—state officials with private company directors in collaboration completed the German civilian adaptations to English rail technology.

Railway Adaptation and Military Management: 1830–1866

This section traces the evolution of the strategic use of railways from an idea in the heads of a few visionaries to its central place in German military policy in the late 1850s. The key puzzle is why Prussia/ Germany was so successful at integrating railroads and grand strategy. The answer has three elements: the character of the Prussian military as a planning institution, the peculiar role of the military in Prussian politics, and an historical turning point—victory over Austria in 1866. Once the military committed itself fully to rail, its dominance in the political system, its close integration with civilian administration, the superior training and organization of the Great General Staff, and the military's commitment to modern planning methods made successful use of rail networks likely. Nevertheless, that success was predicated on victory in war. Until that victory, the military as a whole did not view rail as a tool of military power.

By far the most prescient and influential thinker on the strategic role for the railways in the 1820s and 1830s was Friedrich List. In his theoretical writings, he argued that an intelligently designed national rail network would help bring about a unified Germany, be a great economic boon, and support Germany's strategic position in central Europe. He was quick to grasp the meaning of the Industrial Revolution for German security. He wrote, "War or the very possibility of war makes the establishment of a manufacturing power an indispensable requirement for any nation of the first rank." His vision, sketched in an 1833 pamphlet, bears a remarkable resemblance to the network that developed. He showed a national network with Berlin at its hub, north–south railroads along the Rhine and Vistula, and interior lines connecting Berlin with the eastern and western lines and with the major industrial and commercial centers.[138]

On the other hand, he seriously misunderstood the strategic implications of the railway. He predicted that a rail network would enhance Germany's ability to defend itself and that the superiority of 'interior lines' guaranteed that an attacker using rail would be stretched thin and made vulnerable. He thought that rail was such a revolutionary defensive weapon that "wars would be confined to frontier areas, and once the nations of Europe discovered the impossibility of following up their victories, they would conclude that it would be better . . . for all to live in peace. Thus the railroad would be the instrument which destroyed war itself." He was not alone in believing that railroads would bring an end to wars, but he was wrong.[139] Though mitigated somewhat by advances in rifle and artillery technology, it was precisely rail's offensive capabilities—especially against France in 1870 and in the initial stages of World War I—that made it such an effective and important development.

In Prussia, meanwhile, official embrace of rail's military potential came slowly. When Finance Minister Friedrich von Motz died in 1830, railroads lost the only senior official advocate. And while civilian officials were on the whole converted to rail by the end of the 1830s, opinion remained divided within the military. Conservatives in the officers' corps often evoked Frederick II's dictum that good communications only made a country easier to overrun, and they were pessimistic about growing civilian enthusiasm for railways.[140] Rail lines were too difficult and costly to build, they argued, and neglect of road construction was unwise. The army had already committed itself to a national network of all-weather highways for commercial and strategic purposes. So, in 1835, and at civilian officials' instigation, when the state investigated the military utility of a Rhineland–Prussian rail line, substantial military pressure ensured that the resulting report concluded that such a rail line wasn't really worth the trouble.[141]

Some of the German states expressed an early interest in strategic rail lines. News of a French line to be built from Paris to Metz and Strasbourg threw the southern German states into a panic. They argued with their sometime-protector (Prussia) that a rail line was needed to counter the threat. Bavaria even made an explicit request in the late 1830s for a collaborative steam-rail effort with the Prussian government. The Prussians rejected the proposal on the grounds that rail could only supplement highways and as such were far too expensive.[142]

By the late 1830s, it had become harder for the military to ignore rail. In 1839, eight thousand Prussian guards were transported to Berlin from Potsdam after maneuvers, becoming the first German troops moved by rail. A split developed within the military in the mid-1830s between those (including an enthusiastic crown prince) convinced of the inevitable indispensability of railroads and others who saw them as merely an expensive adjunct to roads. The special commission formed to produce a report for the war ministry pitted an advocate, General Staff Captain and artillery commander Eduard Peucker against a skeptic, General Staff Captain Friedrich Leopold Fischer. The final report was something of a compromise: it acknowledged the military potential of the railroad, but because design and reliability were as yet uncertain, the report recommended that the state allow private rail development to continue, although, "private planning and construction of railroads should therefore receive detailed military scrutiny and approval before concession."[143]

The report was incorporated into the Railway Law of 1838, but railroad advocates had to press hard to achieve anything before the coronation of Frederick William IV in 1840. Minister of War Gustav von Rauch, a staunch pro-rail man, attempted to pass legislation in 1838 and 1839 that would have required private lines to move troops during international crises, and at reduced rates. With the approval of the Crown, his ministry was effectively stopped by Finance and Industry ministers more concerned with economic growth than military necessity. There were some small victories. As per the 1838 law, companies were forced to reinforce tracks near fortresses and, when the army required it, bridges were to be made of wood, not stone.

By the early 1840s, gaps in the nascent national network were a growing source of worry for the railroad lobby in the military. Among this group were a newly converted Fischer, the older cavalry officer Wilhelm von Reyher, and Helmuth von Moltke, then a staff officer and by 1857 the head of the General Staff. The former two were the first important rail supporters from outside the technical and engineering military specialties.[144] Moltke's support of railways resulted from his personal experience. His study of the Russo-Turkish campaign of 1838–1839 impressed on him the possibilities of rail, and while a staff officer in the Rhineland in the early 1840s he was a board member of the Berlin–Hamburg Railway and "even then saw what advantages there were for the State in the proper and judicious building of railways, in a planned network of Government roads, and in respect to military interests." In the same essay, Moltke wrote that the railway represented "a complete revolution of the avenues of communication," and "the government could not be separated from such great undertakings."[145]

Nationalization was the issue for the pro-railway bloc in the military. Many out-of-the-way but strategically significant garrison towns were without rail lines of any kind. Pressure from within the military for nationalization culminated in the Railroad Law of 1842. The law fell short of nationalization of existing lines, but did allow for the possibility of future state-built lines as strategic need dictated. It also provided a generous subsidy in the form of a guaranteed 3.5 percent return to the investors in five struggling rail lines.[146] But despite the interest of rising luminaries like Moltke, and the military's best intentions, the military utility of railways remained open for debate into the 1840s and 1850s. By the late 1840s, German rail had passed France in mileage, but for military purposes the network was still insufficient. The reach of existing lines was limited, and did not always go where it was militarily useful. Economic efficiency often meant equipment insufficiently reliable for military purposes.[147]

The entire network was single-tracked. Double-tracking allowed for continuous back and forth travel that was thought to be essential during wartime. To make matters worse, the lines were all owned by private enterprises with no management expertise in large-scale troop movement (nor did the military have this capability). Without their cooperation and a serious commitment from the military to peacetime planning, they were unlikely to develop such expertise anytime soon. Many in the military began to conclude that, without nationalization, effective military planning was impossible. Carl von Reyher, chief of the Prussian General Staff in 1848, tried to establish coordination between civilian technicians and the military, but attracted no interest.[148]

Some crisis was necessary to clarify to the civilian railway operators and the remaining intransigents in the civilian and military bureaucracies the necessity of coordination. In quick succession, the military had two: the Revolution of 1848 and the 1850 mobilization against Austria. During the revolution, the army did not use the railways, but the rebels did. While the army found their troops on the roads vulnerable to the rather unorthodox tactics used by the militants, they also were somewhat confused by the extraordinary mobility of the rebels.[149] If the revolution was a learning experience, the 1850 mobilization was a disaster. Organization was a complete failure; men, animals, and supplies sat in piles at loading centers or traveled aimlessly from station to station. Afterwards, the General Staff began to look seriously into using telegraph and railroads for troop movements. They discovered that the quick transport of large numbers would require coordination far greater than their current capabilities.[150]

Only with Moltke's ascension to Chief of the General Staff in 1857 did coordination and planning receive sustained attention. Even then, his recommendations for civilian–military planning meetings and coordination with the other German states weren't followed until the eve of the 1859 mobilization in Italy. But Moltke's rise indicated that rail planning was moving toward the center of Prussian army affairs.[151] Before the wars, the military was interested in rail and took steps to ensure some control over the civilian lines (made easier by their powerful position within the Prussian political system), but it had no idea how to use rail effectively. During the wars, Moltke's careful preparation, reshaping of the staff, and military success guaranteed that rail would become a component of the international system as a tool of mechanized, rationalized armies. His rise also marks a transition point in the maturation phase of the railroad as a complex sociotechnical system.

The first step in the railroad case has conformed to the research design laid out in the previous chapter. The railroad developed into a sociotechnical system as part of the transnational process of the development and diffusion of industrialization. Some of the mechanisms for that spread are familiar realist variables—competition for power between states, while others are part of larger transnational economic processes such as the spread of knowledge and the expansion of markets. Along the way, rail's development was subject to political contestation and considerable uncertainty. As we move into the next phase, when military necessity and technological development come more closely together, these disagreements will be heightened, and the developmental paths taken and not taken will become more significant.

THE RAILROAD, INTERACTION CAPACITY, AND SYSTEM CHANGE

The transformation to the international system in the era of the railroads occurred at two levels: changes in the distribution of power, and changes in the nature of the system. Railroad technology altered relative power in the international system by giving an advantage to Germany for a brief time. The new technological environment also changed the force, time, and space dimensions in international relations—that is, it changed the interaction capacity of the system. It altered domestic organization for resource extraction, and, for those societies that wished to participate in great power politics, required great institutional adaptation.

The transformation of the international system differed geographically in ways that warrant separate analysis. In continental Europe, the changes largely affected the relations between states of roughly similar military power, technical ability, and internal political and economic organization. The railroad's effect on the periphery was different, though no less profound. It literally expanded the geographic scale of the international system. Colonizers used rail lines to subdue regions of the periphery that had previously resisted European imperialism, and railroads enabled the extension of effective control into the interior of colonial holdings where prior European activity had been limited to the coasts.

Germany's emergence as a great power in the last half of the nineteenth century was sudden. In two wars over only four years, the Prussian/German army humbled the two greatest armies of Continental Europe. German success was due to a rapidly growing and industrializing economy, Moltke's military and Bismarck's political genius, superior use of rifled firearms, economic and political unification, and railroads.

Railroads were at the center of a host of transformations to Germany and its relations with the outside world. They were the most important element in Prussia's strategic success against Austria and France. The railroads were the only revolutionary *strategic* technology (rifles had a tactical, not strategic, impact). And railroads were critical to German unification—itself critical to the growth of German power.

The changes in the distribution of power in Europe and in the nature of the European system occurred simultaneously, making it difficult to separate the creation of a new technological environment from the benefits that new environment bestowed on Germany. As Prussia and the other powers moved to exploit the promise of the railroad for military affairs (or not, as in the case of Austria), they created the actual technological form. The railroad that Moltke's 'demigods' rode (metaphorically) to Vienna and (actually) to Paris was not the railroad conceived in Britain at the beginning of the century, or even the railroad of the German states in the 1840s and 1850s. It was larger in scope and embedded in a military organization and culture redesigned under Moltke's leadership to use the railroad effectively. The transformed military placed greater importance on planning, and elevated the status and power of the Great General Staff within the army as a whole and the technical and planning sections within the staff itself. A modern army, rational, bureaucratic, and technologically sophisticated, replaced the old one of courage and élan. It had become a "learning organization" in the words of one historian.[152] But this was no inevitable march to excellence. The old army did not disappear quickly or quietly. Disagreement with the organizational changes and strategic innovations was widespread, and only the victories against Austria and France validated Moltke's vision for the railroad. Without those victories, it is doubtful that rail would have played the significant role it did in the international system through to World War I—such is the political nature of technologies.

Chronologically, the transformation occurred in three phases: first, the pre-1866 war preparations to use rail as a military tool; second, the war with Austria and its aftermath; and third, and most decisively, the 1870 war with France—which created unification domestically and continental dominance internationally. The changes to the nature of the international system evolved throughout the three phases and affected three fundamental features of the system: force, time, and space. Railroads enabled the size of armies to increase. More troops could be brought to a potential battlefield in less time, making it practical to bring to battle larger and larger armies. Larger armies, in turn, meant that battles were more destructive and carried out over larger expanses of space. Prussia mobilized nearly 280,000 men for the 1866 war and nearly 500,000 in 1870 over the course of just five months. In contrast, Napoleon mobilized nearly 500,000 during the Napoleonic Wars, but that effort took over fifteen years and several campaigns. In 1914—the last major war without extensive use of internal-combustion powered vehicles—Germany mobilized four million troops, including one and one-half million in the first ten days. Prussia took advantage of this new ability. Moltke's strategy, at least at a theoretical level, depended on superior numbers to ensure victory. Prussia's 294,000 soldiers were met by only 245,000 Austrian and Saxon troops in 1866; the Prussian army's mobilization of 462,000 (to total 850,00 by war's end) well outnumbered the initial French force of 238,000.[153]

The second system characteristic changed by the railroad is time. Even in the earliest days of troop rail travel, when confusion was at a maximum, armies moved by rail traveled anywhere from six to ten times faster than similar troops on foot. Railroads and their intelligent use sped up the process of mobilization. Greater speed in turn shortened reaction time to changing events (this was partially mitigated by telegraph communication). Shortening the time necessary to apply military force changed the nature of diplomacy by reducing decision-making time and altering what military planners could see as possible. Certain maneuvers, once logistically unthinkable, were now possible, and opened up a whole new universe of strategic options. One of the most impressive examples occurred in the 1866 war with Austria. Moltke withheld his troops from the likely battlefield until the last possible moment and carried out a decisive outflanking of the Austrian army.[154]

Finally, the railroad expanded space. A continental railroad network greatly increased the territory armies could cover in a given time. In so doing, it increased the size of territory it was feasible to defend, and the depth to which enemy territory could be penetrated. In the case of Germany, it made the simultaneous defense of both eastern and western borders possible, paving the way for a unified Germany in the 1870s. And without rail, the siege of Paris during the war with France could not have occurred on the scale it did.[155]

Because railroads transform force, space, and time, states had to transform themselves and their relations with their societies. The railroad, the larger armies, and the increased amounts of army materiel placed a premium on planning and organization, both before and during hostilities. If they wished to remain internationally competitive, states had to remake themselves.[156] Beginning with Germany, states that could do so rationalized planning, increased their technological expertise, pushed for greater administrative efficiencies, and increased administrative size. Large-scale organization and planning and extensive peacetime intrusions in the civilian economy became hallmark features of state practice.

In other words, international success was not achieved by merely possessing rail technology. The sociotechnical system was completed by the addition of layers of administration and systematic planning. Thus, the arrival of the railroad produced a fundamental shift in the nature of the units of the international system. States were still territorial, and still claimed internal monopoly of force and international sovereign equality, but their functions and roles both domestically and internationally had been vastly expanded. They became industrial states in order to manage the first industrial-era technological system: the railroad.

Changes to the nature of the system are important, independent of their effects on the distribution of power. Although for a time rail gave an advantage to Germany, once that advantage faded, the environment was still permanently changed. The speed and size of the new armies had to be guarded against. New military and resource extraction policies were devised, maintained, and altered to adapt to the demands of the new environment. Once the form of the railroad—in all its complexity of tracks, locomotives, rules, procedures, schedules, and organization—had been fixed and its military effectiveness validated by the Wars of Unification, states had no alternative other than to choose how to adapt.

RAILROADS AND THE EUROPEAN SYSTEM

In this section, I make two arguments: (1) railroads in late nineteenth-century Europe changed the use and characteristics of force in such profound ways that the international system was fundamentally changed; (2) the primary beneficiary of this transformation—and the driving force behind alterations to the distribution of power in the same period—was Germany. It is impractical to try to separate the two arguments—the processes that demonstrate the one, demonstrate the other.

The Austro-Prussian and Franco-Prussian Wars demonstrated that effective rail mobilization was power. The addition of machine power to international politics and warfare, for the first time in human history, had profound effects. The speed with which huge armies could be brought to battle, and the additional materiel they could carry (an additional by-product of the industrialization of war), meant that more troops arrived faster, better armed, and better rested than before. Such an army was more destructive than armies of previous eras. Of equal and perhaps even greater importance was the effect rail had on organization. As a complex, multifaceted, and not-always-reliable machine, the rail network required an unprecedented level of precision organization and planning. Because rail did not lend itself to improvisation in the course of mobilization, centralized control became a requirement of military strategy.

World War I and the notorious Schlieffen Plan exacerbated these tendencies. In the forty-three years between 1871 and 1914, armies got bigger, the weapons they carried heavier and more numerous, the rail network denser and more complex, and the organizational layer larger, more technical, and more specialized. By World War I, all the participant states had developed elaborate plans for defense or attack; states and military organizations had adapted to the new environment. The overall effect of the transformation was to permanently link industrial production and economic health with war-making capacity and international power. No longer could economically weak states field powerful armies; no longer could non-integrated, disorganized societies hope to be great powers.

Germany, even taking the 1918 defeat into account, clearly benefited most from the industrialization of war in general and from railroads in particular. Railroads spurred economic growth, extended the geographic scope of the economy, and overcame market fragmentation. The railroad also constituted a new international entity—the German state. The 1815 Congress of Vienna created a governance fiction for Germany; hegemony was divided between the Prussian kingdom and the Austrian Empire. The events of the century demonstrated the fragility of the arrangement.[157] Rail facilitated Prussia's two stunning military victories and political unification. The railroads gave Prussians, Austrians, and French alike the ability to move huge armies to the front with unprecedented swiftness. But only Prussian strategy successfully adapted to the opportunity that rail presented and the Prussians used this initial mobilization phase to seize a decisive advantage.

Four factors help explain Prussian superiority. The first is an accident of geography. Germany's geostrategic position between three great powers (France, Austria, and Russia) made Germans recognize the strategic potential of railways quite early on. Second, the extent and nature of the German rail network facilitated successful mobilizations. Although state and military leaders had had some say in the design and construction of the rail network, for the most part the lines were laid by private firms with the aid of government concessions. Nonetheless, the network was well suited to military needs. The lines allowed Moltke to plan and execute a strategy based on rapid concentration of force deployed along interior lines. Third, planning for railway mobilization had been a growing priority for the Prussian General Staff since the 1850s. Several poor attempts at mobilization had convinced the military of the importance of preplanning, and the requisite staff, organization, and expertise were developed. Finally, the actual mobilization strategy devised by Moltke made full use of railroad's potential.

The Austro-Prussian War

In the early 1830s, the private entrepreneurs behind the first railway proposals were always sure to include some mention of the possible strategic benefits of railways. Friedrich List wrote that "each mile of railway which a neighboring nation finishes sooner than we, each mile more of railway it possesses, gives it an advantage over us."[158] A growing group within the military also was convinced of rail's utility. Realizing a working, useful rail network was a lengthy and arduous process. It was not inevitable that civilian lines could work for military purposes. Prussia's earliest experiences with rail during wartime were not impressive. Even leading up to the war with France, it was generally acknowledged that the Prussians lagged behind the rest of the great powers in the use of railroads for war.[159]

The Punctation at Olmütz in 1850 underscored Prussia's continued vulnerability to Austrian power and also served notice to the Prussian military of the utility of rail transport. A confrontation erupted when Prussia attempted to dissolve the German confederation and unite the northern German states under Prussian hegemony. The Austrians responded swiftly. The emperor convinced the Frankfurt Diet to invoke a 'federal execution' to approve the movement of Imperial troops into Hesse-Cassel. The Austrian army moved 75,000 troops from Hungary and Vienna to Bohemia via rail before marching them into Hesse-Cassel. Slow to respond, the Prussians found themselves outflanked. The Austrians' militarily response forced the Prussians to drop their plans and consent to the Austrian occupation of Hesse-Cassel.[160]

The War of 1859 between France and the Austrian Empire was a second learning experience. Both sides used rail to transport and concentrate troops and experimented with attacking rail installations, though not very effectively. The French effort was impressive enough to convince Moltke—newly appointed head of the Great General Staff—that France was Prussia's most important enemy and worthy of emulation. He sent a group of officers to France to study their rail mobilization and others to pore over official reports.[161]

After the 1859 war, the Prussian army under Moltke's guidance turned to devising a coherent and organized railroad strategy. The

General Staff, in cooperation with the civilian ministries and representatives from other German states, began to establish a common rail doctrine for all of Germany and to develop and test in advance a general mobilization plan. The Prussians were the first to systematically prepare for railroad mobilization during peacetime. Their efforts included a survey of the conditions and capabilities of all militarily significant lines, the establishment of officer special training down to the garrison level, and the development of a Field Railway Detachment for rail destruction, repair, and operation—the first country to do so. Finally, in 1861, the army issued a comprehensive set of instructions for rail mobilization including timetables and directions for loading and unloading trains. The era of the military generalist had ended and the era of the specialist had begun.[162]

This activity was in the context of deteriorating relations with Austria. The settlement of the Congress of Vienna in 1816, by splitting governance of the German states between the twin powers of Austria and Prussia, was too mechanical and arbitrary. The two governors engaged in a constant tug-of-war for influence. In 1863, Austria made a final attempt at a peaceful unification of Germany with the Hapsburg Empire. Emperor Franz Josef proposed that federal authority be strengthened and the princes voluntarily surrender some of their sovereignty. Fearing Prussia more than Austria, most of the German princes may well have gone along with this proposal had Bismarck not managed to maneuver William I into rejecting the invitation to attend the assembly of princes at Frankfort (*Fürstentag*). The assembly passed the proposal but when it was forwarded to Berlin, the king rejected it.[163] These events set the stage for war with Austria and, ultimately, German unification under Prussia.

The war began over the breakdown of the settlement that ended the 1864 Danish War. The empire tried to resurrect its prestige with the Third Germany, as the smaller states had taken to calling themselves, by supporting the Duke of Holstein's claims to independent status. The Confederation Diet went along. Prussia responded by moving its Baltic naval base from Danzig to Kiel. The two powers were moving toward confrontation and the Confederation was splitting apart. "Our tickets" Bismarck observed, "are on diverging lines."[164]

By the end of April 1866, Austria began mobilization. Meanwhile, both continued to use the Diet to advance their aims while the smaller states scrambled to avoid the dominion of either. In early June, Austria moved to hear the appeals for self-rule from the Holstein estates, even though this would violate the 1864 agreement. When the motion passed, Prussia declared the 1864 settlement null and moved troops into Holstein. The Austrians withdrew what troops they had, but moved in the Diet that federal troops be sent against Prussian occupation of Holstein. When this motion carried (the "Third Germany" sided with the Austrians), Prussia declared the Confederation dissolved and ordered Saxony, Hannover, and Hesse-Cassel to accept a Prussian proposal for a new German state. When they refused, Prussia invaded them all and in three days completed occupation of each.

In late June, as the Austrians rolled toward Prussia, bets in Paris were running four-to-one in favor of the empire. But in seven weeks the Prussian army decisively defeated the Austrians at Königgrätz and was marching toward Vienna when a truce was called and a peace settled—heavily favoring the Prussians.[165] Schleswig-Holstein, Hannover, Hesse-Cassel, Frankfurt, and Nassau were annexed to Prussia. Several southern states—Saxony, Bavaria, Baden, Württemberg, and Hesse-Darmstadt—were made 'independent' and formed a loose "North" German Confederation.[166]

The war was a watershed in the development of technologies of force and the interaction capacity of the international system. Its scale was massive—the 460,000 troops who participated in the battle at Königgrätz were larger by 30,000 than the largest set piece of the Napoleonic Wars. It was the first significant industrial-era war in Europe.[167] Railroads were the critical enabler of increased army size, though larger populations and greater administrative conscription capacity were also important. Without rail, the huge armies could not be transported effectively to the battle. Industrial technology increased the destructive power of those armies through improved artillery and infantry firearms. As Craig notes, industrial prowess was the new decisive factor, "in an age in which industrial progress was making it possible to arm and transport armies which dwarfed those of antiquity, wars would be won by those nations which could raise, train, deploy and command large armies most effectively."[168] In 1866, that advantage clearly fell to the Prussians, but they were aided by a strategic plan that made the best use of their industrial strength. That plan depended on the extensive German rail network.

Prior experience taught Moltke and the General Staff that railroads had to be integrated into strategic and operational planning. It was not enough to bring troops to the front. Technological advances in infantry weaponry made flanking and encircling movements much harder to carry out on the battlefield on foot, as they had been in Napoleon's time, because fire from new rifled weapons was too devastating. The increased size of armies also made complex, controlled battlefield movements more and more difficult. Instead, as Moltke was the first to realize, rail could be used to accomplish the same objectives but at the operational level. In preparing for war with Austria, he developed a mobilization plan that would use railroads to maneuver armies before the actual battle and save the concentration of the troops for the battle itself. This broke with the fundamentals of Napoleonic-era strategy, which held that concentration must occur before the battle so as to have one's greatest force assembled and ready to deliver a crushing blow. But with considerably larger armies, the advantage of pre-engagement concentration was lost in the sheer crush of men and the time lag between when the first and last troops reach the battle. By delaying concentration until the battle itself, and by using railroads to maneuver troops into position for the concentration, Moltke overcame the limitations of the new larger armies. These plans, not the sheer size or density of the rail net, gave the Prussians a decisive operational advantage in 1866 and again in 1870.[169]

Because the Austrians had several possible strategies available to them, the General Staff needed a flexible defense to meet any contingency. Moltke's plan—first developed in 1860—was for a small force in Silesia and the bulk of Prussian forces on what would be the Austrian western flanks at Dresden near the Elbe bridgeheads of Torgau and Wittenberg. The plan is interesting because it emphasized offense for defensive purposes; as the situation developed, it became even more offensive. It is also interesting because the main concentration points in the plan—Dresden and Görlitz—were chosen not for their intrinsic strategic value, but for their extensive railroad facilities. As the meeting points of several lines, the two junctions would allow rapid redirection of troops should the need arise. Because of the network's layout, they also allowed preemption of any threat to southern Germany should Austria decide instead to try and 'liberate' Saxony, Hannover, Württemberg, or any of the other southern states. The entire plan depended on Prussia's ability to mobilize faster and more efficiently than the Austrians.[170]

Political dithering, the final obstacle to the legitimation of the railroad as the centerpiece of modern military planning, nearly wrecked the General Staff's plans. The fate of the railroad as a component of the interaction capacity of the international system likely would have been different had it destroyed Moltke's plans and the Prussians lost. The Austro-Prussian War is thus a pivotal conjuncture in the development of the railroad system. This is a crucial point. The war tipped the development of the railroad more firmly toward maturity as a sociotechnical system and as part of the interaction capacity of the international system. While in retrospect the development trajectory seems natural or inevitable, it was not.

A risky but successful improvisation was necessary to counter an initial and unexpected Austrian move toward Silesia that went unanswered by the Prussian political command for three weeks.[171] Moltke's response was in keeping with his general principles—separation until the moment of battle—but it was more extensive, and the separation was riskier than he had planned.[172] On his direction, the five armies undertook a massive leftward (eastward) shift and were then spread out along a railway arc of 275 miles along the Saxon, Bohemian, and Silesian borders. From there, the armies moved on the town of Königgrätz in Bohemia for what was to prove the decisive battle.[173]

The ability of the Prussian army to carry out the maneuver is indicative of their preparation and knowledge of the rail network and rail management. As planned, control flowed directly from the General Staff. The Executive Commission, made up of an officer from the General Staff's Railway Section and a representative from the Commerce Ministry, took the strategic plans of the staff and turned them into railway time schedules and requisition orders and passed those directions on to the Line Commissions. Tracks that were designed to carry only eight trains per day were made to carry twelve, and in twenty-one days the Prussians moved 197,000 men, 55,000 horses, and 5,300 vehicles via rail to the front.[174]

The Austrian mobilization, on the other hand, was too poor to take advantage of the exposed Prussian flank during the eastward shift. The Austrians took nearly six weeks (twice as long), to mobilize approximately the same number of men. Because they had only one rail line leading into Moravia, and because they were slow in using it, the advantage of their early start evaporated and the Prussians were able to dictate their meeting place.[175]

Even so, Prussian success was not assured. The Austrian commander Benedek arrived first at the soon-to-be battlefield and had his choice of preparations. Here he made a crucial error and gave the Prussians a piece of luck. He placed his armies on the west bank facing Prussia with the Elbe to his back, meaning that any hard going would make a tactical retreat impossible. That is exactly what happened, as Prussian forces defeated the Austrians, and an inconvenient defeat was made catastrophic by the need to cross the Elbe to retreat. This in turn made the logical next step impossible: holding the Prussian forces (even in the event of a battlefield loss) at the Elbe until the South Army, on its way from Italy, could join. This would have given the Austrians superior numbers and likely would have turned the tide of the war.

The Prussians, too, made a mistake. Moltke's planned strategic envelopment was nearly foiled by the late arrival of the Second Army from the north and by Prince Friedrich Karl's apparent inability to understand Moltke's plan—he pushed the offensive on the morning of the third instead of waiting for the Second Army to arrive that afternoon. But Benedek's graver error allowed the Prussians to avoid the consequences of their mistake. Once the battle was over, and the rout on, the Austrians and their allies proved incapable of preventing the Prussians from using their own railroads against them. The southern German states were unable to keep their lines out of the hands of the Prussians and, within a few days of the occupations, the Prussians had the important Saxon lines nearly up to full capacity. Even in defeat, the Austrians were not thorough in destroying rail behind them.[176] It is not clear if they failed to appreciate the value of their railroads to the Prussians or were simply reluctant to destroy their own infrastructure.

The density of the rail network in Prussia enabled the improvisation on Moltke's plans. Whereas Austria had only one rail line leading north from Vienna into Bohemia, the Prussians had five.[177] Figure 3.5 graphs the growth of the German, French, and Austrian rail networks up to 1870. The chart shows that, for a time, Austria kept pace with the other two continental powers. By the middle of the century, the Empire's rail network had virtually stagnated while rapid network expansion in France and Germany continued (the drop-off in the French network at the end of the graph was caused by the loss of Alsace-Lorraine to the Prussians in 1870).

The Prussian state had nationalized most of the rail network in the 1850s, and the state had repaired and improved many of the lines. On the whole, the lines lay where the private entrepreneurs had placed them in the 1830s and 1840s with no precise military plan in mind. Moltke's plan was driven in large part by where the rail lines were.[178]

Figure 3.5
German, French, and Austro-Hungarian Rail Networks Compared:
1825–1870.

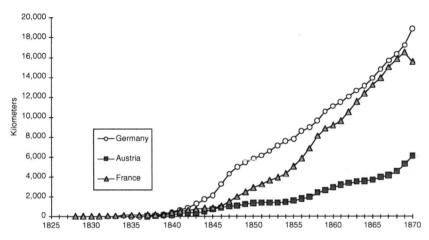

Information source: B. R. Mitchell (1975), *European Historical Statistics, 1750–1970* (New York: Columbia University Press), 581, 583.

In contrast to the success of mobilization and operational maneuvers, the attempt to supply the troops by rail from the rear was disastrous. The army had incorrectly assumed that the combination of supply officers, private rail line administrators, and troops in the field could coordinate their efforts and keep the army supplied. Instead, the supply officers simply directed their supplies toward the front, the rail carriers followed instructions to ship whatever they were told wherever they were told, and no allowance was made for the time it took to unload. Nearly eighteen tons of supplies were trapped on rail lines behind the front. Rotting, spoilage, and—in the case of the livestock—death from malnutrition and dehydration resulted.[179]

On the whole, however, the results of the 1866 war were extraordinary and, as far as Prussia was concerned, positive. Austria's defeat toppled what remained of the Holy Roman Empire from any position of influence in European diplomatic affairs. The outcome also set Prussia up for almost inevitable conflict with France. The war demonstrated the value of the increased firepower provided by new rifled weapons and the importance of a dense strategic rail network to transport and maneuver the bigger armies into battle. Finally, the war represented the end of the era of the romantic soldier—embodied in the Austrian general Benedek—and the rise of the soldier as a professional and a technician—embodied by Moltke.

As the tools of war increased in size and complexity, experts and managers were needed to wield them. Planning, coordination, and regulation would replace élan, bravery, and inspiration. Most important, the fortuitous victory over Benedek at Königgrätz legitimated the Prussian style of rail planning. Over the next half-century, the other great powers would emulate the Prussian system with greater or lesser degrees of fidelity, but the place of the railroad in the international system was now fixed.

The Franco-Prussian War

The war with France in 1870 affirmed the strategic role played by railroads and German superiority. Once again German mobilization was more organized and effective, and the difference gave German forces a decisive advantage. The war also differed from the 1866 conflict. Against France, there was no marked disparity in rail line density or length (see Figure 3.5). At the time, the commonplace view was that the French railroads leading to the Rhineland were of superior strategic design and construction.[180] But whatever advantage the French network had in theory was of little use in practice. With little attention to prewar planning and no central direction when activity began, the French mobilization and concentration were a disaster.

By contrast, refinements to the Prussian plans enabled them to take advantage of the French failures. Moltke planned a defensive action in the Palatinate and positioned the bulk of his armies back from the Saar to absorb the French advance. When the offensive failed to materialize, the Prussians pushed forward and the first encounters of the war took place on the French side of the Saar. The Prussians never looked back. Those early clashes took place at the beginning of August. By the beginning of September, the Imperial Army led by Napoleon III was defeated at Seden (his surrender led to revolution in Paris and the establishment of the Third Republic); by the middle of the month Paris itself was under siege, and by the end of January 1871 Paris had fallen and the war had ended.

Prussian use of rail was not perfect. Troops were at times late in arriving or their commanders ignored the directions of the General Staff. Supply again was poor. Although the staff hoped railroads would aid in the advance through France, delays in capturing fortressed rail lines and sabotage by French troops limited rail's role (until the siege of Paris) to the initial mobilization. But this does not diminish rail's significance. It remained the most important operational technology and affected equally the organization, plans, and fortunes of both states. As to Prussian effectiveness, Showalter has argued, "The challenge of the machine is not to use it perfectly, but to make it perform the work desired."[181] The Prussians did that. The speed and carrying capacity of rail are useless without careful planning, coordination, and regulation. The Prussian's superior organizational adaptation to rail made the difference.[182]

Prussia's decisive advantage came from Moltke and the General Staff's thorough plan for rail mobilization. Some observers were quick to give the breech-loading needle-gun the credit for the Prussian victory against Austria—thereby removing from the Austrians any blame for faulty organization, strategy, or tactics. But others realized that railway networks were now the most important elements in strategic and operational planning. The 1866 war demonstrated that efficient organization could confer a decisive advantage if it allowed the new mass armies—made up of well-trained reservists in their homes instead of fewer well-trained soldiers housed in barracks—to be called up, clothed, equipped, and sent to face a poorly organized adversary.[183]

The addition of Hannover, Nassau, Hesse-Cassel, and Frankfurt-am-Main to Prussia added 400 miles of rail lines and in between the wars the Prussian rail network increased by more than 1,800 miles, or an increase of 40 percent, while the number of locomotives increased by nearly 75 percent. The Prussians also made changes to their rail organization and supply structure. Immediately after the war with Austria, a mixed committee of staff officers and civilian and private railway authorities was appointed to identify faults in the mobilization and supply systems of 1866, to develop plans to avoid them, and to improve on the general efficiencies. The most important organizational task was the integration of the North German Confederation into existing army mobilization plans.[184]

Consequently, the entire system of command and control of communications was reorganized. The mixed civil–military Central Commission—composed of officers from the General Staff and the Ministry of War, and staff members from the Ministry of Commerce and the Ministry of the Interior—was made a permanent organization, not just a wartime expedient. In 1867, the integration planners produced the

"Route Service Regulation" that would govern the use of rail lines and rolling stock throughout Germany in the event of war.[185]

Supply problems also received a great deal of attention. The army created a Route Inspection Department within the General Staff to oversee supply; the removal of the sick, wounded, and prisoners of war; and the maintenance of open communication. This replaced the decentralized system that had failed in 1866. Each army and independent corps was to have its own Lines of Communication Inspectorate to control flow of supplies and reinforcements from the rear. This elaborate organization was placed under the command of an Inspector-General of Communications who had direct lines of communication to the Commander-in-Chief of the army and the War Minister. In the end, centralization was as ineffective as decentralization. The responsibility was too much for one person, and the system broke down.[186]

With Austria defeated and weak, war between France and Prussia was considered inevitable. The precipitant was the Hohenzollern candidature to the Spanish throne. Bismarck had successfully negotiated for the placement of a Prussian Hohenzollern, but the French saw it as a potential disruption of the European balance of power and protested. Their demands for the withdrawal of the candidate and satisfaction for the insult were rebuffed. The war was on and the news was greeted with cheers in Paris and Berlin.[187]

The Prussian army had no delay in mobilization as in 1866. There were six railway lines running to the west—nine if the three from the southern German states were counted—and the General Staff estimated that these could carry 300,000 men (360,000 including the southerners) into the Rhineland in three weeks and an additional 70,000 in four. With these numbers, Moltke concluded that a simple strategy would do. He would leave a small force in the east to check Austria should the Emperor decide to come to the aid of his French ally and push into France between the Rhine and the Mosel.[188] Timetables had been drawn up, reservists knew when and where to report for duty, and, as a 1918 report on the mobilization noted, "proper preparations for the railroad concentration had been made in time of peace, and all that was required in case of mobilization was to carry out the concentration of the field army in accordance with the will of the supreme command."[189] The numbers of troops moved—462,000 in eighteen days—corresponded almost exactly with staff estimates and the army settled in to their planned positions in the Palatinate and Baden.[190]

The French had a denser rail network than the Prussians but had paid insufficient attention to planning. Too few of the strategic railways, those leading from industrial areas and population centers to the front, were doubled tracked—four compared to the Prussians' six. Despite having an analog of Moltke in Marshal Niel (he had added a railroad bureau to the general staff), the French were the opposite of the Prussians when it came to preparation and planning.[191] The 1866 war between Prussia and Austria had made an impression on some influential members of the military and they, with the support of the emperor, made an attempt at army reform. A commission was established in 1867 to reform discipline, training, organization, use of railways, and the machinery for mobilization and concentration since "all were inadequate by Prussian standards."[192] By July 1870, the French military brought an estimated 492,000 men under arms, or more than the initial German mobilization, with an additional 300,000 ready within three weeks.[193]

The numbers were meaningless because the reforms had done nothing to make up for poor intelligence and complete absence of mobilization planning. The French mobilized on July 14, one day ahead of the Germans, but their disorganization and inefficiency quickly removed any advantage. Because the military had no control over the railroads, troop movements via rail were disastrous. Individual officers ended up improvising—requisitioning trains and supplies as they could—and first-line troops were frequently without basic fighting equipment. Reserve corps were especially hard hit and many ended up scattered around France.[194] "The result was that by the sixth of August, the twenty-third day of mobilization, only about half the reservists had reached their regiments, and many of these lacked the most essential items of uniform and equipment. The rest, if they had left their depots at all, were marooned en route by railway delays and spent their days sleeping, drinking, begging, and plundering army stores."[195]

In France, Prussia, and elsewhere in Europe, it had always been assumed that the French would go on the attack. But because of the chaos, the numbers needed to execute French general Leboeuf's planned offensive did not materialize. By July 28, he expected his army of the Rhine to number 385,000—instead it was only 202,000; by the thirty-first of the month, it was still only 238,000. Wisely, he decided not press forward.[196]

Meanwhile, German troops poured into the Rhineland. Concentration also went as planned. Moltke divided his army into two wings separated by 50 miles—the same strategy of separation he had used at Königgrätz. His right wing of 184,000 threatened Lorraine and Metz and the left wing of 125,000 threatened Alsace and Strasbourg— a deployment itself dictated by the French railway network. Their rail layout gave the French the choice of only two bases to anchor their operations: Metz and Strasbourg. When a German offensive into France begun, the two fortressed rail bases would be cut off from each other in short order.[197]

When the French did not attack, Moltke began an encirclement from the north and west. Problems with subordinates—especially Steinmetz, the aged hero of the Austrian war—ruined Moltke's plans for a clinical encirclement and destruction operation, but his forces did achieve two decisive victories at Spicheren and Froeschwiller on August 6. With those two defeats, the French ran out of ideas and morale. Now a French advance into Prussia was out of the question. All that remained to be determined was where and when Moltke would advance, and if the French army could hold out long enough to force stalemate and settlement. The answers: to Metz and Paris, and no. A massive mopping-up operation remained, more akin to a guerrilla war than a traditional military conflict. The French continued to fight valiantly and, after the leaders of the Third Republic created a people's army, made life very difficult for the Prussians. But after the initial encounters, the winner was never in doubt.[198]

Once the Germans moved into France, the shortcomings of their rail planning showed clearly. Both sides' efforts at supply were disastrous. The French army was short of food by July 20, and had the Prussians not been able to live off the land, they would have eaten very poorly if at all on their march through France. Total lack of organization doomed the French efforts, while in the Prussian case overcentralization of command and reliance early in the war on civilians were serious problems. Trains and rolling stock piled up on the tracks well behind the advancing army much as they had in the war against Austria. The problems occurred at the points the technology of the Industrial Revolution—the railroad—met the technology of the previous era—the horse-drawn carts and backs of men used to unload and transport the stores from the railheads. Things improved late in the war when the military took command of the railways. But supply trains were still unable to keep up with advancing troops— who were on foot because the army's failure to capture key fortresses made the use of French rail lines impossible.[199]

The final result—the siege and bombardment of Paris and a humiliating capitulation—was a crushing defeat for France. In the space of five years, the Prussians had fought and defeated two of the three great land powers in Europe. Prussia's sharp rise to a position of dominance on the continent was complete. In a final bit of irony, on January 18, 1871—at Versailles—the assembled princes of Germany proclaimed the King of Prussia the new emperor of Germany. The unification of Germany was completed in French accommodations.[200]

In the war with France, the railways proved their worth as an operational tool to a greater extent than against Austria. A retrospective report by the German General Staff in 1918 declared, "The utilization of the railroads on the part of the German army in the war of 1870–71 is in the same class with the great successes which were achieved by the army leadership under King William I."[201] This was intentional myth making on their part. Nevertheless, in the face of fundamental changes to war fighting the initial deployment of forces assumed great importance. Armies were much larger, troops had considerably less training and experience than armies of the eighteenth century, and improvements to artillery and infantry firepower made traditional offensive tactics ineffective. Both France and Germany had extensive railway networks, and both had considerable experience using those railroads to transport troops to battle. But the Germans had successfully adapted their practices to the operational potential of railroads while the French, indeed the rest of Europe, had not. After the war with Austria, most European observers misunderstood Moltke's contribution to strategy. English military experts argued that his maneuvers had been lucky—as he had violated the principle of concentration before battle—and, if he tried similar maneuvers against France, he would be crushed. Such experts made the same mistake after hearing reports of the initial mobilization in 1870. Moltke's decision to separate into two wings was deemed dangerous compared to France's superior single mass. That Prussia's opponents and independent observers could be so wrong is indicative of how great the adaptation gap was.[202]

To World War I

If the Austro-Prussian War solidified within Prussia the shape of rail as a sociotechnical system, the Franco-Prussian war did the same for Europe as a whole. The technical shortcomings of the Prussian use of rail notwithstanding (supply was still poor), the Franco-Prussian War marked the political maturation of the railroad. Unlike after the Austro-Prussian War, there was no disagreement or misunderstanding about the source of the Prussian victory: it was technological and organizational superiority, in particular in the realm of mobilization. Everyone began to copy the Prussian model: the General Staff, technical proficiency, and the elevation of planning and expertise over élan and bravery.[203] These efforts at emulation meant the gap between Germany and the rest would not last for long. The 1866 and 1870 wars were only a prelude to the apotheosis of the use of rail in wartime—World War I. The most rapid period of economic growth in history occurred between 1871 and 1914. Population in Europe exploded. The railway networks of the Continent more than doubled in size—from 65,000 miles in 1870 to 180,000 miles in 1914 with most of that growth coming in Germany and Russia.[204] In 1914, rail had an even larger role to play. The size of armies, the preplanning and organization, the detail and precision of the nineteenth-century mobilizations pale in comparison to the efforts mounted by the French, Russians, and Germans in 1914. By then, mobilization and movement were the essence of military art. In forty years, Moltke's strategy had been turned into rigid doctrine—superior mobilization was thought to ensure victory.

The Germans took the supply problems they encountered in 1870 very seriously. Moltke concluded in 1870 that the logistical limits of rail technology supply had been reached; the system had been too overburdened and horse-drawn transport beyond the railhead proved a disaster.[205] If, as expected, the size of armies and amount of materiel and the scope and complexity of the rail network would increase in coming wars, then significant measures were needed to ensure that military mobilization and supply systems could keep up.

The new German state pursued improvements in three areas: organization and integration with civilian rail lines; construction of new, state-owned lines along strategic routes; and more nationalizations. Organization underwent a wholesale review. New regulations governing the use of railways during wartime were issued in 1872, 1878, 1887, 1888, 1899, and 1908. The 1908 Field Service Regulations made the case for complete military control over railways during wartime: "Railways exercise a decisive influence on the whole conduct of a war. They are of the greatest importance for mobilizing and concentrating the army, and for maintaining them in a state of efficiency."[206]

Germany also stepped up planning and building new railroads to strengthen interior communication and increase the number and quality of lines to the frontier. In the decade after the war, the German network nearly doubled in length and by 1910 was three times its length in 1870. The number of rails to the French frontier in south Germany was doubled from three to six and all were double-tracked; the number of crossing points over the Rhine was increased from nine in 1870 to nineteen just before World War I.[207]

Finally, the states continued to nationalize railway lines. Before 1870, lines had been nationalized for a variety of reasons, typically poor service and financial troubles. After the war, the reasons were more militarist, as reflected in Moltke's 1889 speech: "Railways have become, in our time, one of the most essential instruments for the conduct of war. The transport of large bodies of troops to a given point is an extremely complicated and comprehensive piece of work, to which continuous attention must be paid. Every fresh railway junction [under state ownership] makes a difference."[208] However, attempts to form a German national rail network failed. To forestall Prussian dominance, Bavaria and Saxony 'nationalized' their entire networks in 1875 and 1876, respectively. Prussia completed nationalization by 1887. By the turn of the century, only secondary lines remained in private hands; 35,500 miles of the 38,300-mile German rail network were owned by the eight states.[209]

The Schlieffen Plan was the most important planning development between 1870 and World War I. Moltke had never been over-enamored of his planning apparatus and had retained respect for the role of confusion, initiative, and creativity in war. He thought that the demands of modern war placed an even greater premium on officer initiative than in previous times. Under Schlieffen, Moltke's successor as Chief of the General Staff, flexibility was abandoned in favor of fixed plans and rigid formulas. Also unlike Moltke, Schlieffen and his acolytes firmly believed that a two-front war fought simultaneously against France and Russia could be won.[210]

Schlieffen's strategy was first to smash France and then quickly redeploy in the East to crush Russia. Because of Switzerland's topographical challenge, and the impressive build-up of French fortifications on their eastern border, Schlieffen chose to rush through Belgium and the Netherlands instead. Eighty-five percent of the German army was to be in the West and 88 percent of that on the right wing.[211] A massive concentration via rail on the Belgian–Luxembourg border (thirty-five corps in five armies) and a much smaller force (five corps and two armies) on the actual French–German frontier would act like a hammer swung across France toward Paris. The plan was daring and logistically complex. For the hammer to swing, the right wing would have to travel considerably faster than the left, and the troops would have to use French railways for much of the time. Herein lay two logistical problems that all the planning by the German General Staff could not overcome.

Even under 1870 conditions, the fast movement of the right wing meant supply, still dependent on horse-drawn carts beyond the railhead, would be overtaxed. But two things had changed by 1914 that made the likelihood of success even smaller. Armies had gotten bigger in the forty-plus years, surpassing in growth both population and industry. Whereas France could only call on 500,000 men in 1870, by 1914 that number had increased to 4 million out of a population of service-aged men of 7.8 million. Germany had a male service-aged population of 15 million. Armies needed more supplies than ever. Advances in weapons design meant that the amount of ammunition the typical corps would need had increased substantially and the critical distance—the distance beyond which an army can no longer be effectively supplied—fell from about 100 miles in 1860 to around half that distance in 1914.[212]

Moltke the younger replaced Schlieffen in 1906 and tried to correct the supply problems. He eliminated the plan to violate Dutch territory. This reduced the distance traveled and number of troops needed, but also cut in half the number of roads available for the advance. He also reduced the size of the western army in favor of a slightly larger defensive force in the east.[213]

The modifications did little to fix the problems. Dependence on French and Belgian rail for transport and supply meant that if the *Eisenbahntruppen* were overtaxed—if the French or Belgians destroyed a great deal of their rail network in front of the German advance— the plan would be seriously compromised. It was still virtually inevitable that the right-wing armies would be too exhausted to fight well when the decisive battle came. Both problems occurred in the war itself. The 1914 battle of Tannenberg, pitting the Germans and the Russians in East Prussia, was the only engagement that even remotely resembled the older Moltke's spectacular battles of movement.[214]

During the war, the German army successfully mobilized over one-and-a-half million men in ten days, but problems with the planned advance developed quickly. Plans had counted on four railroads through Luxembourg and Belgium to keep the right-wing armies supplied, but the railway construction companies could not keep up with the extensive demolitions and out of forty-four major lines in Belgium, only three had been restored by the battle of the Marne. It was only because their advance through France stalled unexpectedly that the Germans were successful at supplying their armies in the field. If the advance had gone as planned, the supply plans probably would have failed.[215]

There was no repeat of 1870, even though the use of rail by the German forces was as impressive as any of their previous achievements. The German advantage had been overcome by sheer size, their opponents' strategy, and the perils of their two-front geostrategic position. Troops needed too much in the way of supplies and ammunition for nonmotorized transport to keep pace with the advance. The Allies effectively destroyed the rail lines in front of the advancing Germans and used their own rail networks to swiftly counter German movements. No longer did Germany's opponents allow it to choose the battlefield based on the availability of converging rail lines. World War I finally revealed the limitations of Germany's geostrategic position. The railroad did allow the German military to consider the defense of eastern and western fronts, but the logic of Germany's diplomacy led the army into a war on both fronts simultaneously. In just four decades, the temporary advantage afforded Germany by superior railroad organization had evaporated.

The moment of rail's greatest triumph also marked the end of its dominance as an operational technology. The introduction of vehicles powered by internal combustion engines in World War I solved the supply problem and freed mobilization and movement from the limitations of rail lines, junctions, and stations. But the transformation to the interaction capacity of the international system was permanent. Army size had increased dramatically and with it army power, the feasible geographic size of states had increased, and the military art had been transformed into a rational, technocratic science. These changes are testament to the enduring impact of the railroad as sociotechnical system on the international system.

THE RAILROAD AND SYSTEM CHANGE ON THE PERIPHERY

The shift in the balance of power to Germany was the most important event in European international politics in the late nineteenth century and, given the two world wars in the twentieth, of considerable importance to world politics as well. The other great event of nineteenth-century international history was the second great wave of European imperialism. Driven by imperial dreams and the force of industrial expansion, the European powers conducted their last and most sweeping makeover of the world and forged the first global international system. Northern European businessmen and engineers revisited the ex-Spanish colonies in Latin America and tied them more firmly to the world economic system. In Asia, European industrial and technological might turned a relationship of relative equality between the Europeans and local rulers in India and China into one of clear subordination. In Africa, steam and modern medical technology allowed Europeans to systematically penetrate the interior of that continent. In 1800, by landmass, 35 percent of Africa and Asia, were European colonial possessions. By 1878, that figure had climbed to 67 percent, and in 1914 it stood at 84 percent.[216]

The railroad (together with the steamship—a maritime locomotive) was the most important tool of colonial expansion in the nineteenth and early twentieth centuries. Railroads tied peripheral markets to the metropole with fast and reliable transport. They were a dramatic physical assertion of colonial dominion and allowed imperial powers ready and effective means of defending their colonies from internal and external threats. In this section, I will briefly sketch the impact of the railroad on the extension of European control in Asia, and Africa, and the effect of rail on the nature of the international system.[217]

The most obvious long-term effect of railroads on the international system was the extension of the European influence and the nation-state form to the periphery. But the railroad also served short-term economic, political, and military purposes. As in Europe, railroads' effects on the international system in the periphery were the result of their effects on time and space: their speed, carrying capacity, and reliability over traditional forms of transport. Rail, together with the steamship and the telegraph, shrunk the world. Time savings reduced distance and effectively brought the rest of the world closer together and gave previously remote places economic and strategic significance to Europe. At the local level, the time and resource savings represented by railways were astonishing. In Uganda, it is estimated that, for freight haulage, railroads were on the order of thirty times cheaper than human porterage. In India, the savings were estimated at between eight and twenty times cheaper than bullock carts.

Railroads reduced the trip from Mombasa to Uganda from one year—on foot—to two to four days. And railroads, unlike Indian roads, do not wash away with each rainy season.[218]

By linking isolated areas, railroads induced political change wherever they were laid. The linking of the eastern and western coasts of the United States in 1869 via the Central and Ocean Pacific Railroads united the continent and made a nation possible out of a handful of separate regions. The Trans-Canadian Railway, finished in 1885, and the Trans-Siberian, completed in 1903, performed the same function.[219] But, more often, railroads were used to absorb small states into larger European empires and bring existing colonial possessions closer to the metropole. Railway loans and concessions were a frequent tool of great power politics. They could knit together spheres of influence, forge subordinate alliances, and keep other European rivals out of the area. Rival concessions could, with luck, peel off desirable territory from another's grasp.

Europeans designed the first rail lines to facilitate raw material resource extraction and manufactured goods importation, not balanced regional economic development. But the rail lines did bring growth and jobs, and their absence could doom an area to economic stagnation. Consequently, local political elites became as dependent on the lines as their economies were. Railroads in the periphery helped create a new national political unit: the underdeveloped modern nation-state. All these effects are evident in the following examples.[220]

India

The Indian railroad network was the largest by far of any colony, and its construction was the single largest technological project of the colonial era. By 1936, the Indian network was larger than the national networks of all but the United States, Canada, Russia, and Germany. The British rulers first realized in the 1820s that railways would "annihilate space" in the vast subcontinent, but it was not until 1853 that the locomotive 'the Lord Falkland' made a short 19-mile trip along the first line between Bombay to Thana.[221]

In the early Victorian era, India was a disappointment to British businessmen and colonial managers. Imperial penetration had not progressed far beyond the coastlines, and what was subject to British incursions was not yet a satisfactory market for imported manufactures. The colony's vast size created an additional problem. The empire was still responsible for defending a huge frontier from Russia and had to cope with the occasional provincial revolt.[222]

These two impulses, commercial and military-strategic, drove British railway investment in India. In January 1844, *The English-man*—a Calcutta journal—outlined the reasons for supporting railroad construction, "The first consideration is as a military measure for the better security with less outlay, of the entire territory, the second is a commercial point of view."[223] And Captain Robert Melville Grindlay—the founder of the banking firm Grindlay and Co. and prominent railroad advocate—wrote, "The political safety of India is intimately connected with its commercial prosperity, and consequently with its commercial value to this country. . . . Our commerce will not survive the destruction of our political power, and Steam Communication will be an important agent in the preservation of the latter."[224]

Railroad advocates first had to face down the de facto rulers of India, the British East India Company, who saw in railroads a threat to their commercial monopoly. The company resisted throughout the 1840s before finally relenting in 1849. The rail advocates turned their lobbying organizations into limited liability companies to raise capital and build the railroads. The contracts were with the company, but the colonial Indian government guaranteed the company and any investors a 5 percent return, with any excess to be split between the two.[225]

The promise of such generous returns sparked the single largest flow of international capital in the colonial era. The railways were built largely on the European pattern. Private companies built with government guarantees and were supervised by government engineers and the military. By 1902, there was 15,000 miles of track, one-third of it government owned. The colonial rulers had discovered in the 1870s that if they wanted the strategically necessary but economically unprofitable lines to the northern frontier, they would have to build them at government expense.[226] The investment in strategic rails more than paid off, however, as it enabled the British to assert military control over the entire subcontinent and protect the colony from Russia. The lines demonstrated their military worth during a nativist uprising in 1857 and again during the Afghan campaign of 1879.[227]

The railways also proved their economic worth to British investors, merchants, and manufacturers. The railways, by their layout and rate structure, encouraged the production and export of raw materials and the importation of finished manufactured goods. They helped establish a century-long pattern of economic development. India is the only country with a network of such size that failed to industrialize during the period of railroad building; at independence, the Indian economy had the same percentage of people in agriculture, industry, trade, and services as a century before.[228]

Finally, the railways spurred nation-building. At the same time they helped the British consolidate imperial rule (there were substantially fewer revolts after the 1857 uprising), they facilitated the emergence of Indian nationalism. The British were astonished by how quickly Indians took to train travel. Long journeys in cramped compartments eroded caste barriers to some extent, and helped turn a patchwork of ancient principalities into a modern, underdeveloped nation-state.[229]

China

China, unlike India, lacked a single colonial overseer. Instead, Britain, France, Germany, Russia, Japan, Belgium, and the United States all battled for influence. For each, railroads were an important means of penetration.[230] Investors from one country or another would secure a concession and build a line that they would then run for their benefit. The resulting railway network was underdeveloped, but not without pattern. It mapped onto, and helped create, the spheres of influence of the foreign powers.

The bulk of railway construction took place between 1895 and 1939. In 1876, the British firm Jardine, Matheson & Company built the Shanghai–Woosung railway, but the Chinese so distrusted the new technology that they tore it up, dumped the parts in the ocean, and reimbursed the foreign investors. As reluctance gradually waned, the Chinese tried, with limited success, to use railway concessions to play one power off against another.[231]

Foreign merchants who wanted to expand trade were the primary advocates for railways in China. The first lines connected major commercial points. In almost all cases the financing was of foreign origin and control remained in foreign hands. The dominance of foreign finance and ownership made Chinese attempts to forge something like a national network impossible. Instead, the patchwork of lines tended to reinforce the positions of influence enjoyed by foreigners while it integrated China into the global economic system. A typical example was the French built and run Yunnan–Indo-China Railway.[232]

The partition of China by railroad rights had security implications as well. The Russians built the Chinese–Eastern Railway in Manchuria at the turn of the century to facilitate the political and economic penetration of northeast China. And once the Trans-Siberian and Berlin–Constantinople to Baghdad were completed, the railways stretched from Europe to Asia, and brought the entire supracontinent into a single railroad network.[233]

Africa

The coming of the railroad to Africa was even more chaotic and scattered than in China, but also brought with it European economic and political influence. Preindustrial commercial traffic in India or China relied on beasts of burden for their motive power, but in Africa the best available means of transport was the human porter—an expensive and inefficient method.[234]

The European powers at the 1876 Brussels Conference recommended building a continental railroad network on the model of India's. But the lack of concentrated traffic and major population centers made such a system impractical. The first African railroad—built in the 1850s by the British—connected Alexandria and Cairo. By the 1860s, South Africa had a few short lines. The French were very active railroad builders in the 1870s through the 1890s—building several lines in the Sudan and in the Niger and Senegal river valleys. Most of the lines built in this period fit a particular pattern: they were short (less than 200 miles) and ran inland from harbors to mining or agricultural areas without connecting one to the other in a network. Railroads connected groundnut and palm oil plantations in West Africa with the Coast; lines ran from Katangan and Rhodesian copper mines to the ocean; and others connected cotton plantations in the Sudan and Uganda with port cities. Some lines were planned to link inland rivers and lakes with each other and those with the coasts, but these plans were too risky for private capitalism and were left to the states and colonial governors and most languished. Several ambitious projects—such as a planned British military railroad from the Cape Coast to the River Prah and a French plan to span the Sahara from Algeria to the Niger—were never built.[235]

The Europeans also built a number of military railroads. The British laid lines in Sudan, the Italians in East Africa, and the French from the Senegal River to the Upper Niger. An example of great-power rail realpolitik took place in southern Africa over the second half of the nineteenth century. The British built an extensive network of railways for the economic exploitation and strategic defense of the valuable colony. The Germans wanted to establish their own colonial empire in southern Africa—one that would rival Britain's India—and, with luck, expel the British from theirs. Africa colonization societies formed in Germany as early as the 1850s, and schemes were proposed to flood South Africa with German immigrants. The competition, which extended into World War I, was fought largely with railway lines.[236]

The German plan was to exploit the Boers' growing distrust of the British. Through joint projects, they hoped that three strategic rail lines—leading to the Cape, Bechuanaland, and Rhodesia—could be built and then used to take South Africa from the British by force. The first—a Boer-German railway across the Kalahari into Bechuanaland—failed when Britain annexed Bechuanaland in 1885. Next was a joint Dutch, German, and Transvaal project to build a railway from Delagoa Bay to Pretoria. It would have been a trans-African railway, but the agreement fell through. Nevertheless, by 1914, the Germans had four major lines and 1,300 miles of railway in southern Africa, two of which (and better than half the total) were mainly or exclusively strategic railways, designed to allow a simultaneous attack on British possessions. The investment was for naught and the German conquest of southern Africa never happened.[237]

The African experience replicates on a smaller and more fragmented scale the pattern of railway development and European expansion in the periphery. The impulse behind the construction of railroad lines in the colonies was usually economic, and railroads were a necessary tool to exploit the potential economic wealth of the colonies. Colonial rulers found that strategic railways leading to and from frontiers were sometimes necessary whether or not private industry was interested in building them. In such cases, the colonial or even the home governments would finance the construction alone. But, in all cases, state support of private enterprise was significant. Government loan guarantees in India, for example, were necessary to spark sufficient investor interest in that rail network.

Thus, railways were a necessary part of late nineteenth-century colonial expansion. They also performed a unique and vital political function. Rail lines followed political boundaries or created new ones, and everywhere bound colonial territories with their European patrons. In terms of interaction capacity, rail lines shrank distance, extended the reach of European states, and literally expanded the size of the international system.

CONCLUSION

The railroad was a critical enabling element in the creation of the late nineteenth-century global economic and political system. Its introduction as a tool of war and conquest, and its rapid spread, are marked by all the features associated with a shift in the interaction capacity of the international system: a change in time–space relations, an increase in speed, an increase in destructive power, and a qualitative change in the manner in which international actors interact with each other (and prepare to interact). The industrial revolution generated unprecedented productive power and energy for political and economic expansion. The railroad (and its oceangoing version, the steamship) was the industrial-era tool that enabled expression of that power and expansive energy. Without the reach, speed, and capacity of the railroad, industrial enterprise would have been substantially reduced in scale and limited to local materials for production and local markets for consumption.

Railroad had a fourfold effect on the international system: it increased and altered the character of the military power states could mobilize. It enabled the most dynamic industrial economy on the European continent to unify into a nation-state and to wrest political supremacy from older, less adaptive continental powers. Outside Europe, it helped unify previously disparate territories under European political control, and integrated them into a global economic system of European design and domination. In both places, it deepened the state's participation in peacetime planning and industrial organization. In other words, for states to adapt to the complexity and organizational requirements of rail, they had to increase their penetration into their own societies and expand their resource extraction.

The four transformations are all products of the Industrial Revolution. Technologies often swap human labor-power for machine labor. This was certainly true of the steam engine and its associated technologies. At a certain point, the increase in power is so large that a quantitative difference becomes a qualitative one, and entirely new tasks and new realities emerge. The same holds true for the geopolitics of the railroad.

The speed and carrying capacity of the railroads reduced space (in relation to time) and enabled armies to grow in size and destructive power. They also complicated logistics and changed the nature of strategic planning and execution. Predictably, those who adapted best to the new environment achieved better results. The superior adaptation of rail technology into a militarily useful system by the Prussians proved to be a decisive advantage in two wars. Austria had failed to adapt to the new industrial economy, and France did not in regard to industrial-era organization

Before the Industrial Revolution, Germany could never have hoped to outpace France, Austria, and Russia in population, the most important power resource. But the railroad erased the simple equation between population and military strength. If the three could be faced one by one, the railroad would give Germany a technologically enhanced strategic advantage.

This analysis holds for the periphery as well. The railroads allowed European imperialists to create and secure markets and pacify large expanses of territory. Without it, the extension of European political and economic influence into the interiors of Africa, Asia, and Latin America (and settlers of European origin into the North American and Australian interiors) would have been all but impossible. The Europeans could never hope to match the native populations in numbers, but the railroad eliminated that disparity. European dominance came from the replacement of human power with machine power, the threat of overwhelming violence, and from the opportunity connection to the European economic system promised. The railroad helped manage the problem of conquering and administering vast spaces and huge populations within the context of an industrial world economy.

Lastly, the changes to the state marked a turning point in the evolution of the state as a domestic and international actor. To adapt industrial technology to state practices, the state had to transform itself into an industrial organization by expanding its size, scope, and functions.[238]

How was it that the railroad came to occupy such a position? This would be a trivial and apolitical question if railroad technology were a found object like gold or kindling for a fire. But since it was built over many decades within a complex set of social structures, the question needs a careful, political answer. The railroad was not an inevitable by-product of the Industrial Revolution, nor was a unified Germany an inevitable by-product of the railroad. The railroad used by the Prussian army in the 1860s and 1870s did not result from the inherent nature of iron rails and locomotives. Instead, the immature technology migrated to Germany via two mechanisms, the spread of industrial technology and geopolitical competition, where it was (semi) consciously constructed into a system built to satisfy certain ends (in this case military victory, unification, and security).

The shape of the railroad was not predetermined. Its development was pushed in one direction and not another by the outcome of nontechnical debates, economic events, political controversies, coincidences of timing, and the unforeseen outcomes of historical conjunctures. The public relations victory of George Stephenson's *Rocket* at the Rainhill Trials cemented the steam locomotive as the choice for rail technology. A cable-driven rail technology might have suited a civilian economy, but would not be well suited to warfare—destruction and reconstruction would have been enormously complicated, for one. The collapse of the railway boom in England pushed capital and technical expertise abroad and accelerated the pace of diffusion.

The timing and pace of diffusion coincided with the breakdown of Austro-Prussian relations; had industrialization spread later, the Prussian system might not have been available for the 1866 war. Nor was the victory over Austria inevitable. Benedek's blunders compensated for the mistakes Moltke's generals made in following his plans. Prussia's victory allowed the emergent technocrats to defeat the traditionalists in the Prussian military and give their ideas about the proper use of rail freer reign. It also established the Prussian military rail "system" as the international standard for emulation. Without these developments, the railroad as a tool of war and conquest might not have emerged at all, and certainly would have taken a different form. This series of contingencies and conjunctures shows the path-dependent nature of technology—it is a process in which branches taken rule out some possibilities but open up others.

The development of railroad as a component of the international system was also clearly a global, political process as well. International economic and political competition shaped the diffusion of rail technology from Britain to Germany, and Prussia's strategic ambitions drove it to innovate. In the absence of those pressures and ambitions—along with important domestic resources and institutional capacities—the "railroad" doesn't happen. It transformed the system by altering interaction capacity, but it emerged out of the system itself—shaped by it and molded to it. Railroad and international system were mutually constituted.

CHAPTER 4

THE ATOMIC BOMB
AND THE SCIENTIFIC STATE

INTRODUCTION

From World War II onward, nuclear weapons made great powers great, structured great power strategic interaction, and redefined the meaning of security. Together with the bipolar distribution of power, they defined the character and logic of the cold war era. The simple strategic calculations and the presumed tendency toward stability of a bipolar world are as much or more the product of the bomb as any happy accident of political arithmetic. The simple strategic calculations, the extreme heightening of risk, and the unacceptable costs of escalation and all-out war caused by nuclear weapons profoundly shaped the nature of the international system. This chapter traces the origins of nuclear weapons, sketches their role in the transition from the pre-cold war system, and outlines their significance to the cold war international system. Discoveries in nuclear and quantum physics before World War II were forged in the crucible of war into a nuclear explosive device. That device altered the interaction capacity of the international system and in turn transformed the system. But the development of the bomb was not inevitable. It depended on sufficient scientific capacity in the United States, accumulated over decades of institution building and international borrowings, and a series of chance conjunctural events: the 1933 Law for the Restoration of the Civil Service in Germany, and World War II. The bomb was a product of political forces—both international and domestic—and the bomb remade the international system. One does not exist without the other.

115

It is impossible to explain the impact of nuclear weapons on the international system without understanding how the international system participated in making nuclear weapons in the first place.

My examination of the bomb's origins stresses three factors. First, institutions—both domestic and international—were of central importance to determining what was and was not possible in the scientific or technological environment. Debates and scientific investigations were structured by institutional settings to favor one type of outcome over another or to favor one line of scientific research over another— in other words, nuclear weapons are a complex sociotechnical system interwoven indistinguishably with politics. Second, two pieces of evidence indicate that unintended consequences played a very important role—underlining this study's central point about the historical, path-dependent nature of technology. Third, autonomous historical agents had a significant role in determining outcomes. Individuals operating within given institutional settings pushed to deform or even escape those settings in pursuit of a variety of objectives. Concretely, innovation and institutional transformation (and international transformation) were the result of efforts to establish research universities in Germany; efforts to build a strong research base in the American universities; efforts to expel Jewish academics from all German state-appointed posts in 1933; and efforts to organize scientific research for war in the United States beginning in the late 1930s. These moments of institutional change are where institutions become less rigid—where more is left to chance and human will.

This chapter, as with the previous one on rail, follows the bomb's origins through four distinct stages. The first stage fixes Germany's institutional setting. The relevant events and features involve the institutional evolution of German science; its relationship to the German state and military; the successes, contradictions, and stresses that led to the diffusion of institutional methods, scientific knowledge, and a large percentage of its scientific talent to the United States over the course of the 1920s and 1930s; and finally, the failure of the German scientific system to develop the atomic bomb during the war. The task of the Germany section is to show how the evolution of the German system provided the setting in which the physical theory that came to underlie the atomic bomb was produced; how this institutional framework—when imperfectly copied by the Americans— greatly facilitated the American bomb project; how this system in the 1910s and 1920s generated great scientific talent that would later be crucial to the development of the bomb; and finally how the same system failed to fulfill its own promise and develop the bomb during the war. The relationship between science and the state was the key institutional reason for German scientific success. The state supported institutional and disciplinary innovation for reasons that about equally mixed international prestige, international great-power competition, and domestic economic development. The same relationship was responsible for the decline of German science and its abandonment in the 1920s and 1930s by many of its most skilled and innovative practitioners.

The second stage examines the United States' institutional setting before and in the initial stages of the diffusion of methods, knowledge, and talent from Germany. The central players are the scientific establishment and the federal government, military, and industry. The most important institutional development in American science before the World War II was the building of a world-class scientific educational and research system in the United States. Foreign models, in particular Germany, heavily influenced the construction of the American university system. Americans admired and studied at German universities in large numbers from the 1870s into the 1920s. Any American scholar of note in the early 1900s had spent time pursuing advanced research in Germany. Then, beginning in the 1920s, American university presidents and enterprising department heads in physics began luring German theoretical physicists away from their German appointments to permanent posts in American universities.[1] The mixing of American and German scientific institutions created the fertile American scientific environment of the 1920s and 1930s. Competition, institutional flexibility, and encouragement of innovation were hallmarks of this new system. The federal government, military, and industry contributed their organizational and administrative experience to the bomb project. The government gained important experience during World War I and managing various New Deal programs—especially the Tennessee Valley Authority. Beginning in the 1890s, the chemical and engineering industries developed rationalized scientific production techniques, which later made a necessary contribution to the success of the bomb project. The bomb itself was not simply a scientific achievement. It required a massive organizational and production effort made possible by the accumulated expertise of the state as well as private industry.

The diffusion of the émigré scientists marks the third stage. When the Nazi regime promulgated the Law for the Restoration of Career

Civil Service on April 4, 1933—and thereby expelled all Jewish academics from their university posts—it dispersed most of its cutting-edge physics talent. This was the first of two critical conjunctures without which nuclear weapons would never have emerged in the form and at the time they did. The United States benefited most from this rich immigration of scientific talent. Enterprising American and British academics, civil servants, and employees of philanthropic institutions established international exchange and placement programs for the refugees. In the United States, physics departments could contact the American refugee service and 'order' a scientist to fit their institutional needs. The diffusion of the scientists connects the institutional borrowings from Germany to the American bomb-building institutions and the émigrés themselves to the successful design and construction of the atomic bomb. Without these émigrés, the development of the bomb would have been delayed by months, if not years, making its use at the close of the war very unlikely.[2]

The fourth stage traces the construction of the institutional framework within which the atomic bomb was built. The Manhattan Project integrated theoretical and experimental scientific activity with engineering and large-scale construction and production techniques—all managed by the federal government—to undertake a project unprecedented in scope, scale, and comprehensiveness. No other state, industry, or firm had ever embarked on a technological project of such magnitude. The result of these efforts was the atomic bomb and a set of institutions and practices that would have a profound impact on cold war international relations.

The resources and organizational effort necessary to develop the bomb dovetailed with the capabilities and institutions in the United States. Only the United States—with its peculiar political and scientific institutional structure and vast collection of scientific talent—could have developed the bomb under wartime conditions. But these were not sufficient conditions for the bomb's emergence. The development of the atomic bomb was not inevitable, and the intensification of bomb research in 1942 did not happen automatically. Strong disagreement accompanied the decision to increase the commitment to wartime atomic bomb research in the United States. Only intervention by Vannevar Bush, director of the Office of Strategic Research and Development (OSRD)—the organization in charge of wartime uranium research, as it was then called—ensured that an expanded commitment was made.[3] Historians and firsthand observers alike have noted that the United States, given traditional congressional restrictions on federal spending, could never have built the bomb in peacetime. The war was necessary to remake American scientific, military, industrial, and state institutions and their interactions. Without that institutional revolution, the bomb could not have been produced.[4] Similarly, the nature of German state-science-industry interactions made the wartime development of a bomb highly unlikely, but the trajectory of German nuclear research in the 1930s suggests that the bomb would have been developed in Germany during peacetime.[5] The war itself was the second critical conjuncture affecting the development trajectory of nuclear weapons.

As for effects, the bomb did not cause the momentous shifts in international political and military power that accompanied World War II—these only developed as the war came to a close. It did, however, solidify those shifts, and was responsible for two other features of the postwar international system as well. By raising the costs of war to their theoretical maximum, it altered the interaction capacity of the international system and the nature of the system itself. Second, the scientific and technological institutions that made the bomb possible were themselves partially constitutive of the emerging American base of power. American postwar hegemony was built in part on this economic and scientific-technological prowess and great power aspirations necessitated the acquisition of an analogous scientific-technological and industrial production apparatus.

At a minimum, the bomb introduced an element of caution into great power competition. At a maximum, the bomb has laid the groundwork for the disintegration of the nation-state system.[6] The bomb has fundamentally altered notions of security. Its incredible destructive power ensures that any nuclear exchange of even moderate size will result in de facto mutual destruction. Its speed, range, and reliability of delivery have erased traditional meanings of front, noncombatant, and mobilization of manpower.

The bomb also had a profound impact on the institutions of state, military, and scientific interaction. The Manhattan Project established the paradigm for what came to be known as the military-industrial complex. Large-scale scientific research during peacetime became a permanent part of great powers' security practices. The bomb transformed the state and state–society relations just as the railroad had more than a half-century before.

Through the presentation of these four stages, and their culmination in the atomic bomb, I argue that the interplay of domestic and transnational institutions and international diffusion brought about a massive reshaping of the logic of the international system. While it makes sense to say nuclear weapons transformed the international system, we must also ask which nuclear weapons? Nuclear weapons are a sociotechnical system. They emerged shaped by a highly politically charged international and domestic environment and developed via a path-dependent process with two significant conjunctures that shaped the 'nuclear weapons' that emerged.

GERMANY

There are three facets to the German contribution to the atomic bomb. First, German science provided an institutional model for the practice of academic science based on two ideas: independent research and academic freedom. Second, the German educational system produced a group of exceptionally talented scientists. This talent was a vital part of both American and British atomic bomb projects (as well the Germans' own project). Third, the theoretical and experimental findings made by German scientists were of paramount importance to the development of the atomic bomb. All three facets of the German contribution were diffused from Germany to the United States over the first four decades of the twentieth century. This process was not some inevitable trajectory of science and engineering, but a product of conscious institutional design by the state, which supported almost all German science, and the scientists themselves. The diffusion of scientists and science was also a political process, taking place as it did within a transnational knowledge community[7] and in the context of international political competition for economic competitiveness and national prestige.

This section will outline the development of the German systems of academic and scientific research. It will also offer an explanation for the development of atomic physics in Germany in the early decades of the twentieth century. Finally, it will begin the process of explaining the diffusion of atomic talent and knowledge from Germany to the United States (and elsewhere) through a detailing of the 'push' factors—that combination of market, institutional, and political factors that drove many scientists from Germany in the 1920s and 1930s.

Why is it that the German-speaking world[8] developed so many talented scientists in the late nineteenth and early twentieth centuries? And why is it that those scientists were at the forefront of the development of the atomic bomb?[9] Only Prussia-Germany (and later the United States) had the educational infrastructure, the attitude toward the funding of scientific work, and the wealth to train dozens of world-class scientists and support their research. But why then did such educational and scientific systems develop in Germany? The answer lies in the peculiar relationship that evolved between state, university, and private industry in Germany in the context of late development. German science rose to dominance through the intersection of preindustrial academic practices and a rapidly industrializing German economy based on the systematic application of scientific discovery. A powerful central state oversaw the relationship between academy and industry because it was very interested in the exploitation of its industrial and intellectual resources for purposes of enhancing national power and prestige. The particular relationship between state and science was the core institutional reason for German scientific success.[10] No other state created the same set of institutions and incentives.

GERMAN SCIENTIFIC PREEMINENCE AND THE RISE OF THE RESEARCH IMPERATIVE

Germany was the archetypal late developer in Alexander Gershenkron's scheme: successful in the industries and technologies that made up the second industrial revolution. These industries—chemicals, electrical, aeronautics, precision mechanical, refrigeration, optics, and others—were crucial to German economic development.[11] They were also dependent on organized science for their development (unlike the first Industrial Revolution's textile production and light manufacturing), so a preeminent scientific infrastructure was a prerequisite for economic success.[12] As the twentieth century began, German science was universally recognized as the world's finest. German scientists won fully one-third of all Nobel prizes awarded in chemistry and physics between 1901 and 1914. Almost all of the newest and most significant discoveries and innovations in the physical sciences between 1900 and 1930 either took place in Germany or in countries within the broader German cultural and linguistic sphere.[13]

German universities (and German science) were the world's finest for two reasons: a commitment to research excellence in the universities, and a superior organization for linking scientific research with economic and political goals. In the eighteenth century, little original scientific research was done in universities, or any other institutionalized setting for that matter. France and England, the leading scientific countries, had a long and successful tradition of independent, aristocratic science. In the absence of institutional support, science was left to those of the independently wealthy with the time and inclination to pursue a life of scientific research, or those the aristocracy saw fit to support. As the nineteenth century began, the university professor was still only a transmitter of existing knowledge. The university was not the place for the production of new knowledge. Over the course of the century, the professor's responsibility to engage in original research replaced this conception.

Professionalization happened first and most rapidly in Germany. Other countries were much slower to adopt a commitment to research excellence—or the research imperative, as one historian of the phenomenon has termed it. The English viewed the imperative as antithetical to the aims and customs of their universities; the Americans admired it but were reluctant to adopt it; the French ignored it.[14]

As science gained a greater role in economic matters, Germany gained an advantage over its European rivals. The absence of scientific practice outside the universities and the strong links between the universities and the state actually encouraged professionalization and adoption of the research imperative. There were no other societal groups to compete with the university for a monopoly on scientific research. Generous state support meant more funds were available for scientific research than in other countries. And the existence of a competitive structure between universities for scholars made research the determinant of scholarly success.

The research imperative was not simply a state- or competition-induced goal. It was closely tied to the peculiarly German scholarly ideal of *Wissenschaft*, which is usually defined as learning in a universal, totalizing sense. Its most important proponent, F. W. J. Schelling, described the process of learning advocated by *Wissenschaft*, "Every thought not conceived in this sprit of unity and totality is intrinsically empty, of no account."[15] The ideal of *Wissenschaft* was created and advocated by a group of academics in the early nineteenth century to counteract the erosion of the universities in the late eighteenth century.

One result of this structure was a novel notion: academic freedom. The pressure to publish could easily coexist in an authoritarian research atmosphere. But German scholarly accomplishments of this period were characterized by their high quality and independence of thought. The research imperative was thus the product of a combination of factors more or less unique to Germany: the interests of a modernizing, unifying state; the economic needs of a late developer;

an ideology of learning that idealized abstract knowledge; a competitive structure between universities; and the pressures of the professionalization of knowledge production.[16]

Superior organization—the second factor explaining German scientific excellence—linked academic research and industrial need. The technologies of the second Industrial Revolution were science-based and required systematic investigation to reveal their potentialities. In the imperial period, German science was specifically directed at industry. The interaction between pure and applied science was institutionalized first in the universities, and later in the profusion of technical and research institutes that sprung up in response to growing industrial demand. The foremost example of this latter phenomenon is Werner Siemens's involvement in what became the *Physikalisch Technische Reichsanstalt* (PTR).[17] In the other European countries and the United States, the links between university, state and industry were nowhere near as institutionalized. This gave the Germans a tremendous lead in science that was erased only in the 1930s. What is most important about the two factors explaining German scientific success (the research imperative and institutional integration) is their political and path-dependent nature. The two were tied directly to state incentives, and they were also unique to Germany because of its peculiar set of state–society relations.

EARLY STATE–ACADEMY RELATIONS

The early imperial period in German science is marked by three trends: increased involvement of industry with scientific research, the refusal of the universities to adapt to the need for greater attention to applied science and engineering, and the rise of independent research and technical institutes to fill the gap left by the universities.

The German state supported higher education and science in the imperial period because of increased demand for higher education from students and from government bureaucracies for trained civil servants. But the state was also motivated by global political and economic competition. The Reich supported science because it considered science and university achievement important for military, economic, and even diplomatic purposes.[18] The German university was both a source of scientific innovation and a politically safe beneficiary of state attention and money. University professors saw the emerging, politically conscious bourgeoisie as a threat to their special privileges and were thus unlikely to join in the demand for expanded political rights. Their reward was substantial increases in government expenditures. The state received something in return and relations with the academy were structured around three institutions: control over academic careers, professional exams, and ideological legitimation.

Over the whole imperial period, spending by Prussia on its universities (which totaled more than half of Germany's total) stayed a relatively constant 0.4 percent to 0.7 percent of the state budget; a figure that disguises the effects of a general increase in state expenditures. Between 1865 and 1914, the *Länder* (federal states) added new facilities to preexisting research institutes and founded twenty-three new institutes of science and technology. Within the universities, salaries for professors and spending for research facilities also increased. Student enrollment in universities grew. There were approximately 14,000 students in German universities in 1870, 34,000 by 1900, and 61,000 in 1914. Between 1870 and 1905, the professoriate doubled in size from a little less than 1,500 to a little less than 3,000.[19]

All universities in the German states were government institutions; there were no private universities as in Western Europe and the United States. The university professor was therefore a salaried civil servant.[20] This relationship was a double-edged sword. It ensured that the professor was isolated from social disapproval, but it tied the professor's fortunes directly to the state.

The state had control over appointments and funding of research and used those tools to create a strong competitive environment for the universities. A peculiar structure, part design and part accident,[21] helped stimulate scientific excellence in the German universities. In Prussia, between 1817 and 1900 there were 1,355 theology, law, and medicine appointments made to senior faculty positions. In each case, an independent review of the candidates by their peers was made, but in 322 cases the Ministry of Education determined the final appointment without or against faculty recommendation. The awarding of research institutes was the preferred manner for funding university scientific research. In almost all cases, the institutes were awarded to individual professors. Neither university nor department had any official say and consequently little influence over the nature of research that went on within it.[22]

Access to higher education, graduate education, and all manner of careers including the professoriate, the civil service, the law, and medicine were governed by a wide variety of examinations administered at various stages by the universities. Exams determined advancement from secondary school to undergraduate university, from undergraduate to professional school, and from professional school to professional practice. As specialization increased and the number of professions grew, the number and type of exams increased. The system of exams gave the state (with the aid of the university) a fine degree of control over the distribution of privilege in German society. Unlike in other societies, independent professional organizations had no control over the process of professional certification.[23]

Ideological legitimation flowed from the university to the state. The university's research and scholarly excellence—tied in with its dependence on the state—generated the presumption of harmony between the idea of scholarly research (*Wissenschaft*) and state interests. The relationship worked as planned. The excellence of the German universities bought the ambitious German state badly desired international prestige. "For many in the scientific, technological, and industrial worlds, [German science] came to symbolize, in another sphere, the young German Reich's newly acquired political power and authority."[24]

Ideally, the state's role in university life was to support the development of science and—by ensuring that the competitive mechanism functioned smoothly—to prevent the ossification of the academy. In practice the system worked, but an unintended consequence was a strengthening of the individual researcher at the expense of the university. Within the universities, faculties held power over appointments, salaries, and research facilities (within limits set by the state); university administrators had little authority.[25]

Beginning in the 1890s, the period covered by in the next section, the scientific environment became more complex. Engineering and applied science rose in importance and government-sponsored, independent, and university-allied research institutes proliferated to meet demand. Here the adaptability of the university ended. The emphasis on practical research directly conflicted with the university's identity as producer and guardian of universal, pure knowledge. The university retrenched. It refused to offer engineering or technical education and was bypassed by the state and private interests. Funding for science shifted from universities to research institutes and technical schools, and individual scientists gained great influence over the evolution of science. Senior physicists, most safely in their research institutes, decisively influenced the direction of the discipline from 1900 to 1920—a period when physics was the most rapidly expanding of all academic disciplines.[26]

STATE–INDUSTRY–ACADEMY RELATIONS: THE INSTITUTIONAL REVOLUTION IN GERMAN SCIENCE, 1870–1933

Political unification brought the research imperative and industry together in pursuit of systematic innovation. The development of the independent research institutes was the second phase in the development of the system that would produce the atom bomb. It was a largely unintended consequence of the peculiar relationship between universities, scientists, and the state. As research demands from industry increased in the last decades of the nineteenth century, the universities (mostly) successfully resisted. The German states, German industry, and individual scientists interested in advancing science responded by ignoring them. Instead they created new scientific institutions or elevated existing ones in funding and prestige. The two most important of these were the research institutes and the *Technische Hochschulen* (THs—technical institutes). Scientific practice in these institutions was spread across the scientific disciplines, but to trace the institutional history of the atom bomb, in what follows I will restrict my analysis to institutes and labs devoted to physics.

The research institute was the most significant new setting for the physical sciences. Research institutes had existed throughout the nineteenth century, but until the 1880s they had been attached to universities and were rather small in scale. In the early 1800s, what became the institutes were referred to as collections—literally collections of experimental equipment gathered when professionalization demanded that equipment to be moved from professors' private homes into university facilities. By the 1840s, institutes absorbed a greater percentage of university budgets than salaries. University research institutes were separate facilities, later even separate buildings, usually given to a prominent faculty member to pursue independent research and advanced training of graduate students. McClelland observes that it "was these institutions [seminars and institutes], a sort of university within the university, that gave the German higher education system much of its world renown in the late nineteenth century."[27]

Yet by the early 1880s, some in industry, state, and academy thought that the demands of graduate training in the university institutes were preventing physicists from devoting enough time to research. In 1882, Field Marshal Helmuth von Moltke and Gustav von

Gossler, the head of the Prussian *Kultusministerium* (Culture Ministry), convened a committee to consider the establishment of a physics institute funded by the state of Prussia and devoted exclusively to advanced basic research. One important advocate of such an institute was the industrialist Werner Siemens. Siemens argued before the committee that university physics lacked the equipment and time for important research. What was needed, he contended, was an institute—supported by the state—devoted to basic research to fulfill the needs of science and industry.[28]

A proposal to fund the institute was submitted to the Reischtag in 1886. Initially, opposition in the legislature was overwhelming. Conservatives were reluctant to commit the necessary funds so they welcomed the complaints of engineers—who argued that the focus on basic research excluded them—and the observations of university physicists—who argued that the institute was unnecessary. The debate was finally resolved by the intervention of the crown prince in 1886. Construction on the PTR began in Berlin in the same year. Much of the work at the institute was focused on measurement and equipment issues, or metrology. This activity was key to the systematization and the advancement of physics as a discipline. Important findings on black-body radiation made at the PTR helped lay the experimental groundwork for quantum mechanics.[29]

The research institutes were complemented by the rise in prestige and size of the THs. The THs had trained engineers and applied scientists since the eighteenth century. They did no research, but the increased demand for applied research scientists in the 1880s and 1890s, and the universities' unwillingness to help fill the gap, led to an elevation in their importance and prestige. Consequently, they were deeply resented and mistrusted by the university professoriate. In 1899, Friedrich Althoff, a Prussian administrator of university affairs, and Felix Klein, a math professor at the University of Göttingen, recommended that the THs be allowed to award a Ph.D. in engineering. Althoff thought to use the award as an example to the THs' university colleagues to incorporate technology into their curricula. The fierce opposition of the professoriate was only overcome through the personal intervention of Kaiser Wilhelm II. Twenty-two years later the THs received the right to award the Ph.D. in physics.[30]

The transformation of German science in the late nineteenth century has been called an institutional revolution.[31] This revolution successfully merged applied and pure science and academic research with economic need. This combination propelled Imperial Germany to the front ranks of economic development and world scientific achievement. The revolution in science was a product of the conservative modernization strategy pursued by crown and Reich and endorsed by both university and industry. Kaiser Wilhelm and Bismarck wanted the army and weapons a modern economy could provide, but not the modern society that went with it.[32] Generally, their partners in the academy and in industry concurred.

The link between scientific achievement and international economic and political competition was quite explicit in the debates over institutional modernization. Anxiety about growing American scientific competitiveness was effective in motivating government action on behalf of German science.[33] Indicative are the intervention of the kaiser to grant the THs the right to award the Ph.D., and the involvement by Bismarck and the crown prince in 1887 to secure funding for the PTR. All three were ultimately convinced to intervene by the argument that, without their help, Germany's competitive position internationally would be compromised.

Two pieces of documentary evidence make the point even more explicitly. In arguing for the *Kaiser Wilhelm Gesellschaft* (KWG—a chemical research institute), three politically active chemists wrote in 1909 that "the military and science are the two strong pillars upon which Germany's greatness rests." And a joint memo drafted by the Prussian Ministry of Education and the Reich Interior Ministry in 1911 argued that "for Germany, the maintenance of its scientific hegemony is just as much a necessity for the state as is the superiority of its army."[34] This relationship between the state and science was the core institutional reason for German scientific success. State leaders, motivated by their modernizing, national mission provided the funds and the insulation from economic and social pressures. Scientists within the universities and institutes supplied the advanced training and created a research ethos that placed the formulation of new knowledge above simple transmission. The social position of the scientist—economically and socially wedded to the state and insulated from the private economy and society—created a political ideology that supported the empire's modernizing project.

Support for the imperial institutions of science continued unabated in the early years of the Weimar Republic and several new funding sources and scientific institutions were created. The most important new institute was Max Planck's *Institut fur Physik*. Theoretical physicists thought the PTR was too applied in its orientation. As early as 1914, a group of Berlin physicists including Planck, Fritz

Haber, Walther Nernst (the discoverer of the third law of thermody-
namics), and Emil Warburg (then president of the PTR) proposed to
the Prussian government institutes for physics and cell physiology (for
Warburg, who was retiring from the PTR). Both institutes were approved in 1917, but government opposition stalled the building of
either institute until after the war. The small sum of money did allow
the Institute for Physics to begin support for physics research. The
Institute in the 1920s supported important research in theoretical and
atomic physics, including work by students of Max Born at the University of Göttingen on quantum and statistical mechanics, and research into the interaction of radiation and matter.[35]

Warburg's Cell Physiology Institute was built in 1931, but problems caused by the Nazi takeover delayed completion of the Physics
Institute. In 1930, Planck got the Rockefeller Foundation—which
had supported much work in German physics in the 1920s through
graduate fellowships and grants for institutes—to agree to underwrite
the construction of the institute for RM1.5 million. Coordination
took some time, so, in 1933 when the Nazis came to power and the
institute was still not built, the foundation began to have some serious
doubts about their participation in Nazi science. In the end, Rockefeller
president Max Mason decided to fulfill the foundation's obligation
and in 1937 the institute was opened. The institute was in operation
for only two years before it was taken over by the German army for
its nuclear fission research.[36]

As with the imperial government, the Weimar state's interest in
supporting science grew out of a concern for the economic health and
political and cultural status of the German nation. And, as during the
empire, the universities were an obstacle to be evaded, not a partner.
This time, instead of building new institutional arrangements to avoid
the universities, the state developed a new method for funding scientific research—one that went directly to the individual researcher.
The ostensible reason for this change was to increase research productivity to boost the prostrate German economy. But German science
played another, far more ambiguous cultural role for Germany. Faced
with the decline of German military power, scientists and state bureaucrats collaborated to use Germany's international scientific prestige in an attempt to prop up waning perceptions of German power
and importance abroad.[37]

Funding for physics alone was nearly twice—in real terms—
what it was before the war. The Weimar government also created two
new funding sources that offered a significant change from prewar

funding patterns. The *Notgemeinschaft der Deutschen Wissenschaft* (NGW) and the *Helmholtz-Gesellschaft zur Förderung der Physikalisch-Technischen Forschung* (HG) offered funding to individual research projects picked by expert panels of active scientists. In practice, this meant that the powerful directors of institutes had complete control over the research done in their institute—a development that would have ramifications for the German atom bomb project during World War II. With the new procedures, the funders judged the quality and promise of researchers and individual projects, and not simply the reputation of the institute director.[38]

The NGW was by far the more important of the two—providing between four and six times as much support for physics over the Weimar period. It made a concerted effort to fund young scientists and break the latter's traditional and harsh dependence on their advisor. It was—from the scientific perspective—quite progressive. Berlin physicists and theoreticians dominated the physics and math-physics referee panels. To an emerging conservative, antitheoretical, and racist backlash within physics (led by the Nobel laureates Johannes Stark and Philip Lenard), these panels and the NGW itself were Jewish and Berlin-centric, which they were.[39]

Politics profoundly shaped the institutions of German science in the later imperial and Weimar periods, just as it had earlier. The consequence, as the National Socialists came to power, was a peculiar system for producing scientific knowledge that would prove dysfunctional with the needs of a wartime atomic bomb project.

ATOMIC SCIENCE

This institutional history has emphasized the systems' strengths in three areas: the production of large numbers of talented scientists, the generation of an atmosphere that encouraged original research, and (to a point) institutions flexible enough to accommodate changes in scientific practice and possibilities. I now focus on the scientific 'outputs' of those institutions. What was the German scientific contribution to atomic science and what was the role of the institutions of German science in that development?

In the winter of 1938–1939, Otto Hahn and Fritz Strassmann, both chemists at the KWG for chemistry, discovered nuclear fission. The two had only a vague sense of the importance of their findings. Lise Meitner and Otto Frisch, her nephew and a theoretical physicist, made the interpretation. Meitner was also a chemist who for many years had shared a productive partnership with Hahn in Berlin where they had worked on radioactivity and beta decay. As a Jew, she was forced to leave Germany in 1938,[40] and it was while at Niels Bohr's Copenhagen physics institute that she and her nephew grasped the implications of the Hahn–Strassmann experiment. Their conclusions were so important, that the nucleus could be split, that Bohr could not await publication of the findings in the February 1939 edition of *Nature*. While on a trip to the United States, he leaked news of their discovery to the atomic physics community in New York and it quickly spread south with him to Princeton and Washington, DC.[41]

This anecdote neatly places the German contribution to the atomic bomb at the moment of its conceptual birth in its broader international scientific context. German scientists did not monopolize the series of discoveries, theoretical breakthroughs, and adjustments and corrections that made up the creation of the atomic bomb. Nevertheless, their contribution looms larger than scientists from any other country (before the 1933 diaspora and the Manhattan Project).

There is no precise way to evaluate the importance of hundreds of individual contributions to a collectively held body of knowledge, but a variety of measures can make an approximation. Forman, Heilbron, and Weart's comprehensive quantitative survey shows that, in 1909, Germany had 962 physicists, Great Britain 282, France 316, Denmark 21, and the United States 404.[42] These figures give Germany 30 percent of the world's physicists and, if physicists in the Austro-Hungarian Empire are included (a reasonable assumption as the finest, such as John von Neumann, tended to end up at German universities), the figure rises to 38 percent. The same study sampled four physics abstracts and found that around the year 1900 approximately 29 percent of physics papers were of German origin, 21 percent from the British Empire, 18 percent from France, 12 percent from the United States, and 6 percent from Italy.[43] The use of these figures is problematic as they provide only a snapshot of one year and give no weight to quality. But, as a crude measure, they offer important evidence for strong German leadership in physics.

To measure influence, a biographical history of atomic science intended to single out the most important achievements gives an overview of the national distribution of atomic scientists from the discovery of X rays by Roentgen in 1895 to nuclear fission.[44] Sixty-seven scientists are profiled. Of the sixty-seven, twenty-two (nearly one-third) are German. The United States and Great Britain tie for second with fifteen (or 22 percent) each. From there, the numbers fall off dramatically: six French citizens, two from Italy, two from the Netherlands, two from India, and one each from Denmark, Japan, and Russia.

The German contribution is also particularly long lasting and especially broad. It extends from Roentgen's discovery in 1895; through Planck's quantum theory of radiation around 1900; Einstein's theories of relativity published in 1905; quantum, statistical, and wave mechanics developed by Heisenberg, Wolfgang Pauli, and Irwin Schrödinger in the mid-1920s, to Meitner and Frisch's insight in 1938. In contrast, the British contribution is more experimental in nature, dominated by J. J. Thompson and Ernest Rutherford, and clustered in the 1900s and 1910s. The most important exception to this generalization is James Chadwick's discovery of the neutron in 1933. Of the fifteen Americans in the sample, only three made their contributions before 1930.

This is an admittedly crude measure (Bohr, for example, is the only Dane represented, but his contribution in qualitative terms far exceeds the $1^1/_2$ percent of the sample he represents). It does, however, confirm the broad picture: German contributions dominate, Bohr's Institute and Rutherford's Cavendish lab are important but isolated pockets of excellence, and American atomic physics emerged only in the 1930s.

Theoretical physics, the intellectual backbone of the atomic bomb, was part of a general trend within the physical sciences that relied more and more on an explicit division of labor between theoretical and experimental work. Experimentation in atomic physics especially needed to be guided by theoretical research. The intellectual labor necessary for producing the theoretical explanations for experimental results and new theoretical models of atomic and nuclear behavior to guide experimentation was a full-time endeavor for the greatest scientific minds of the era. It was all but impossible to be a first-rate experimentalist and theorist in atomic physics. Enrico Fermi comes closest to that ideal, but his achievements were still largely experimental in nature. No national scientific community had as many theoretical physicists as Germany, and no community had the ability to train new theoretical physicists.

In 1900, Germany had sixteen faculty posts in theoretical and mathematical physics or 15 percent of all physics posts in the country.

Austria-Hungary had eight, or 17 percent of the total. Great Britain had two, who accounted for only 3 percent of the kingdom's physicists; France 4 or 8 percent; and the United States 2 or 3 percent. Ten years later, the figures were all but unchanged, although the two senior faculty in the United States seem to have retired. Papers on relativity provide another perspective. Up to 1922, 30 percent of all papers on relativity were produced by German scholars while half that amount were attributed to physicists within the British Empire and 13 and 11 percent to French and American physicists, respectively.[45]

The individual contributions of the greatest among their number underline the central role played by German scientists.[46] Max Planck's discovery of the quantum of action and the photon was the first theoretical challenge to classical physics. Albert Einstein's theories of relativity allowed scientists to think of matter and energy as two forms of the same fundamental phenomenon. Wolfgang Pauli's exclusion principle—describing the necessary distribution of electrons within the levels of the atom—is one of the most fundamental theoretical underpinnings of atomic physics. Erwin Schrödinger, Werner Heisenberg, and Max Born developed the mathematical tools used to solve the dynamic problems of the behavior of electrons: wave and quantum mechanics, respectively. Heisenberg's great contribution was to move quantum and atomic theory beyond the rather metaphysical contributions of Bohr to a theory that stressed, and made use of, actual measurement and experimentation.

German science held this lead for three reasons. German universities trained more atomic scientists than any other national system—often training students from other countries (the U.S. case will be discussed later). In the early decades of the twentieth century, there were four institutes of theoretical physics in the world; three of these—Göttingen, Berlin, and Munich—were German (Bohr's Copenhagen institute was the fourth). The Munich institute, directed by Arnold Sommerfeld, trained fully one-third of all the theoretical physicists in Germany, including four Nobel Prize winners, between 1906 and 1928.[47]

Second, the research ethos was stronger in German universities. This ethos, with its Hegelian tenor, encouraged the pursuit of abstract knowledge for its own sake and, as a consequence, the German academy was the first to embrace theoretical physics. Of the world's seventeen theoretical physicists in 1909, ten were German and five of the remaining were Austrian or Swiss. There were no theoretical physicists in Great Britain, France, or the United States.[48]

Third, the flexibility of German scientific institutions allowed scientists to be more innovative. The institutional structure was able to break down or circumvent the inherent conservatism of the professoriate. Famous, talented physicists could get separate institutes for theoretical physics founded in their honor, frequently with no intervention or influence on the part of their colleagues. Once the institutes were established, the institute directors had complete control of the nature of research that went on within their institutes. Therefore, despite resistance from experimentalists, the young field of theoretical physics was able to find a home in German universities as it emerged in the 1880s. This is in marked contrast to the situation elsewhere. One of the shortcomings of the British, French, and American universities was the ability of the professoriate to stifle disciplinary innovation. In England, France, and the United States at the same time (and well into the twentieth century), theoretical physics was shunned by mainstream physicists and shut off from independent support.[49]

The institutional environment of German science was a remarkable and unique breeding ground for innovation in science, and physics in particular. The institutional design—the emphasis on research, the independence of researchers, and support for a large number of physicists—is directly connected with the outputs. German scientists dominated physics, particularly theoretical and atomic physics. But the same features that were sources of strength in the 1910s and 1920s broke down in the 1930s.

THE DECLINE OF GERMAN SCIENCE

In an atmosphere of war, institutional innovation, social and political upheaval, and economic depression, German physicists made their greatest contributions to atomic physics. Einstein's theory of relativity, Planck's quantum theory, Heisenberg's quantum mechanics, Schröedinger's wave mechanics, and many others were all produced in the turbulent early decades of the twentieth century. But the same decades also signaled the eclipse of German science and the replacement of the German model for scientific organization with the American. The rise of American science accounts for much of Germany's decline. The failure of the German model to adapt to changing social and scientific circumstances explains the rest. The loss of German scientific leadership internally has three facets: the conservatism and independence of the professoriate stalled needed institutional adaptation, demographic pressure on resources in the form of increased student enrollments only exacerbated the failure to adapt, and the historical conjuncture of the Great Depression doomed any attempts at adjustment.

The continued success of a national scientific enterprise depends on dual excellence in scientific research and in the training and integration of the next generation of researchers. In pre-World War I Germany, the close relationship with the state and the social, political, and economic insulation that relationship provided had allowed the scientific community to develop relatively independently. The research ethos and competition between universities and professors for students and researchers alike guaranteed a high quality of instruction and research. But it also institutionalized the power of the individual senior faculty member and eroded traditional corporate identification and solidarity within the university.

Applied sciences and engineering were the most important disciplinary developments of the second Industrial Revolution. But the research ethos enshrined in the universities disdained them, and the professoriate refused to teach or practice the applied sciences. The institutional evolution of the institutes and THs bypassed the professoriate instead of forcing it to adapt. But the academy through its long relationship with the state retained the advantage of salaries and prestige. The university remained the only place a young scientist could make his or her name and aspire to a lucrative and prestigious position in a university or research institute. Neither institutes nor universities could satisfy the career demands of the scientists they were producing. The demographic explosion and the Depression only exacerbated this problem.

Between 1870 and 1905, the university population trebled, with the bulk of the increase coming in the last decade. The general growth of the population, the expansion of careers requiring a university degree, greater societal wealth, longer courses of study, and the attractiveness of the university to women and foreigners all contributed to the increase. In the same period, from 1870 to 1905, the professoriate (meaning those with civil service standing: full and associate professors) only doubled.[50]

Through sheer numerical pressure, the teaching load on the faculty increased and the time available for research decreased. The growing ranks of junior faculty took up the bulk of new teaching duties, but the successful resistance of the professoriate to expand its ranks made the employment prospects for these new faculty grim.

Elevation to the senior faculty ranks was very unlikely, but there was little opportunity to perform the research necessary to attract outside attention (from a research institute or foreign university). The junior professor was stuck in genteel poverty by a conservative oligarchy of older professors. This situation was made only worse by the Depression. Because universities were already losing research prestige to the independent institutes, research funding was cut back and teaching appointments reduced.[51]

The Depression sped up processes already under way. The university gerontocracy caused, and graduate student unemployment exacerbated, the decline of German science. But bad conditions for scientists would have been meaningless without significant options. In the 1920s and 1930s, a brilliant alternative to employment in Germany, especially for atomic scientists, existed: the United States. The effort to build American science begun in the 1900s had paid off handsomely by the 1920s. The fantastic experimental machinery (such as cyclotrons, which did not exist in Germany as yet) and the high salaries lured several German theoretical and atomic physicists to the United States before the 1933 expulsion of Jewish academics from the universities and government employment.[52] The center of scientific activity shifted from Germany to the United States. In the absence of Nazism, many German scientists probably would have found their way to American universities in the 1930s and 1940s anyway.[53]

THE FAILURE OF THE GERMAN BOMB PROJECT

The expulsion of Jews from all civil service positions in April 1933 set the stage for the final phase of pre-bomb German science: the failed Nazi atomic bomb project. Since the war ended, a lively debate has ensued as to the precise causes of that failure.[54] My task is not to evaluate the truthfulness of the various competing claims for the failure—they deal in too great detail with the twists and turns of individual psychology and intellectual capability. I only need to evaluate the consequences of the institutional devolution of German science on the project. In brief, the scientific institutions that had served Germany so well for more than half a century had ossified by the 1940s. The resultant structure—which concentrated so much influence over the direction of research in individual institute heads—was unable to produce the required synergy between theoretical and experimental physics, and then both with industry. The necessary institutional design for a successful bomb project was simply not there.

After an initial flirtation with *Deutsche Physik*—an anti-quantum mechanics, anti-Jewish version of physics—the Nazi regime turned quickly to "Jewish" physics.[55] But the toll of the 1933 dismissal order on the sciences was great, and greatest of all in physics. Of the twenty Nobel Prize laureates removed from their posts, eleven were physicists, but enough physics ability remained to make an atomic bomb project feasible. The top scientists on the German bomb project were a talented group. They included Otto Hahn, a radiochemist at the KWG; Max von Laue, a nuclear physicist also at the KWG; Walter Gerlach, a physicist at the Institute of Physics in Munich; Heisenberg, physicist and then director of the KWG; Paul Hartek, a physical chemist from Hamburg; and Carl Friedrich von Weizsäcker, a theoretical physicist at the KWG. A number of these men (most notably, von Laue and Heisenberg) were important figures in prewar quantum and atomic physics.[56]

The problem was not inadequate talent. Instead, the bomb project suffered from insufficient integration of pure science with applied science, engineering, and industrial production—an organization that would prove so important to the success of the Manhattan Project. David Irving has argued that the German effort was slowed down significantly by excessive attention to the theoretical implications of their bomb project, a trait long characteristic of German science.[57] However, the institutional legacy of German science only begs the question: why was there not a revolution in the organization of science during wartime as there was in the United States? At the moment when Americans were remaking science–state relations, the Germans were making do with old forms and methods. The Nazis did enjoy some success with their wartime industrial policy, but they were either engineering or scientific achievements. The integration of theory and applied science with engineering and mass production so important to the atomic bomb and radar projects were American and British achievements. Why wasn't such an integration made by German science?

In the winter of 1941–1942, the American and German bomb efforts were remarkably similar. The amount of money spent was all but identical and the scientific results were similar. Then the American effort began to pull ahead. Part of the explanation for the change was superior American technology. Experimental tools like cyclotrons allowed the American project to discover properties of plutonium and uranium faster than the German attempt. But a science policy decision made that winter by the German army officials overseeing the bomb project was a more significant factor. They decided not to push the project into industrial production but instead scaled the program back—essentially keeping it in the lab. They concluded that production of a bomb during the war was unlikely. Although they thought a bomb feasible in principle, changing war fortunes and growing economic hardship within Germany combined with pessimistic reports from the atomic scientists convinced the army that there was no point in pursuing the bomb with any greater commitment of resources. The war in Europe had changed that winter from one that seemed likely to end quickly and in Germany's favor, to one that seemed likely to end later rather than sooner. Every German scientific resource was needed on programs with obvious and clear benefit to the new circumstances. In this context, the bomb was irrelevant.[58]

The United States, on the other hand, had decided that the bomb was both feasible during the war and potentially relevant to American war aims. American scientists were as pessimistic as their German counterparts about construction of a working bomb before war's end, but their pessimism existed in a different context. The Japanese bombing of Pearl Harbor and American entry into the war only reinforced the decision to move the bomb project into the industrial production phase and made speed more of an issue. A decision was made in the winter of 1941–1942 that the OSRD should push as fast as possible on the bomb and with full-scale construction on the horizon, the project could be turned over to the army—an event that took place on August 13, 1942.[59]

Scientific leadership passed from Germany to the United States. The institutional revolution necessary to bring the atomic bomb into being was an unprecedented melding of state–military direction with scientific freedom; theoretical physics with applied engineering; and all of these with industrial mass production. The United States was better positioned to make this revolution, but the Germans also had to choose not to try. This they did in 1941–1942 under a confluence of factors: loss of scientific personnel, inadequate institutional links between the pure and applied sciences, declining economic conditions, and an important shift in the course of the war, with the first two the more crucial elements.

CONCLUSION

The flexibility of German scientific institutions, the quantity of funding for science, and the dominance of the research ethos created ideal conditions for the flourishing of theoretical physics. These three factors ensured that the highest quality advanced training in theoretical physics was available, that research in theoretical physics was funded as it was nowhere else, and that theoretical physicists enjoyed sufficient prestige and influence to pursue their research agenda.[60] The evolution of a distinct subdiscipline of theoretical physics in turn made atomic physics possible. The investigation of the structure and behavior of the atom and it parts was unprecedented in the history of science because it depended so heavily on theory. Theory, for the first time, directed experiment and verification rather than being created post hoc to account for experimental results. This section has tried to account for the emergence of theoretical physics in institutional terms—by forging a link between the institutions and funding of German science and the actual atomic science that was practiced within the institutions. However, institutions can only restrict options and enable action—they are never completely determinative. The creative genius of Einstein or Heisenberg is not accounted for in this analysis.

The broader argument for this section is that conditions unique to Germany created a climate ideal for the development of atomic physics. The same conditions, added to a changing international situation, made it unlikely but not impossible that Germany would build an atomic bomb. A set of scientific institutions and modes of scientific practice were the creation of interested state managers, industrial leaders, and scientists. Concerned, respectively, with an international competition for power and prestige, international and domestic economic competitiveness, and the development of the scientific disciplines; this triumvirate built an exceptional university system in the nineteenth century and an ideology that favored research. When the university system proved resistant to accommodating the changes deemed necessary for the continued development of science, the same triumvirate collaborated on new institutional arrangements and simply bypassed the conservative university departments. These new arrangements were especially beneficial to the new fields of nuclear and quantum physics. In most instances, the new subdiscipline flourished not in university departments, but in institutes created to safeguard it from jealous university colleagues.

The same institutional structure and disciplinary ideology proved to be the German system's undoing. The system failed on three levels: political ideology, the sharp division between theory and experiment, and the absence of scientific collaboration. All three were necessary in the emerging age of 'big science,' and all three were present in abundance in the American institutional setting. The dependence on the state and the disinterested, 'apolitical' quality of *Wissenschaft* turned the academy into a refuge of reaction and bigotry. Even before the 1933 Civil Service law went into effect, anti-Semitism had driven many scientists from Germany. Although disappearing senior positions (relative to the number of aspirants) and declining salaries were of course a factor, it is no accident that most of the early émigrés were also Jewish. While not (yet) barred from holding university positions, unspoken quotas at times blocked appointments or promotions; having too many Jews in one's department was something to be avoided.[61]

The institute structure—individual academic 'stars' isolated and all-powerful in their own domains—while a useful and necessary innovation, made it impossible for German science to create the interchange and collaboration that was to characterize American science. This created a sharp division between theory and experiment and collaboration in the discipline more generally. German scientists spoke with one another. Absent was collaboration on a single project; theorists were not available in the lab to answer questions about an experiment in progress, nor was joint authorship promoted.

The German system created the necessary scientific preconditions for the atomic bomb, but that system lacked the capabilities to capitalize on its achievements. The expulsion of the Jews from the academy in 1933 was but the last act in the diffusion of the system's achievements to the United States. German science would never recover from the loss of the émigrés and the devastation of World War II.

AMERICAN GROUND

European science, European scientific training, and European scientists were a necessary component of the atomic bomb project, but science and scientists entered into an environment that was highly receptive and capable of exploiting that knowledge and talent. In the previous section, I explained the first half of this equation: the excellence of German science and the initial reasons for pre-Nazi era emigration to the United States. In this section, I discuss the American environment. Two institutional features explain its receptivity: the strength of academic physics and its ability to absorb quantum physics, and the development of the management and systems engineering techniques necessary to plan and administer the Manhattan Project.

The transmission of quantum physics depended on the development of great universities with graduate schools committed to research, and a discipline of physics strong and flexible enough to accommodate the new subdiscipline and its practitioners. A small handful of academic entrepreneurs, in collaboration with the major American philanthropic organizations, built the American graduate school heavily reliant on foreign, especially German, models and without any significant state role (sharply distinguishing the American case from the German one).

American physics' receptivity to quantum physics was surprising in light of an impoverished theoretical tradition. Yet, in the 1910s and 1920s, a generation of experimental physicists emerged who grasped that the new developments in physics then taking place in Europe would dominate all further developments in the discipline. Out of character with their institutional position, this group of academic entrepreneurs strongly advocated the strengthening of theoretical physics. This impulse to reorient the discipline came at a key moment in the history of science funding in the United States. After World War I, both the major universities and the large philanthropic organizations began to fund scientific research. Physics was one of many academic disciplines to benefit from the new, research-oriented largesse, but physics was especially well placed to make effective use of these huge increases in funding.

International interactions were essential to the development of American physics. Academic entrepreneurs in American physics worked hard to recruit German physicists, to expose their departments to a steady stream of foreign visitors, and to send their most promising students and junior faculty abroad on fellowships. American physics was also uniquely successful at melding theoretical and experimental physics. Unlike the European centers, theorists and experimentalists worked side by side in most American physics departments.

The second part of the explanation for American receptivity was large-project management expertise. The Manhattan Project was immense and unprecedented in its scale. Without sufficient management expertise by state and military managers, the project would have been impossible—especially given the restricted timeframe imposed by the war. Government experiences in World War I and implementing New Deal programs were the foundation of federal expertise. The army in particular, which would run the Manhattan Project, gained invaluable experience managing the Tennessee Valley Authority in the 1930s. Private industry had a role to play as well. It applied to the

Manhattan Project the management and engineering techniques developed in the years since the Civil War. The abilities of private firms to create hierarchy, standardize, and integrate in their sections of the project were critical to the project's overall success.

The diffusion of quantum physics from Germany to the United States entered an environment in which the lines of communication between science, technology, and the American state were rapidly being opened and transformed—largely through the experience of war and the moral equivalent of war, the Great Depression.[62] The transformation created the immediate preconditions for the rapid transition of quantum physics from theoretical science to applied science to technology to weapon to industry.

THE CREATION OF THE GRADUATE SCHOOL

The research-oriented university was a latecomer to the United States. There were institutions of higher learning that granted the Ph.D., but until the 1870s doctorates were awarded in the absence of a formal graduate school or organized graduate program. For some time after 1870, the Ph.D. was used more as an honorary degree than as an award for academic achievement. Princeton, for example, began awarding honorary Ph.D.s in 1866, twelve years before the college gave them for course work and research. The Ph.D. was still a general-purpose degree well into the twentieth century and its connection to research accomplishment tenuous.[63]

Academic science in this environment was weak and poorly institutionalized. Increased specialization in the late nineteenth century, and science's increasing level of difficulty, destroyed the gentleman-scientist tradition in the United States and turned science into an esoteric, isolated pursuit. Yet without either institutional or social support, funding for scientific research was a significant problem. The improvements in American universities and foundation funding in the late nineteenth century did not touch the sciences until several decades later.[64]

The federal government (and until the Morrill Act of 1862 the states as well) had little or nothing to do with the country's universities and colleges and even less to do with what little scientific research went on within them. Yet, by the 1870s, all the institutions of the federal science policy of the post-World War II period were in existence: universities and government and private laboratories.[65] Over the next half-century, these institutions were integrated and universities were transformed from sites for moral instruction to the centers for scientific research.

The construction of American research universities is the first element in the integration of academy, science, and government. The inspiration for the research university came from abroad—specifically Germany—and the resulting combination was a peculiar German-American hybrid. To a person, the university-builders of the post-Civil War era had all spent time studying in Germany and there observed the model of the research university.[66] They admired the colloquia, the emphasis on independent research, the academic freedom, and the scholarly discipline of German universities. Beginning in the 1860s and 1870s, when these men came to positions of authority in the United States, they modeled the nascent American graduate schools on the German universities.[67]

The thousands of American students who studied in German universities between 1860 and 1920 were the agents of transmission for the German model. Between 1850 and 1914, nearly 10,000 Americans went to Germany to study. In nineteenth-century America, the German university enjoyed unquestioned prestige. Most in a position to know or care felt that adequate professional training in the scholarly disciplines could not be had at American universities and colleges—experience at a German university was essential. Career success reflected this view.[68]

Figure 4.1 gives a graphic sense of the popularity of German universities to American students—though the data are far from exact.[69]

Figure 4.1
American Graduate Students in Germany: 1820s–1910s.

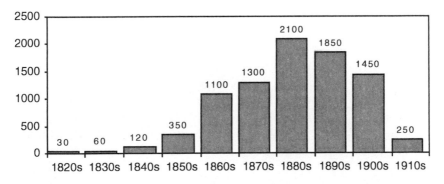

Information source: Charles F. Thwing (1928), *The American and the German University: One Hundred Years of History* (New York: Macmillan), 42.

For aspiring scientists, Göttingen was far and away the most presti-gious location. Students were attracted to Carl Friedrich Gauss in the mathematics department, Wilhelm Weber in physics, and Friedrich Wöhler in chemistry. Attendance figures at Göttingen show 167 Americans studied there in the 1870s, 225 in the 1880s, 316 in the 1890s, and 230 in the 1900s. Neither the French nor English univer-sities held similar appeal to Americans interested in an academic career. French programs were too long (nine years) and disorganized, while advanced education in England had yet to absorb the research ethos. Both were more riven with what to the American eye were distasteful class distinctions than German universities.[70]

By the turn of the century, the appeal of the German universi-ties had for the time being worn thin. The American graduate school, exemplified by the University of Chicago, was well established, and the German-educated students of an earlier generation were now professors directing those same graduate schools. This new generation was proud of their accomplishments and reluctant to allow their stu-dents to receive foreign training. World War I shook confidence in the German model even further. Americans reinterpreted the Ger-man university as elitist, authoritarian, and a possible training ground for imperialist ideas. The attitude changed rapidly once the war ended, however, and yet another generation of American academics made the pilgrimage to German universities. Aspiring scientists were the bulk of this later immigration in contrast to the more humanistic and social scientific backgrounds of the first generation.[71]

The institutions the educational entrepreneurs built, based on the German model, stressed research, placed less emphasis on teach-ing, and reformed the traditional curriculum. Classical education in Greek, Latin, literature, and theology were demoted in importance. They were replaced by subjects more in keeping with the industrial age: the social and natural sciences. In the period from the end of the Civil War to World War I, the universities beat out the competi-tion—the research amateurs, the independent research institutes, li-braries, technical institutes, and liberal arts colleges—because they both taught and did research. They reproduced themselves, were com-prehensive in terms of the services they offered, and worked on fun-damental problems. Research amateurs could do little to withstand the pressures of professionalization. The independent research insti-tutes—such as Wood's Hole Marine Biological Laboratory, the Smithsonian Institution, the New York Museum of Natural History, and the National Geographic Society—were unable to make themselves comprehensive enough. Technical institutes, such as the Massachusetts Institute of Technology and the California Institute of Technology, responded to competition from universities by becoming more like them. Liberal arts colleges survived by avoiding direct competition with universities.[72]

The Johns Hopkins University in Baltimore—which opened in 1876—was the first German-style research university to be founded in the United States. Others quickly followed. Few of the elite colleges were unfamiliar with graduate education. Most had a law school and divinity school, and perhaps even a medical school. Some even granted Ph.D.s and/or offered graduate instruction. But they were not integrated institutions like the German universities. They had multiple, highly independent faculty (especially in the 'professional' schools) and centralized command and control were infrequent at best. The graduate 'programs' were not distinct schools with standards, requirements, codes of conduct, or programs of study but small collections of interested faculty and students. This situation changed rapidly in the 1870s and 1880s. Harvard, Columbia, and Princeton, among others, consolidated control and established distinct graduate programs among other reforms. Their achievements were marked symbolically in 1900 with the founding of the Association of American Universities. With this note of institutional self-consciousness, the research university formally emerged.[73]

American physics emerged in the early twentieth century in this reformed educational environment. The early generation of German-influenced reformers had established the importance of research and placed the natural sciences firmly within the universities. But the transfer to the United States of German methods was not precise—a condition that devolved to the benefit of American science. The American version of the German university avoided reproducing the independent institute with its lone, all-powerful professor. Instead, the institute and the department were rather unconsciously merged. This had a number of advantages. Concentration of power was avoided; American science departments were more egalitarian inasmuch as they possessed several professors of equal, senior rank instead of one professor of greater institutional and rank-based power than his or her peers. In similar fashion, research and teaching were concentrated within the same institution, and it was difficult—again different from the German institutes—for one task to gain clear precedence over the other.

Another feature of the German university that did not take root in the American environment was the primary identification of a professor with a university. Instead, the American professoriate viewed themselves as part of their discipline first, with fealty to their university secondary. This tended to strengthen the power of the university president, but it also increased the overall level of competition in American higher education—both between and for professors. The gerontocracy of the late nineteenth- and early twentieth-century German universities was, for the time being, impossible in the American context.

The successful melding of German and American institutions shaped the institutional framework in which the scientific entrepreneurs in the 1910s and 1920s would operate. The decentralized, competitive university system increased the flexibility of science and made it highly innovative. The universities educated the scientists and supported their research (with theirs and others' funds), but the nature of university governance and of the scientific disciplines gave American scientists a degree of flexibility and freedom that had by the twentieth century largely vanished from Germany. While the situation in Germany obviously did not prevent the remarkable scientific work that went on in German universities in the 1920s and 1930s, it did stall the careers of many young German academics and caused them to look elsewhere. The center of dynamism and innovation had shifted with the changes to the educational systems.[74]

THEORETICAL PHYSICS IN THE UNITED STATES

The interwar years were ones of spectacular growth in American physics in general and in nuclear physics in particular. The Great Depression, despite its impact on the rest of the economy, had little effect on expenditures in physics departments, employment in physics, and even industry and government research in physics. The United States went from being a physics backwater (or "provincial outpost" as one historian put it[75]) to international preeminence. It would likely have attained this position even without the influx of talent from Nazi Germany in 1933. Among the many reasons for this development, I would single out four institutional factors as particularly important.

The first was the conscious attempt by the leaders of American physics to improve the state of their discipline. Second was a dramatic shift in the amount and direction of funding for research in the physical sciences. A change in the funding of the natural sciences after

World War I initiated by the major philanthropic organizations had a dramatic impact on the development of atomic physics. Third was the unique melding of theoretical and experimental physics that had been developing in the American university since the turn of the century. The final factor was international scientific exchange. The circulation of nuclear physicists around the world was a particular boon to the United States. American physics benefited from the constant stream of eminent visitors who came to the new American centers for physics for visiting professorships, lecture series, and the like. Physics also benefited from the fellowships that allowed an entire generation of American theoretical and atomic physicists to be educated at the centers of European physics, mostly in Germany. These four factors, and the growth in prominence of American physics that they explain, indicate the importance of institutional context and innovation and international exchange to the development of the atomic bomb.

Quantum Physics in the University

Until the 1920s, when they consumed at all, American scientists used European scientific theory; they were rarely producers. This attitude toward theoretical science was driven by the strong experimental tradition in American physics, the lack of tolerance for scientific work that was not immediately profitable for science and industry, and the general low regard for university scientists as researchers. The larger environment for physics began to change dramatically in the 1880s. The number of students and faculty in physics departments increased considerably, making specialization possible. Membership in the American Physical Society, of which more than 80 percent were educators, increased from around 250 in 1905 to nearly 1,300 in 1920 to more than 3,500 in 1939. Universities with an emphasis on research were established, and funds for research were made available on a large scale.[76]

Increased funding was also driven by changes in the material environment of physics itself—changes that were making physics more expensive. Electricity, vacuum lines, refrigeration, and gas and water lines were all new around 1900. But, driven by new experimental demands, all were rapidly becoming essential to the well-equipped physics laboratory. Expenditures on physics reflect this. Around 1900, approximately $2.5 million was being invested in physics research worldwide. The United States was spending one and one-half times that of Great Britain, twice that of Germany, and three times that of France. The rate of growth of expenditures in the United States was twice that of the second two and five times that of France.[77]

The relationship between applied physics and industry was also transformed around World War I. The universities began to produce more applied physicists—industrial physicists made up only one-tenth of membership in the American Physical Society in 1913 but 25 percent in 1920—and more papers began to filter out of industrial labs and into applied physics journals. Strong ties were developed between industry and academy, because, in a time when the universities were producing more and more physicists, industry was frequently the only source of employment. Funding was being made available to American physicists in the 1920s and 1930s in quantities not possible in Europe.[78]

Theoretical physics was slower to develop. Before 1925, it was essentially mathematical physics. But beginning in the 1910s, a small group of prominent experimentalists began a concerted effort to strengthen theoretical and quantum physics in their departments. This group included Robert S. Millikan of Chicago (later of Caltech), Arthur H. Compton of Chicago, Harrison M. Randall of Michigan, Karl T. Compton of Princeton, Raymond Birge of Berkeley, and George W. Pierce and Percy Bridgeman at Harvard. Despite being experimentalists, all saw that American physics was seriously deficient in theory, and all were firmly convinced that without an adequate base of theorists, experimental physics would languish and American physics would not fulfill its promise. In a letter recommending a student for a graduate fellowship in Germany, Karl T. Compton wrote of quantum mechanics, "There is no field of physics at the present time which is of such great importance."[79]

Growth in the undergraduate and graduate populations between the wars, along with growth in the number of doctorates, meant more than simple increases in faculty rolls; it pushed departments over a qualitative edge. Before, all that even a relatively well-off department could afford was four or five professors with enough general knowledge to teach an entire physics curriculum to undergraduates and graduate students alike. With increased enrollments, many departments reached a point at which it was possible to have one or two specialists in each of several expanding subfields, including quantum and theoretical physics.[80]

Physics also benefited from a new source of funding. Beginning after World War I, the major philanthropic organizations reoriented their funding from general education to research. Instead of working to raise the overall level of research quality, the philanthropies sought, in the words of Wickliffe Rose, president of the International Education Board (IEB) and the General Education Board (GEB) of the Rockefeller Foundation, to "make the peaks higher."[81] Private funding between the wars was almost exclusively targeted to the twenty top physics departments.

The strengthening of theoretical and quantum physics in American universities was the result of conscious policy of the entrepreneurs at each of the major departments. Recruiting and training of scientific talent was, with fund-raising, the most important task. But those were not the only challenges they faced. A good-sized segment of American physicists were opposed to making too much room for the new physics. But, by the 1920s, even if they were opposed, most influential physicists had realized that without quantum theorists, their experimental sections would languish.[82] Heisenberg et al. had given the experimentalists the mathematical tools necessary to study atomic and subatomic physics. But few of the older experimentalists—including many of quantum physics' greatest advocates—had the math skills necessary to do anything more than follow the debates. This necessitated a conscious policy favoring the younger scientists. American physics was also helped by its historically more pragmatic sensibility. Debates over the philosophical implications of the new physics hampered the field's acceptance in Germany. In the United States, however, the possibility of particle-wave duality had no such troubling philosophical or spiritual implications. It was experimentally proven, so the metaphysics were unimportant.[83]

Nevertheless, quantum physics was far from universally triumphant; the transformation of the discipline was carried out almost exclusively at the elite schools. They trained the first generation and dominated developments in the field. In Katherine Sopka's biographical appendix, only four of the thirty-four quantum physicists listed (a sample determined by ranking their significance to the field's development) were not affiliated with one of the top twenty.[84] At each of these elite departments, an identical pattern held: funding increases, close relations with the major philathropies, recruitment of European theoretical physicists, and encouragement of foreign training for promising American students. The most spectacular example of this pattern is Robert A. Millikan at the University of Chicago and then Caltech.

Upon arriving at Caltech from the University of Chicago in 1920, Millikan immediately set to work attracting world-class quantum physicists. Caltech quickly accumulated the best and highest concentration of quantum physicists in the United States and was a perpetual and lavish host to the world's finest physicists—including Albert Einstein who, before accepting an appointment at the Institute for Advanced Studies in the fall of 1933, spent 1930–1931 and the winters of 1931–1932 and 1932–1933 at Caltech as a visiting professor. In 1921, Millikan successfully wooed Paul Epstein from Leiden to a permanent appointment at Caltech and followed that in 1925 with the recruitment of Fritz Zwicky from Zurich.[85] In addition to Einstein, the list of prominent visitors included Arnold Sommerfeld as a lecturer in 1923 and as visiting professor in 1928, Max Born as a lecturer in 1926, Erwin Schrödinger as lecturer in 1927, and Niels Bohr as lecturer in 1933. The American faculty and graduate students in quantum physics at Caltech were equally prominent and internationally trained. Faculty included J. Robert Oppenheimer, Carl Eckart, and Linus Pauling (technically a quantum chemist).[86]

In collaboration with new funding initiatives from private foundations, academic entrepreneurs in the 1910s and 1920s like Millikan consciously strengthened physics in general and theoretical and quantum physics in particular. They did this in the face of opposition from the public at large that thought science overly materialist and godless, and from older experimentalists threatened by the new physics. Their determination and the resources of the foundations made them successful, but they were also able to draw on an international physics discipline and weaknesses in the German academic market.

Changes in Funding

The second factor in the rise of American theoretical physics was a change in the pattern of funding for science. The major philanthropic organizations, which had been very influential in the building of the American higher education system in the Progressive Era, began to directly support scientific research for the first time in the 1910s—a development that has been called one of the most significant events in the history of learning in the United States. Foundations financed the fellowship programs that sent young American quantum physicists to Europe to complete their educations; they supported the hiring of European theorists, along with summer programs and symposia for international exchange; and they funded the purchase of new laboratory equipment. Foundation support for the natural sciences enabled American physics to make a giant leap forward in organization and quality.[87]

This was a major break with past practice. Before World War I, the major philanthropic organizations preferred to support the general endowment funds of colleges and universities and avoided direct funding of scientific research.[88] After the war, this attitude began to change. The financial position of universities had improved to the point where general endowment help was not urgently necessary as it had been a few decades earlier. More important, the growth of American universities and colleges in human and financial size reduced the impact the relatively static foundation funds could have had.

Several institutional innovations also drove this change in emphasis. The experience of World War I brought many academic scientists in contact with government and industry. They emerged from the war with a new set of contacts and a new appreciation for the benefits that collaboration with extra-academic organizations could bring to science. Likewise, foundation managers got a glimpse of the impact science could have on economy and society. It is no accident that almost all the major innovators on both sides of the academy–foundation relationship had experience inside the World War I mobilization effort. After the war, new leadership emerged within science and in the foundations. The scientists pushed for more research funds. The new foundation administrators for their part took from their wartime experience the desire to play an active role in the development of American science.

The first step in remaking financial support for the natural sciences was taken by the Carnegie Corporation. Its most important benefaction was to the National Research Council (NRC). The NRC was a sort of trade association for the National Academy of Sciences. George Ellery Hale created the council during World War I to organize scientists for the war effort. In 1919, the corporation gave it $5 million to expand its wartime activities for the coordination of the training and development of science as a whole.[89]

The Rockefeller Foundation was the most important American philanthropic organization to refocus its giving efforts on research in the natural sciences. Through all its various programs, the foundation gave over $19 million to American physics departments in the years 1925 through 1932, and nearly 190 fellowships for physicists in the period between the wars.[90] The foundation also supported physics in European universities and facilitated foreign travel by physicists so that the atomic physics community enjoyed the greatest quantity of international interchange of any scientific discipline.

The key figure at the foundation was General Education Board (GEB) head Wickliffe Rose. By 1925, Rose had completely shifted the GEB's funding orientation; they ceased giving to endowments and had proceeded on a program to boost key departments. The strategy was to boost the top departments in each field even higher. In physics, the primary beneficiaries were Caltech, Princeton, Berkeley, Chicago, Harvard, and MIT. Some of the gifts included $2.5 million over four years to Caltech for teaching and research in the sciences, and $2 million to Princeton over the same period for physics.[91] The International Education Board (IEB) was the foundation's international analog to the GEB. Bohr's Copenhagen Institute and physics and math institutes at Göttingen are just two examples of the many IEB projects.[92]

One of the great innovations of the period between the wars was the funding of promising graduate students and young faculty members with fellowships for study at another institution. It was probably here that the activities of the philanthropic organizations had their greatest impact on American science. The fellowships gave the most talented young scientists one or two years of time for intensive work at a point in their careers when most would be overwhelmed by teaching requirements.[93]

The National Research Council (NRC) fellowship program was established in 1919. The Council was concerned that existing programs and resources could not ensure an adequate and talented supply of scientists, so it collaborated with the Rockefeller Foundation on a program, the National Research Fellowships, to fund the recruitment and training of young scientists. Initial capitalization of the program was $29,000, but that figure rapidly grew to over $300,000 per year by 1925 and continued at around that level until World War II. By 1950, more than 1,100 scientists had been trained under the program, and the foundation had spent more than $4 million. Of those, Robert Oppenheimer and Edward Condon were but two of the quantum physicists who used NRC fellowships to complete their studies in Europe.[94]

The Guggenheim Foundation's sole contribution to the funding of science was a fellowship program begun in 1923. But its impact on theoretical physics was greater than its size. From the start, between one-third and one-half of all the fellowships awarded went to the physical and biological sciences. Among these were at least twelve graduate students in quantum physics who used their awards to study at the centers of European physics. The group includes several who were later active in the Manhattan Project and/or made substantial contributions to atomic physics. The most famous recipients of Guggenheim fellowships include Carl Eckart from Caltech, Robert Mulliken and Frank Hoyt from Chicago, Edwin Kemble and John Slater from Harvard, and Linus Pauling from Berkeley.[95]

Several features of this transformation in scientific funding stand out as particularly significant. The first is the importance of institutional innovation. Changing social and economic conditions allowed individuals devoted to scientific research and shaped by the war to seize control of an obsolescing giving apparatus. The intentions and actions of these key administrators were also important. Rose and the rest were most interested in building American science in institutional terms: training enough scientists as well as possible, and having as many centers of scientific excellence as possible. They were not advocates of any particular line of scientific research, but instead wished to bring organization, centralization, and modern efficiencies to scientific research. Their international orientation was part of the same general objective. Rose in particular reasoned that if the finest scientists and institutions were abroad, then strengthening them would redound to American science through programs of international exchange supported by his and other foundations.

These twin objectives had the effect of quickening the pace of development in atomic physics. By sponsoring their circulation, the foundations increased the exposure of American physicists to the best work in the field. The system of sponsorship also tended to favor the same institutions pursuing the development of programs for quantum physics most aggressively. The most dynamic departments were those with an entrepreneur at their head and a minimum of problems with older faculty, trustees, and administrations. They also were more amenable to making the kinds of adjustments the foundations required to secure grants—in other words, more likely to make the sorts of institutional innovations the foundations were interested in. Those departments or universities dominated by groups resistant to change or suspicious of this new source of funding, and there were plenty, did not benefit much from foundation largess, nor were they the departments pushing for the advancement of atomic physics.[96]

Experiment and Theory

The third factor in the rise of American quantum physics is the unique melding of experiment and theory. American physics had traditionally been largely experimental. This tradition lingered among physicists even as theoretical physics became an American specialty. Samuel Goudsmit, who came from Leiden to Michigan in 1927, remembered his first contact with American graduate students: "all the students at Michigan had at one time or another taken the family car apart and had put it together again. . . . At Michigan the students had contact with the machine shop, everyone knew how to use his hands. . . . Nobody in Europe would have known to do that." The theoreticians the American system produced had a greater knowledge of experimental technique than other countries and were more prepared to collaborate with their experimentalist colleagues. In Germany, by contrast, theory and experiment were usually in separate research institutes, each controlled by a single scientist. This feature of American scientific practice was unique to the American educational system.[97]

The development of atomic physics caused a huge change in the practice of physics in a way that uniquely benefited the American style. The scale, complexity, and cost of experimental equipment increased substantially in the early part of the twentieth century. Before the 1920s, scientists made most laboratory equipment in the lab themselves. Even the equipment Rutherford used to discover the atomic nucleus was largely homemade. But further investigation of the nucleus required a more sophisticated piece of machinery—like the cyclotron, which was crucial to the electromagnetic separation of Uranium-235 from Uranium-238.[98]

Ernest O. Lawrence developed the first cyclotron in 1930 with financial help from the Rockefeller Foundation's Research Corporation. The foundation was later heavily involved in supporting cyclotron construction, including ones built at the University of Minnesota and the University of Copenhagen in 1937. By the mid- to late 1930s, the United States had built between two and three times as many cyclotrons as the rest of the world. This dominance reflected both the change in the practice of physics and the suitability of American physics to this new science.[99]

The American centers of theoretical physics were characterized by strong collaboration between experimentalists and theoreticians. The two most striking examples of this phenomenon were the departments at Berkeley and MIT. The leading theoreticians at the two schools, Robert Oppenheimer at Berkeley and John Slater at MIT, were both graduate students at Harvard. There they had worked with Percy Bridgeman, one of the great physics educators of his generation. Though an experimentalist, Bridgeman was keenly interested in theory, and he made certain that theorists trained by him were well versed in experimental technique.[100]

Oppenheimer joined the Berkeley department a year after Lawrence in 1929. The two became close friends and proceeded to build a department simultaneously strong in experimentation and theory. Lawrence kept Berkeley at the center of work in experimental nuclear physics for many years. Oppenheimer, for his part, became the outstanding educator of theoretical physics in the United States, but with a remarkable gift for understanding experimental work. He single-handedly made Berkeley the center for training in theory during the 1930s—in Hans Bethe's words, "the greatest school of theoretical physics that the United States has ever known." In the decade of the 1930s, his renown as an educator attracted more NRC theoretical physics fellows to Berkeley than to any other university.[101]

Oppenheimer and Lawrence developed a very close working relationship. In some respects, it was a necessary result of fundamental changes in the nature of physics research. The cyclotrons on which Lawrence built his reputation were generating huge amounts of often confusing information about the atomic nucleus. For the first time in the history of physics, the experimentalists were dependent on the guidance of theorists to interpret their data. Stanford experimentalists were very pleased when Felix Bloch arrived from Germany in the wake of the 1933 dismissals. Now they no longer had to wait for Oppenheimer's visits for theoretical consultation.[102]

At MIT, Karl Compton arrived as the president in 1930 and immediately set to work repairing the school's declining reputation in engineering. He pushed the school aggressively into modern physics and tried to utilize the school's traditional technological expertise in a more scientific setting. He transformed the physics department by eliminating older faculty and hiring John Slater from Harvard to be chair of the department and George Harrison from Stanford as head experimentalist.[103] Slater and Harrison formed a relationship similar to (though not as celebrated as) that between Oppenheimer and Lawrence.

International Interactions

The entrepreneurial energy of the department builders, the money poured into physics by the foundations, and the peculiarly American combination of theoretical and experimental atomic physics gradually raised the United States in the estimation of the international physics community. Physics, and especially quantum physics, in the 1920s was an international discipline in the sense that the scientists formed a transnational community of practitioners with shared understandings and frequent communication. This was truest for atomic physics at the time of its most rapid development since there were relatively few scientists with expertise in the field. International collaboration and constant communication were therefore necessary for rapid and efficient progress.

In Europe, a circuit developed between the main centers of physics: Munich, Leipzig, Göttingen, Leiden, Zurich, Cambridge, Copenhagen, and Berlin. For the young physicist eager to learn the latest techniques and absorb the latest theories, stops at each of the major centers were required. This was as true for American physicists as for Europeans. I. I. Rabi remembers that in the two years between 1925 and 1927, virtually the entire younger generation of American quantum physicists—Edwin C. Kemble, Edward U. Condon, Howard P. Robertson, F. Wheeler Loomis, Robert Oppenheimer, William V. Houston, Linus C. Pauling, Julius Stratton, John C. Slater, and William W. Watson—were in Europe.[104]

Slowly, the physics centers in the United States became a part of the tour. John Slater recalls a moment at the 1933 meeting of the American Physical Society when he realized that the American scientists were at last the equals of their European colleagues. Europeans had always come to these meetings as honored guests to impart the latest knowledge from Europe. But, at the 1933 meeting, Slater observed "that the young American workers on the program gave talks of such high quality on research of such importance that for the first time the European physicists present were here to learn as much as to instruct."[105] American physics had, in John Van Vleck's words, "come of age" in international reputation as well.[106]

This two-part international interaction—visiting Europeans in the United States and European training for young American physicists—was central to the development of American physics before World War II. The international circulation of physicists allowed the Americans to observe the atomic revolution firsthand.[107] Most of the visitors were German, and Americans went mostly to Germany universities and institutions.

The fellowship programs for young American physicists were of great importance to atomic physics. Fully 15 percent of all physics Ph.D.s in the 1920s and 1930s received NRC fellowships. Fifty of these fellows in physics went to Europe between 1920 and 1932. Many of the same scientists would work together again during the war at Los Alamos, Chicago, or at other atomic program sites.[108]

Conclusion

The four features of the development of atomic physics I have singled out for analysis interrelate rather neatly. Each of the four is based in a particular social universe or social structure: the university, the discipline of physics, the philanthropic foundation, experimentalists, theoreticians, and finally the system of nation-states. The discipline of physics—both as a body of knowledge and body of practitioners—capable of making the bomb depended on developments, or institutional innovations, within each of these social systems. Of equal or greater importance was the communication, or translation in Hugh Aitken's phrase, between these social systems.[109] For any of the scientific discoveries or the innovations to institutional form or practice to have meaning, it had to be transferred from one system to another. At each step along the path I sketched there have been 'translators' who have done this work. While individuals are important in the development of twentieth-century atomic physics, the institutions themselves have been communicators and translators as well.

The role of individuals in this analysis is clear. The system-building college presidents drew inspiration for their efforts from the German university and modern American business organization. They also communicated the new relationship of the university to research above—to the university's trustees and the broader economy—and below, to their faculties. The department-builders in physics were all scientists, but they also had great social engineering skills. They were able to communicate with their colleagues in the department and agree on scientific goals. They were also able to communicate what they saw to be physics' needs to those outside of science: the universities, philanthropic organizations, and industrial corporations who might choose to help fund their plans for physics. Finally, the interaction of experimentalists and theoreticians within the discipline of physics depended on talented individuals on both sides of the divide seeing the gains to be had from collaboration and a way to bring it about. Oppenheimer and Lawrence at Berkeley, Slater and Harrison at MIT, Hans Bethe at Cornell, Felix Bloch at Stanford, and I. I. Rabi at Columbia were the most prominent agents of the translation process.[110]

The institutions were also important translators and communicators. With the professionalization of science, the universities and the foundations were the bridge between the outside private economy (and later the state) and the practice of science. Bridging the international gap are institutions on a global scale. The university linked the German model and the American reproduction, and international science linked physics in Germany with physics in the United States. These sets of institutional relationships—university, foundation, discipline—were half the context of the American bomb effort. The next sections deal with the other half, state and industrial technology management. Both are necessary to explain the successful atomic bomb project in the United States.

THE MANAGEMENT OF TECHNOLOGY: PUBLIC AND PRIVATE

The development of atomic physics in the United States in the 1920s and 1930s and the talent of the Manhattan Project scientists were critical to the Manhattan Project's success. Once at work on the bomb, the scientists made astounding progress in an extraordinarily short period of time. The pressure of the war deserves some credit for this. But, more important, the scientists worked within a massive, complex scientific–technology–industrial system designed and overseen by project managers from both government and industry. The ability to successfully manage such a large project was by no means inevitable. Only hard-won experience, and many prior mistakes, ensured that the U.S. government and firms like Du Pont had the managerial ability to organize and direct the Manhattan Project. The contribution of management expertise to the development of the atomic bomb emphasizes one of the central themes of this study—the importance of institutional setting and innovation, and translations

between institutions (domestic and international) for the development of new technologies.

Development of Federal Management Expertise

World War II is commonly seen as a watershed in American science
policy. Some have argued that before the war there was no such thing
as American science policy and that the war precipitated its invention.[111] It would be a mistake, however, to conclude that the innovations of the war years were created from institutional whole cloth. If
the federal government and the military had remained as ignorant of
large-project management and planning techniques as they had during World War I, the near disaster of the bungling in 1917 1918
would have been repeated as true disaster in the 1940s. In the period
between the wars, the federal government gained expertise in managing large-scale technological systems and directing scientific research—
areas in which they had no prior experience. In this section I trace
the evolution of management and planning techniques in the federal
government beginning with World War I and ending with analyses of
three specific areas: science policy, the National Advisory Committee
for Aeronautics, and the Tennessee Valley Authority. This evolution
explains the accumulation of management expertise in the institutions immediately relevant to the Manhattan Project: the army and
federal science managers.

The experience of World War I was critical in changing attitudes about central management. The mobilization plan for the war
was a product of the then-dominant conservative, associationalist
approach to planning identified with Herbert Hoover and the heads
of many U.S. major industrial concerns. It was a disaster. The institutions formed during the war were premised on a collaborative, vol-
untarist ideal that denied to the government the authority and
centralized power necessary for effective management.

Public and private planning for the war was made up of committees and boards. Government initiatives included the Food Administration, the Aircraft Production Board, the Emergency Fleet
Corporation, the War Industries Board, and the Exports Council. The
government also took over the railroads and coordinated raw materials production with private firms and associations. Yet neither the
civilian boards nor the government had (or could get from Congress)
authority appropriate to their tasks. The more than 150 autonomous

procurement bureaus of the War Department began in early 1917 a wholesale and often brutal competition for progressively scarcer resources. The bureaus arranged for their own transportation of goods. The resulting congestion of the country's transportation system included 45,000 rail cars of coal stretched motionless from New York City to Pittsburgh and Buffalo. Wood for shipbuilding waited on the Philadelphia docks for unloading until after the war. In January, Harry Garfield, the chairmen of the Fuel Administration (with authority from Congress via the 1917 Lever Food and Fuel Act) was forced to shut down all factories east of the Mississippi to break the transport bottleneck to the eastern ports.[112]

The confusion and waste of the mobilization effort convinced many that planning and centralization were necessary not simply for the running of a war, but for the running of an economy as well. Wartime experiences brought business and government permanently together for the first time. Both now shared similar organizational structures, and—through congressional committees, cabinet departments, and executive agencies—regular and close relations. Several of the wartime administrative devices would be revived, some on a permanent basis, during the Great Depression. The War Industries Board, for example, was the model for the Roosevelt administration's National Recovery Administration (NRA).[113] So while the mobilization and planning efforts for the war were less than a success, they laid the groundwork for science planning, technology project management, and institutionalized public–private cooperation on large-scale projects.

The development of federal science programs is a microcosm of the effects of World War I and bears directly on the Manhattan Project. Before the war, government involvement in science was limited to a handful of military arsenals, testing grounds, and agricultural research bureaus. In general, the government and the military had little to do with the innovating elements of the private sector—either industrial or academic. The war changed the relationship between government and the private sector. Scientists, engineers, and corporate managers eagerly offered their services to the war effort. In 1915, Secretary of the Navy Josephus Daniels asked the inventor Thomas Edison to work on the problem of submarine detection. Edison responded by forming the Naval Consulting Board to address the problem. George Ellery Hale convinced President Wilson in 1916 to charter a new agency of the National Academy of Sciences, the National

Research Council, to manage the collaboration between government and the scientific community.[114]

The arrangements made to mobilize science did not survive the war intact. Advocates of a federal science policy were caught in a web of conflicting objectives and competing interest groups within and between the scientific community and the government. The NRC, the most important state–science collaboration of the war, survived as an administrator of private philanthropic funds. But Hale's attempts to extend the council's coordination activities with the government after the war came to nothing.[115]

Two new government–science organizations, the Science Advisory Board (SAB) and the National Resources Planning Board (NRPB), fought bitterly over objectives and procedures and the result was stalemate. The NPRB could accomplish little in the face of opposition from the bulk of scientists and from Congress. The SAB faced opposition from within its sponsor the National Academy of Sciences and could not agree on what the board's relationship to the government would be. The board's attempts to formulate science policy on associationalist grounds were "sputtering" and largely a failure.[116]

After World War I, scientists had come to accept the inevitability and desirability of planning and centralized management of scientific research. They were not yet prepared, however, to accept government management. In this they were in agreement with many national leaders in government and industry. Millikan wrote, "It may then be set down as a fact fairly well established by the experience of the Great War that rapid progress in the application of science to any national need is not to be expected in any country which depends, as most countries have done in the past, simply upon the *undirected* inventive genius of its people to make these applications."[117]

Two interwar institutions were important for building government large-project management expertise. The first was the National Advisory Committee for Aeronautics (NACA). Founded in 1915 in the midst of worry about the war in Europe, in the 1920s and 1930s and into World War II the NACA carried out cutting edge research in aeronautical engineering. The country's most sophisticated wind tunnels were at the NACA laboratory in Norfolk, Virginia. Experiments conducted in the tunnels by NACA engineers were responsible for major alterations in airplane design including significant increases in engine efficiency and power, the development of retractable landing gear, wing design, maneuverability, and safety. The commission's constituencies were the private aerospace industry and airlines, and the military—especially the navy.[118]

Advocates for the NACA were concerned about World War I, but were motivated primarily by the widening gap that separated aeronautics in the United States from Europe. In 1914, the Secretary of the Smithsonian Institution Charles D. Walcott sent Albert F. Zahm, a physicist from Catholic University, and Jerome C. Hunsaker, an aeronautical engineer from MIT, to Europe on a fact-finding tour. Their visit established many important contacts with Europeans and the resulting report provided a blueprint for NACA's organization.[119]

After the war, NACA leadership reduced its contacts with Washington and withdrew to the Langley lab in Norfolk and to research. The concentration on research paid off handsomely. Like their counterparts in physics, the NACA and the aeronautical engineering community invested in foreign scientists. Max Munk, a student of Ludwig Prandtl's at Göttingen, was the Lab's director from 1921 to 1929. With the Guggenheim Foundation's help, Caltech was able to attract Theodore von Kármán—one of the most important and influential aeronautical engineers of the century—from Germany to Pasadena. And, in the 1930s, the NACA Lab added a theorist—the Norwegian Theodor Theodorsen—to help the largely experimentalist staff with the increasingly complex mathematics necessary to the emerging discipline.[120]

The most important work done by NACA itself was at the Langley Lab. There, NACA scientists built the wind tunnel that made them famous. The lab operated much like the large-scale, directed, and collaborative scientific projects that began to appear in the 1920s and would characterize wartime and postwar science. Successes, such as an engine cowling design that saved fuel and increased air speed, made the idea of government-sponsored research palatable to Congress and public and ensured that the military was a happy and loyal customer.[121]

The NACA was a training ground for one of the Manhattan Project's most important managers, Vannevar Bush. He became the commission's director in 1939 and, for him, the NACA represented a model for his first World War II-era federal science agency, the National Defense Research Committee (NDRC) and its successor, the OSRD.

Bush was drawn to the NACA's independent administrative status, its budgetary independence, and its authority to conduct military research on its own initiative. He also drew on the NACA's procedures for organizing and funding research. Using the contract, he was able to support both individual grant research and large-scale managed projects. He was also keenly aware of the need to avoid conflicts with other federal bureaus and agencies if his organization's autonomy was to be maintained. Bush's initial plans for the NDRC included the stipulation that the committee's research would supplement, not replace, any ongoing research in other government technical bureaus.[122] Finally, Bush adopted the odd governance-by-committee structure of the NACA into his organization of the NDRC and the OSRD. All three organizations had semiautonomous committees defined primarily by functional area. Project design and personnel were the province of the committees with the executive committee and/or chief executive providing general direction.

The NACA thus served as an important precedent for the Manhattan Project. It was a highly successful demonstration project of sorts for the benefits of government-sponsored scientific research. And it was the model for the federal agency that directed the scientific research on the bomb before the project was turned over to the army.

The Tennessee Valley Authority (TVA) is the second institutional predecessor of the Manhattan Project. It was the largest federal technological management project yet undertaken by the Army Corps of Engineers, the army branch that administered the Manhattan Project. It was also a demonstration project for the kind of technocratic economic and social planning advocated by progressives. True to the spirit of the times, Roosevelt campaigned heavily against private power companies in the 1932 presidential election campaign, and he signed legislation establishing the TVA in May 1933.[123]

The legislative victory delighted progressives, regional planning advocates, and opponents of private power. The first directors did not disappoint this constituency. Arthur E. Morgan, an engineer and planning zealot; Harcourt Morgan, president of the University of Tennessee and a progressive; and David Lilienthal, an attorney, were the first commissioners. The directors were a similar-minded collection of engineers, educators, agricultural researchers, and lawyers.[124] Arthur Morgan was in charge of the technological project. Lilienthal and Harcourt Morgan were responsible for selling the project to the region's inhabitants and the country and directing the authority's legal and legislative battles (the constitutional challenge to the TVA by Wendell Wilkie, owner of the Tennessee Electric Power Company, was not resolved until 1939).[125]

In a decision of significance for the Manhattan Project, Morgan took the unprecedented step of not relying on private contracts for the authority's engineers and managers. Consequently, the authority built a highly skilled and competent base of engineers and laborers within the organization itself. The TVA was a success. Their rates for the first 100 kilowatts were 55 percent of the average national price for electricity from private producers and after 200 kilowatts the price dropped to 7.3 percent of that average.[126]

The TVA demonstrated two things about large government projects, both of which proved useful to later federal project managers. First was the importance of relative autonomy from the rest of the federal political system. The TVA was a uniquely independent project. There was some interaction with other government bureaus—for example, the Bureau of Reclamation designed the Norris and Wheeler Dams—but the authority was not subordinate to any other federal agencies, nor did it rely on them for personnel or administration. The directors were chosen by the president and the board by the three directors. This autonomy allowed the TVA to avoid damage to their mission from Congress and the agencies. Vannevar Bush expended a considerable amount of energy and political capital maintaining a similar degree of insulation for the OSRD.[127]

Second, the TVA proved that the federal government could design, build, and operate a large technological project without either running the concern into the ground or destroying potential private competition. The authority, as production and price figures demonstrate, was an efficient producer.[128] And, despite the worries of private power and years spent in court trying to dismantle the TVA, the provision of electric power by private firms did not suffer appreciably from the additional competition.

For my purposes, the TVA is most important as a precedent-setter for large-scale government projects. I have not found in the historical record anyone who strongly questioned the wisdom of putting the Manhattan Project in government hands. The opposite appears to be the case; it was naturally assumed that the government would bear the burden.[129] Had the same opportunity emerged during World War I, there doubtless would have been a different outcome.

Along with the two examples above of the NACA and government support for science, the evolution of the TVA points to a profound transformation in the ability of the American federal government to gain political support for, and to successfully manage, large scientific and technological projects. The mobilization failures of World War I and the experience of the Great Depression irrevocably changed government capacity and government–science and government–industry relations. State authority, and centralized authority,[130] were now appropriate tools, and the government was well equipped to wield them. A similar transformation was also under way in the private sector, the subject of the next section

Systematic Management and the Industrial Corporation

In December 1942, President Roosevelt approved the expenditure of $400 million for uranium separation plants and a plutonium-producing pile. The Manhattan Project had entered its industrial phase. Under the direction of Brigadier General Leslie Groves, plans were quickly made for the construction firm of Stone and Webster, the Du Pont Corporation, the Kellex Company, the Tennessee Eastman Corporation, the J. A. Jones Construction Company, and the Carbide and Carbon Construction Company to share in the design, building, and operation of the massive industrial facilities necessary to produce the enriched uranium and the plutonium for an atomic bomb.[131] In the project's final stages, the makers of the atomic bomb had to rely on the accumulated managerial and technological expertise of the United States' huge private industrial and construction firms to attain the scale necessary for a working bomb.

The size of the Manhattan Project plant was massive, easily outstripping the next-largest federal construction project to that time, the TVA. Yet, as Hounshell and Smith point out, the Du Pont Corporation was large enough—in terms of plant, employees, and so on—to contain the entire project.[132] For a firm of Du Pont's size, the Manhattan Project did not require any major adjustments. This is the context for the second half of the development of the management expertise necessary to administer the bomb project. Du Pont and the rest of the private sector firms brought with them the size and administrative and engineering experience essential to move the bomb project from a large-scale scientific research program to an industrial product engineering and manufacturing program. As with the federal government, the firms' expertise was a product of an earlier adaptation to circumstances and crises. Using Du Pont as an example, this section shows how managerial expertise and an organization for product-driven, scientific research was developed between the years

1902 and the late 1930s and how these two featured in the success of the Manhattan Project.

Du Pont is an excellent example, both for its important role in the atomic bomb project and its prominent place among American industry's innovators. The development of the large industrial corporation was one of the distinguishing features of American political economy in the last quarter of the nineteenth and first quarter of the twentieth centuries. Du Pont was the first large firm to adopt the 'modern,' multidivisional organizational structure in the 1910s and 1920s and was very influential as an organizational innovator.[133] Its history, and its role in the Manhattan Project, illustrate the importance of historical conjunctures for the accumulation of technological expertise in institutions and the importance of those particular institutions to the development and manufacture of the atomic bomb.

For much of the firm's nearly century-long history, Du Pont had been a manufacturer of gunpowder exclusively. The firm had been quite successful. The son of the company's founder, Henry, used his firm's dominant position to concentrate and rationalize the industry during the depression of the 1870s. After the end of World War I, industry concentration had proceeded about as far as possible and the U.S. Justice Department had already brought several actions against the company to break its monopolist position in the industry. With forward and backward integration precluded, the only feasible strategy was diversification. In 1908, during a crisis over military supply (the government temporarily canceled a large part of its gunpowder order), the firm had investigated the production of artificial leather, artificial silk, and celluloid-type products. All these products were well within Du Pont's sphere of expertise and made use of production by-products from the manufacture of gunpowder.[134]

During World War I, in the rush to fill government orders for gunpowder, Du Pont built up massive excesses in production capacity, managerial talent, and production-process by-products. To compensate, beginning in 1917, the company went on a buying spree. It expanded simultaneously into the artificial leather, pyroxlyin (celluloid), dyestuffs, vegetable oil, water soluble chemicals, cellulose and cotton purification, and varnishes and paint industries by acquiring several firms in each category and set about making their new diversified firm profitable. The centralized command structure that had worked so well for a single-product firm proved incompetent for handling the multitude of differing demands and needs of the new divisions. For four years, Du Pont lost money in every category. After a systematic review of their organizational options, the executive committee opted for a reorganization along divisional, product-oriented lines. Under the new system, the general manager at the head of each division was responsible for the operations of that division and all but autonomous from the Board of Directors. The board's relationship to the divisions was analogous to banker and accountant, no longer manager or administrator.[135]

The establishment of autonomous divisions allowed Du Pont's already strong predisposition for industrial science to blossom; new product development based on laboratory research became the central feature of the firm's continued success. The case of nylon is particularly instructive. The synthetic fiber originated in a new industrial research environment that combined autonomy from the central office with careful planning and control at the project level. The objective of this new organizational scheme was to shepherd new materials developed in the lab to mass-manufacture with a maximum of efficiency. This method was the model used by the firm for its Manhattan Project responsibilities.

Nylon emerged in 1930 from a small research lab in the Rayon Department run by an academic chemist, Wallace H. Carothers, recruited from Harvard with the lab's founding in 1927. The nylon lab was the first industrial lab managed by systematic corporate management techniques. The lab's founder, Du Pont's director of central research George Stine, tried to make it a basic research installation. When Carothers discovered nylon in 1930, the lab's 'academic era' ended. A new director, Elmer Bolton, pushed to bring the promising fiber to production. Once production was imminent, the nylon project took on all the features that would characterize Du Pont's involvement with the Manhattan Project. Several possible mechanisms for spinning the fiber at mass-production levels were considered simultaneously. The project was managed in parallel, not linearly. Development of the production process was not held up if certain parts were falling behind. Space was simply set aside in blueprints and on the factory floor. As it was, nylon took fully ten years to bring to market, an indication of the extent of Du Pont's commitment to the product and the transformation in science and technology management the project represented.[136]

Du Pont was brought reluctantly into the Manhattan Project in late 1942 to design and build the plutonium pilot plant at Oak Ridge (it was to be operated by Chicago scientists) and to design, build, and operate the plutonium production plant at Hanford, Washington. The company gathered a team of nylon project veterans—Stine, Bolton, and Crawford Greenewalt—and imposed the nylon research program model. The physicists at the Chicago laboratory (which at that point included lab director Arthur H. Compton, Enrico Fermi, James Franck, Leo Szilard, and Eugene Wigner, among others) had to live uncomfortably through a reorganization of research reporting, weekly steering committee meetings, and the 'freezing' of certain design features of the proposed plant so that progress on the whole project could proceed.[137]

The experience with Du Pont was a touchstone for most of the complaints from academic scientists on the project. They ridiculed the idiocy of the engineers, worried that their expertise was being ignored, and charged that their work was being turned into a marginal branch of the Du Pont Corporation's operations. But the company's achievements on the project were the result of their conservative and systematic engineering methods. Du Pont engineers' expertise at scaling processes up from the lab to mass-production was unavailable to the scientists. For example, the Hanford plant was the largest single construction project of the war; it employed over 60,000 workers and was built with astonishing rapidity. A crucial oversight by the scientists in designing its coolant system was successfully overcome by conservative redundancies Du Pont had automatically included in the plant's construction despite the derision of the scientists.[138]

Du Pont could not have stepped in to the bomb project so quickly and so successfully had the conjunctures of the post-Civil War transformation of the American political economy and World War I not prompted reorganization and diversification. These conjunctures were the same ones that prepared the physics discipline and the federal government for their roles in the atomic bomb project.

Conclusion

When theoretical and atomic physics made their way from Germany to the United States in the 1920s and 1930s, they entered an environment rich in the right sort of resources. The new sciences were intensely abstract and mathematical disciplines, and the young American theoreticians were skilled in the language of abstract mathematics. Investigation of the atomic nucleus required large and expensive experimental equipment, and the practical, engineering-like tradition of American experimental physics made it the creator of the massive cyclotron. The United States's immense wealth coupled with the interest of the major philanthropies in funding large scientific projects made it comparatively easy to afford the machines. Running these machines required not just skilled experimentalists, but equally skilled theoreticians to interpret the huge quantities of data the cyclotrons spewed out. Experimentalists and theoreticians were required to work in tandem to make the most productive use of the new machines. The large, comprehensive American research universities gave departments the concentrations of physicists and graduate students needed for the task. And the open nature of the scientific disciplines in the United States—in which a scientist identified more with his or her discipline than with a particular university—valued disciplinary standing over standing within the university and fostered a tolerance for large, organized research projects.[139]

The year 1932 has been called a miraculous year for physics. It saw five monumental discoveries—the neutron, deuterium, the cyclotron, the positron, and the Cockcroft-Walton accelerator—that pushed nuclear physics into the unquestioned forefront of physics research and set it on a solid experimental footing. Of the five discoveries, three of them—Urey's discovery of deuterium, Lawrence's cyclotron, and Carl Anderson's discovery of the positron—were the work of Americans. These discoveries show that American physics had indeed come of age, but they also demonstrate the importance of the American organizational environment. The cyclotron was the product of a massive, organized research project occupying several physicists and countless more graduate students. The positron was a joint project of Anderson and Seth Neddermeyer, and both deuterium and the positron were the work of young American physicists at the new centers for physics (Columbia for Urey, Caltech for Anderson).[140]

The bomb was both a scientific and an organizational accomplishment. Hence, this section has also focused on the development of the technology management expertise in the public and private sectors. Their histories show that the requisite expertise grew out of an enthusiasm for planning and rationalization that accompanied the American rise to industrial and economic preeminence in the late nineteenth century, and the experiences of crisis-induced state management attempts.

Two components to this story remain—one scientific and the other organizational. Both repeat the themes of crisis or conjuncture and organizational innovation in response. The organizational component involved the innovations that attended the NDRC/OSRD's uranium project management and the Manhattan Project. The scientific component was provided by the dozens of physicists who found their way to the United States after being expelled from their positions in Germany. Émigré physicists played vital roles in the Manhattan Project. But before the project itself was even considered by the American government, it was the émigrés—with their firsthand knowledge of the dangers of the Nazi regime—who pushed hard to bring the feasibility of the bomb to the government's attention.

DIFFUSION

MASS DIFFUSION

When the National Socialist government promulgated the Law for Restoration of Career Civil Service on April 13, 1933, German dominance of international scholarship was effectively ended. In sheer numbers, the losses to the German academy were not that great—particularly in a period of reduced employment opportunities for young scholars. But with a national share of less than 1 percent of the population, Jews held over 12 percent of university professorships and had won one-quarter of the country's Nobel Prizes. The qualitative loss, particularly in physics, was staggering. By exiling Jews from the universities, Germany stripped itself of more than half its most influential and widely published leaders in the new fields of quantum and nuclear physics—fields that would shape the development of physics in the 1930s, 1940s, and beyond.[141]

The response to the expulsion law from the international academic community was immediate. Clearinghouses and placement organizations in Great Britain, the United States, and Switzerland sprang up within months of the law's passage and many continued operation through the war and after. The process of "rescuing science and learning,"[142] as one of the contemporary accounts put it, was huge, international in scope, high-minded and high profile. In Great Britain, the Royal Society and its luminaries—including Lord Beveridge, Lord Rayleigh, and John Maynard Keynes—sponsored the British effort and in the United States the same educational–philanthropic complex that had boosted American science in the 1920s helped establish the American effort.[143] Firsthand accounts of the various rescue enterprises relate their actions in the language of high moral purpose.[144] But the most interesting facet, from the standpoint of the development of the atomic bomb, is the almost total absence of state involvement in the rescue effort. The British, American, and Swiss agencies that coordinated the rescue and (when they could afford it) helped support the refugees financially were wholly private in affiliation and means of support.[145] International institutional involvement was also minimal: the League of Nations was heavily involved with the reception, treatment, and placement of refugees from Central Europe from 1933 and on through the war, but had little to do with the efforts to aid scholars and professionals.[146] This was largely due to the already well-developed transnational links among scientists; they moved so swiftly and effectively that state or international organization involvement would have been redundant.

This section outlines the institutions of rescue and their achievements. Here the mechanism for diffusion of scientific talent was not state emulation of successful practices, as neorealists would argue. Instead, it was a transnational institution—an academic discipline—that organized itself to manage the flow of refugees and find them suitable academic homes. The same set of factors that determined the success of American science in the 1930s aided in the absorption of the refugees. They entered an institutional environment developed in the 1910s and 1920s and fairly rapidly found places within that environment. The same institutions that had supported the growth of American science also supported the placement of refugees. The Rockefeller Foundation and other philanthropic organizations financed a good share of the placement effort in the United States. Because of superior resources, the refugees flowed predominantly to the United States and almost without exception to the elite centers of American physics. Once there, they did not transform the system, but enhanced it. The refugees embraced the theoretical–experimental synergy that was already a distinguishing feature of American physics. Their addition was an essential boost to the system that in less than a decade would be at work on the atomic bomb.

The Diffusion Organizations

Two main agencies—one each in Great Britain and the United States—and a host of smaller efforts sprang up in the 1930s to aid the academic refugees. The British agency, the Academic Assistance

Council (or AAC), renamed itself the Society for the Protection of Science and Learning in 1936. The AAC/SPSL's American counterpart was the Emergency Committee in Aid of Displaced German (later Foreign) Scholars (or Emergency Committee). The British and American efforts differ markedly in their intentions and effects. The differences underscore not the geopolitical, but geoscientific strengths and interests of the two countries and precisely mirror the benefits each gained from the expulsions.

The AAC/SPSL was designed as a clearinghouse for information for potential refugees and sponsors. The council collected personal statements from dismissed scholars detailing educational background, work, publication history, interests, and so on and tried to match them with interested philanthropists, universities, industrial firms, or research institutes. The AAC/SPSL would usually pay to transport them from the Continent and give them a small sum, on the order of £250 per year for a married scholar and £180 for an unmarried scholar (compared to the £310 per year a British lecturer could expect in salary), to help them continue their research. If necessary, the AAC/SPSL would also pay for the applicant to deliver a lecture to a British, or even American, scientific audience. These procedures reflected the British belief that few if any foreign scholars would find permanent positions in Great Britain. The purpose of the stipend and funded lectures were to expose the refugee scholar to a British audience so that recommendations from British scientists could accompany the refugees to the United States.[147]

These policies reflected the fact that the British university system—still heavily oriented to undergraduate education and deeply affected by the Depression—could simply not absorb many refugees on a permanent basis. Instead the council directed British resources to preparing refugees to enter the American academic market. The rather small and upper-class nature of the British academy and British physics in particular was an additional factor. Physics in Britain was almost wholly contained in Cambridge and adding to such a small community would doubtless have proved difficult. Lastly, quite conscious anti-Semitism in the academy led Rutherford, for example, to avoid adding refugee scientists at the Cavendish for fear of provoking an anti-Semitic backlash.[148]

The AAC/SPSL's analysis of the situation created its own reality. The society had one hundred sixty-five physicists on file, of whom sixty-seven actually came to Britain for some period of time. Of those, the SPSL offered grants to forty of them. Only three of the sixty-seven received permanent positions before the war and an additional sixteen after the war. Forty-three received temporary posts and thirty-two (or nearly half) reemigrated after a short stay in Britain. Among those who passed through Britain on their way elsewhere were Albert Einstein— who briefly considered an offer from Oxford before heading for the United States—Erwin Schrödinger, Hans Bethe, and Fritz London.[149]

The Emergency Committee (EC) in the United States played a smaller role than the AAC/SPSL, especially where physics was concerned. Nonetheless, the EC was the 'official' placement organization and an important indication of the style of the American effort. It began by assuming that the United States would be the refugee's permanent home—explicitly the reverse of AAC/SPSL policy and their placement procedure was also the opposite. The committee solicited applications from universities or college who wished to add a displaced scholar. The returned applications would indicate the field and specialty desired. The EC placed 335 scholars in permanent posts in the United States and Palestine. Despite a list of 107 available physicists, the EC itself placed only sixteen in American universities.[150] This did not mean that physics suffered in the diaspora. Instead it shows that it was much easier for physicists to make arrangements outside of these formal channels. A cumulative count from several sources has at least 127 placements in physics in the period after the 1933 expulsions, of which the Emergency Committee's sixteen is obviously a tiny portion.[151] Physics, with its old and dense international connections, already had an informal network in place. For example, from their posts at Princeton, Eugene Wigner and Rudolf Ladenburg drew up a list in December 1933 and circulated it along with a letter requesting help. On it, the two listed twenty-eight physicists and chemists they knew who were in need of a position. I calculate that using a completely refugee-based network, Wigner and Ladenburg's list resulted in American jobs for eleven of the twenty-eight and a post in Britain for a twelfth.[152]

Though the largest, the AAC/SPSL and the EC were not the only organized efforts to rescue scholars and scientists from Nazi persecution. In the United States, the most important non-EC organization was probably the Rockefeller Foundation. In addition to its support of the Emergency Committee, the Foundation supported their own fund—the Special Research Aid Fund for Deposed Scholars—from 1933 to 1939. The fund spent $775,000 on refugee placement—a figure that exceeded by several factors the amount given by the foundation to the EC—with more than a third of that going abroad. The foundation also helped underwrite the placement of many scholars at the New School for Social Research. In all, the foundation supported jointly or alone 178 scholars from 1933 to the end of the war, of whom 155 were placed permanently. Of these, more than forty were mathematicians or physicists.[153]

This survey of refugee organizations and placement efforts demonstrates that a quite well-organized international effort followed the expulsion of Jews from the German (and then Austrian and Czechoslovakian) academy. This effort was by and large contained within the international university community and its satellites (such as the philanthropic educational institutions) and was funded by academics and Jewish philanthropic organizations. The benefits of the expulsions—due to a combination of resources, educational infrastructure, and intentions—redounded overwhelmingly to the United States. This was especially true in physics. American universities were treated to a phenomenal infusion of talent and experience. Just how critical a loss it was to German physics, and how significant was this infusion, are my next subjects.

Germany's Loss

The losses to Germany's physics infrastructure by the expulsions were final and fatal. The achievements of Jewish scientists and their concentration in the most active and innovative sectors of the sciences made the loss great. Physics, with the highest percentage of Jewish scientists, suffered the most.[154] No agreement will likely ever emerge on a precise numerical figure for dismissals and emigration. A firsthand observer—the American sociologist Edward Hartshorne—counted 106 dismissed physicists in 1936. The Emergency Committee records 107 physicists in the United States alone, a figure repeated in two secondary accounts of the immigration to the United States, and the SPSL had 165 physicists on file. Beyerchen concludes that an accurate count is impossible, but that displacement of one-quarter of all physicists employed in Germany in the years 1933 to 1934 is a conservative estimate.[155]

A qualitative evaluation of the refugees provides a more accurate picture of the true losses to German science. The conservatism and traditional anti-Semitism of the German academy meant that Jews were concentrated in physics, and within physics in the more marginalized (but more innovative) areas such as quantum and nuclear physics. For similar reasons, Jews were overwhelmingly concentrated in the larger, big-city universities where new and innovative research could find a niche. Finally, the age of the dismissed (and the subsequent refugees) was heavily skewed toward the younger end of the scale. Twenty current or future Nobel Prize winners were among those expelled, of whom eleven were physicists. Although only 20 percent of all German physicists taught either in Göttingen or Berlin, fully 40 percent of those who emigrated (or 32 and 19 percent of the respective faculties) came from those two universities. The University of Frankfurt also suffered the loss of a huge (32 percent) portion of their faculty. Meanwhile, nearly half of all universities suffered the loss of a single physicist—a condition explained by their provinciality and small size. As for age, fully half the pool of refugee physicists and mathematicians that flowed through the SPSL's database were in their early thirties.[156]

A comprehensive picture of the qualitative loss to German physics is found in Fischer's statistical work.[157] By surveying international physics citations, Fischer compiled lists of the top fifty most-cited nuclear physicists in different periods leading up to and after the 1933 expulsions. In his first period—1926 to 1930—German dominance of nuclear physics was unquestioned: twenty-six of the fifty most-cited physicists were German and/or teaching in German universities. But of the twenty-six, three had emigrated before the 1933 expulsions and eleven more emigrated after the race law was passed (including the Nobel laureates Erwin Schrödinger, Max Born, and James Franck, and Lise Meitner who with her nephew Otto Frisch would publish the first papers announcing the existence of nuclear fission). This left twelve of twenty-six of Germany's top nuclear physicists still in Germany in the mid-1930s. By 1935, the figure for most cited had fallen to five.

Fischer's data demonstrates that Germany lost most heavily in nuclear physics among the productive rank-and-file scientists as well. While future emigrants accounted for 10.7 percent of all journal articles published in the three most prominent German physics journals from 1926 to 1933 (this, despite being only 6.2 percent of the publishing population), their share in the 'atom and molecules' category (roughly nuclear physics) was 22.6 percent and in the 'quantum theory' category 25.1 percent. Future emigrants were, for a whole host of reasons intellectual and sociological, not only on average more productive than their non-Jewish colleagues, they were also heavily concentrated in nuclear and quantum physics.[158] Thus, the expulsions had the effect of hollowing out the most innovative fields at a crucial time in their development. The expulsions had a substantial impact on the Nazi bomb project.

The United States' Gain

The addition of the post-1933 refugees to American physics was a great boon. The discipline received over one hundred relatively young scholars heavily concentrated in an area of physics of looming importance and in which the Unites States was underpopulated. The universities saw the expulsions as a great opportunity to add to their talent pools. On July 25, 1933, a Berkeley administrator, Monroe Deutsch, wrote in a letter to university president Robert G. Sproul that he welcomed the chance "to profit by the stupidity and brutality of the German government."[159]

To convey the magnitude of the additions, I combined the information on physics refugees from a variety of sources.[160] Schweber lists thirty-four American quantum physicists at major American universities in the 1930s.[161] I count at least forty-two theorists in the wave of post-1933 refugees of one hundred twenty-eight—a figure that exceeds the total number of theorists currently at work in American universities. This figure does not include the acquisitions by Caltech, Princeton, and so on of the 1920s and early 1930s such as Samuel Goudsmit, George Uhlenbeck, Otto LaPorte, and Paul Epstein. Of the one hundred twenty-eight, at least fifty-six were nuclear physicists. Of the seventy-four total theoretical and/or nuclear physicists, only ten were not from Germany, Austria, and Hungary—these ten included one French physicist, five Italians, two Poles, a Swiss, and a Russian.

An even more compelling picture emerges when the war service of the post-1933 refugees is considered. At least twenty-five of the refugee physicists participated in the Manhattan Project. These included some of the most important scientists of the project: Eugene Wigner, Victor Weisskopf, Leo Szilard, Enrico Fermi, Edward Teller, and Hans Bethe. Most of them served in some capacity at Los Alamos; some, such as Bethe, were full-time while others, such as John von Neumann, were part-time consultants. Since Los Alamos employed only about one hundred scientists, the refugee contribution—numerically and qualitatively—was great.[162]

A further twenty-three were involved in some other aspect of the government's wartime science effort including the Radiation Laboratory at MIT, as civilian consultants to the NDRC and OSRD, or in other military or civilian government research. These latter counts no doubt underestimate the role of refugees in the wartime science effort, as only physicists were investigated, and they do not include counts of any scientists who may have remained within an academic environment conducting war research (such as through an OSRD contract).

The data present a general picture that underlines the importance of diffusion to the bomb project. But none of the émigrés would have found a useful home had the American universities not undergone such a dramatic transformation in the prior decades. By the 1930s, the American physics discipline had created an environment in which theoretical and experimental physics productively coexisted. The refugees, many of them theorists, entered this environment and immediately made a unique and valuable contribution. This point resists demonstration through aggregated evidence, but it has been made often enough in the secondary literature.[163]

A final example reinforces the point. Hans Bethe was hired at Cornell on the expectation that they would aid the department's experimental nuclear physics programs. Bethe made what was probably the most important and lasting contribution to the symbiosis of theory and experiment in nuclear physics. Working with two young American experimentalists at Cornell—Robert F. Bacher and M. Stanley Livingston (the latter having just come from graduate training under Lawrence and Oppenheimer at California)—Bethe published a monumental survey of knowledge in nuclear physics in three articles. With Bethe writing the theoretical sections and directing the project, the three systematically investigated every aspect of nuclear physics. They synthesized theory, reanalyzed experimental data, and in come cases even reran experiments. The three articles—which were collectively known as the Bethe Bible—ran in total nearly five hundred pages and were the standard reference work in nuclear physics well into the 1950s.[164]

The diffusion process completes the development phase of the technology life cycle of the atomic bomb. The conditions necessary for the atomic bomb were created by a convergence of four forces in the American environment: the maturation of the American university and American physics, the accumulation of state management expertise, rationalized industrial management techniques, and the refugee physicists.

While the four developed somewhat independently, they evolved together during wartime to form a unique organizational entity. The next section traces the maturation of the technological system during wartime and afterward and its effects on the international system—where the sociotechnical system stops being molded by international politics and becomes a part of the interaction capacity of the international system. At this point, the system trajectory was still open-ended. Some scientists thought that nuclear explosion was theoretically possible, but few thought it actually attainable and certainly not in the space of a few years. The crush of war pressurized the development of atomic science and fixed its form in the bomb. Its meaning was made solid by its wartime use and postwar decisions on nuclear strategy. These determined, in the end, the effects of nuclear weapons on the international system, not anything inherent in nuclear physics itself.

TRANSFORMATION

CREATING THE NUCLEAR SOCIOTECHNICAL SYSTEM: THE URANIUM AND MANHATTAN PROJECTS

The development of the atomic bomb in the United States between 1939 and 1945 stands as one of the greatest scientific and technical achievements in human history. It also marks the beginning of the maturation of the bomb as technological system—the beginning of the fixing of its form and political meaning. The program brought together all the institutional and innovative strands developed in the previous sections: scientific excellence; academic and research infrastructure; administrative, engineering, and manufacturing expertise; and vital 'international inputs' all met and mixed during those six years in an extraordinary combination of creative scientific research and rationalized, centralized mass control and manufacture.

The project itself evolved in two parts: first, the pre-1942 scientific efforts overseen by the National Defense Research Council (NDRC) founded in 1940 and its successor, the Organization for Scientific Research and Development (OSRD) founded the next year, and, second, the Manhattan Project proper. The NDRC/OSRD were both founded and directed by Vannevar Bush. The idea was to mobilize American science but avoid the mistakes of World War I by keeping scientists in their own university labs and free of unnecessary bureaucratic entanglements. The mechanism for this agenda was the contract for research activities in a specified area, not a particular product. This allowed the government to control basic research adroitly: a hand light enough to not kill science's creative spark, but heavy enough to avoid directionless puttering by the scientists. The Manhattan Project consisted of army-directed research laboratories at the University of Chicago, Columbia University, and the University of California, Berkeley (among other places); plutonium and uranium manufacture at Oak Ridge, Tennessee, and Hanford Washington; and bomb research, assembly, and manufacture at Los Alamos, New Mexico.[165]

The bomb project began with three physicist refugees: Albert Einstein, Eugene Wigner, and Leo Szilard. In mid-1939, Szilard and Wigner—responding to the Hahn-Strassmann experiment and the Meitner-Frisch interpretation of the fissioning of barium—pressed Einstein to help them draft and sign a letter to President Roosevelt warning him of the strong possibility of a fission bomb. Roosevelt was sufficiently impressed to order the creation of the Uranium Committee, under the directorship of the head of the National Bureau of Standards Lyman Briggs. But with an initial budget of $6,000 yearly and a conservative director (Briggs), the committee accomplished very little, frustrating scientists, such as Szilard, Teller, and Lawrence, working independently on nuclear fission.[166]

After Pearl Harbor, Bush and the other members of the Uranium Committee had to decide to push forward with a massive commitment of resources to create a bomb before war's end or to kill the project and allocate its resources elsewhere. At Columbia, Fermi, Wigner, and especially Szilard had been pressuring for more resources. Lawrence, meanwhile, had been convinced of a bomb's feasibility through conversations with Ralph Fowler, the British scientific liaison in Washington, and Mark Oliphant, an Australian physicist working on the British MAUD (atomic bomb) project. He too pressured the National Defense Research Council (NDRC) through Karl Compton to "light a fire under the Briggs Committee." Several positive reports from MAUD in April and October 1941 also helped sway Bush in favor of the project.[167]

He convened an independent advisory committee to evaluate American progress, and also on the reports from the British project (headed by two refugees, Rudolf Peierls and Otto Frisch). In November 1941, the Uranium Committee was drastically reorganized. Conant, Arthur H. Compton (University of Chicago physicist and older brother of Karl), and Lawrence were added to the committee that now reported directly to Bush instead of the NDRC head (Conant), and Briggs was shunted aside. The project was divided into three parts—the last two were redundant research projects: Arthur Compton was in charge of building a fissible uranium pile at Chicago, Lawrence of producing enriched uranium through electromagnetic separation at Berkeley, and Urey of producing enriched uranium through gaseous diffusion at Columbia.[168]

The Chicago team succeeded in generating the first sustained nuclear reaction on December 2, 1942. Thereafter, the problem became the production of an adequate amount of fissible material. Fear of a German bomb was driving decision-making at this point, however, and everything had to happen at once. Brigadier General Leslie R. Groves began arranging for the industrial, engineering, and construction firms to plan and build production plants for processes that the scientists had yet to determine. Beginning in October 1942, research was centralized under Robert Oppenheimer at Los Alamos.

Production of fissile materials was a major stumbling block, so research proceeded along multiple lines simultaneously. It was hoped that one of the at first six, then four, separation methods would prove to be the better process.[169] In the end, all four were used since none was (during the war) obviously superior. They were employed in tandem: U-235 purified through the gaseous diffusion plant at Oak Ridge was then passed through the thermal diffusion plant before final purification at the electromagnetic separation plant and shipment to Los Alamos.[170]

The choice of extraction methods reveals the project's structure. Time pressure and the economic and scientific resources available to the United States made the extraordinary step of simultaneous, redundant research programs possible. The coordination of the various procedures and their ultimate use was emblematic of the flexibility and improvisational character of the project. In research and through plant construction and production, the academic scientists remained closely involved in the project.

The Oak Ridge electromagnetic separation plant, built by the Stone and Webster Construction Company and operated by the Tennessee Eastman Corporation (a newly created subsidiary of the Eastman Kodak Company), typified the extensive science–industrial collaboration. Lawrence's group designed the plant at his Berkeley laboratory and personally supervised construction. The magnets that were to power Alpha I Racetrack for the separation project failed on installation. Electrical and vacuum tank failures caused by the same high-powered calutron magnets made production on the second Beta Racetrack seem highly unlikely. Lawrence was intimately involved in the attempts to repair the damaged magnets and bring the two racetracks to operation—a role presumably better suited to an engineer or factory foreman than a physicist.[171]

The scientific work at Los Alamos brought all the strands of the argument to this point together: it was highly collaborative, carefully planned, precisely timed and executed, yet haphazard and unpredictable. It gathered together in one place and for one intense project theoretical and experimental science and industrial mass-production. At its simplest, the Los Alamos scientists had to determine the properties and behavior of the fissionable material (uranium 235 and plutonium 239), and figure out how to bring the material to its critical (fissioning) stage fast enough to create an explosion. Experimental nuclear physicists such as Emilio Segrè and Otto Frisch worked to determine the properties of plutonium (uranium 235 had been more or less fully investigated before Los Alamos) and its critical mass. Metallurgists, such as Cyril Stanley Smith, were needed to turn the uranium and plutonium—usually embedded in graphite or some other crystalline solid, or suspended in liquid—into solid metal. But the most complex and vexing problem was the design of the explosive device needed to bring the fissionable material to critical mass. This project involved the intensive collaboration of all manner of scientists and engineers. Sometimes the Los Alamos scientists went outside the compound to find the needed expertise. Seth Neddermeyer—the physicist who first thought of using implosion for the atom bomb and directed the initial research efforts—traveled to Bruceton, Pennsylvania, in 1943 to learn more about high explosives from the engineers at the Navy Explosives Research Lab. Implosion perfectly exemplifies the culmination of the scientific and administrative trends I have been tracing.[172]

Two main methods for triggering a nuclear chain reaction were considered: the 'gun' method in which a conventional charge would fire a shell into the radioactive material, and the 'implosion' method in which a spherical-shaped conventional charge would compress the fissionable material. Despite the theoretical elegance and efficiency of the implosion method, many problems, conceptual and practical, made it a second priority. The enthusiasm of occasional Los Alamos consultant John von Neumann, however, convinced Oppenheimer to keep the method's creator, Seth Neddermeyer, and the Harvard chemist and explosives expert George Kistiakowsky working on the problem. By July 1944, time had run out on the gun method. Decay had caused the Hanford-produced samples of plutonium 239 (the fissible isotope) to become contaminated by plutonium 240 (which is nonfissible), leaving the more efficient implosion method the only workable triggering mechanism for a plutonium bomb. Oppenheimer relieved Neddermeyer, placed Robert F. Bacher at the head of a Gadget Division for implosion, and appointed Kistiakowsky to the head of a new division within the Ordnance Department. Both new groups had to work closely with the Theoretical Division, whose share of time devoted to implosion work saw a marked increase.[173]

To solve the riddle of spherical implosion, the Theoretical Division under the direction of Hans Bethe made a systematic exploration of all possible shapes and forces of an implosion, and then calculated the forces, waves, and vectors implied by the theories—all under considerable time pressure. The computational effort alone was enormous, and Bethe had to organize his group much like a general or an industrial manager.[174]

Kistiakowsky's group within the Ordnance Department was expending nearly one ton of high explosives per day in search of the correct shape and composition of the charge. Sufficient improvement began to show in all aspects of the implosion project in the winter of 1945, so on March 5 of that year Oppenheimer froze research on the implosion device. Bomb assembly and a test firing were imminent, so, much like a Du Pont managing engineer, Oppenheimer had to ensure that the rationalization of the research was preserved and delays avoided. The first atomic test at Trinity took place on July 16 and the two bombs were dropped on Hiroshima and Nagasaki on August 6 and 8, respectively.[175]

The experience of the scientists in the project shows how science, industrial and state management, and the diffusion of scientific knowledge and scientists themselves came together in this historical conjuncture. Lawrence's work with the electromagnetic separation project, Arthur Compton's management of the Metallurgical Laboratory, and Oppenheimer's achievements at Los Alamos are examples from the highest levels of the bomb project of the manner in which techniques and imperatives of management and planning invaded the academic scientists' realm. The translators who navigated between science, industry, and government in the early part of the war were academic scientists such as Vannevar Bush and James B. Conant. But once the project was fully under way, all who participated were forced to become their own translators (or leave the project, as many did after disputes with the military over security measures or with industry over creative control). Academic scientists not only learned to coexist with government and industrial management hierarchies and procedures, but they learned to manage themselves.

The émigrés also played a vital role in the bomb project. While not quite the "city of foreigners" described by Victor Weisskopf, Los Alamos nonetheless was heavily populated with refugees from German, Austrian, and Italian universities and research institutes.[176] Even in the brief version of the bomb's creation I offer, it is clear that their contributions were essential. Several of them (Hans Bethe, Eugene Wigner, Enrico Fermi, and Otto Frisch among them) administered important parts of the project.[177] Because of their abilities and their commitment to defeating fascism, the U.S. government was forced to ignore the refugee's enemy alien status and override the army's normal security procedures to allow them to work on a secret, wartime military project. The bomb emerged out of this symbiosis of science, industry, government, and foreign borrowings. It laid the foundations for cold war-era technology development and transformed the international system.

INTERNATIONAL SYSTEMIC EFFECTS

Nuclear weapons transformed security and the nature of state interaction in three ways. First, they altered the interaction capacity of the international system by changing the role of force, time, distance, the meaning of the front, and mobilization. This argument recasts the familiar "nuclear revolution" thesis in explicitly technological terms. Second, the Manhattan Project transformed state–society relations—changing the nature of the state and the manner in which it extracted resources and knowledge from society. If the Industrial Revolution pushed the state into the management of industry, the atomic age extended that reach into science. The project left an institutional residue on the new great powers and on those who tried to follow in their footsteps. This residue is varyingly called, beginning with Eisenhower, the military–industrial complex the scientific state, the science-intensive state, or simply big science.[178] Lastly, nuclear weapons had a secondary effect on the traditional distribution of power between states. The war toppled Germany, Great Britain, and Japan from the ranks of the most powerful states and consolidated the United States and the Soviet Union as two superpowers. Nuclear weapons did not make them powerful, but they confirmed their status and cemented the gap between the two and every other state. But because changes to the distribution of power are not the focus here, the emphasis will be on the first two transformations.

Interaction Capacity

The most obvious feature of nuclear weapons is their incredible destructive power. Their power is more than simply a quantitative increase over conventional explosives. This was apparent to the first observers to consider their strategic and security implications. In 1946, Bernard Brodie wrote, "No conceivable variation in the power of the atomic bomb could compare in importance with the disparity in power between atomic and previous types of explosives."[179] Since the 1940s— with the development of the hydrogen bomb; more sophisticated, longer range delivery systems; and more powerful warheads—the gap between nuclear and conventional explosives has only increased. Nuclear weapons are thus a very efficient military tool. Nuclear threats are easy to make credible (at least in theory) because so few are actually required to deliver the promised destruction, a fact also noted by early observers. Most important, the destructive power of nuclear weapons makes, as Robert Jervis puts it, mutual destruction of nuclear adversaries nothing less than a fact of contemporary international politics.[180]

A less-apparent effect of nuclear weapons, one in keeping with the focus on interaction capacity, is the shrinking of time. Traditionally, the use of strategic weapons included a time element of sufficient duration to allow the parties time to react, even to communicate. None of this is true in the same way for nuclear weapons. Even allowing for their delivery by long-range bombers (the original delivery method), the suddenness of the destruction meted by nuclear weapons makes communication or counterstrategy irrelevant. Thomas Schelling makes the point nicely, "To compress a catastrophic war within the span of time that a man can stay awake drastically changes the politics of war, the process of decision, the possibility of central control and restraint, . . . and the capacity to think and reflect while war is in progress."[181] This technological feature of nuclear weapons has clear security implications. Because delivery is so rapid and destruction immediate, nuclear states have shifted their security strategy from mobilization capacity to deterrence capacity—including surveillance capacity, spurring more technological development, deepening state penetration into society, and altering state–society relations.

Because of the changes to the time element, states prepare for nuclear war by trying to prevent it, rather than mobilizing the necessary resources to fight it.[182]

Similar to its effects on time, nuclear weapons have transformed the meaning of geographic distance to national security. With nuclear weapons, any nuclear power has the ability to destroy the cities of its rival(s) from its own bases on its own territory. Technology replaces geography as the arbiter of secure 'distance' between threats or rivals. This has enhanced the role technology plays in obtaining security and reduced the importance of more traditional geographic measures of security such as isolation, fortifications, naval deployments, forward presence, and so forth. The replacement of technology for geography was realized by American strategy-makers even during World War II. The U.S. military's report on strategic bombing outlined a strategy for the postwar world that explicitly recognized this change.[183]

The combination of changes to the meanings of time and distance and the nature of the delivery of nuclear weapons has removed the concept of the front from the nuclear strategic universe. Defense of a traditional border from nuclear attack is nonsensical, as the nuclear weapon by its nature sweeps over such defenses to penetrate directly to the core of the territory under attack (or threatened with attack). Thus, defensive strategies for the nuclear age must either be comprehensive—meaning extended over the entire globe to detect nuclear attack from the moment of launch—or deterrence based, or both. Once again, nuclear weapons demand a technological response for security (such as surveillance technologies or enhanced nuclear capabilities) instead of a geopolitical one (such as alliance-making or conquest).

Finally, nuclear weapons changed the meaning of mobilization. Before the nuclear age, war or the threat of war required the mobilization of the resources and population of a territory in anticipation of armed conflict. The ongoing industrialization of war was steadily increasing the amount of resources and people necessary for effective mobilization, along with the complexity of their extraction. But mobilization was only a plan until war or the direct threat of war. The nature of nuclear weapons requires permanent 'peacetime' mobilization of a significant proportion of society—and not simply those traditionally understood as warriors, but scientists, engineers, technicians, factory workers, bureaucrats, managers, and administrators, too. These nuclear warriors are not simply involved in the design of new or improved weapons—such activity has always gone on during peacetime—

but in the permanent planning and maintaining of a technology-based mobilization system with nuclear weapons at its center.

These five effects of nuclear weapons on the international system combine to change the role of technology itself. This is less a direct change in the international environment and more a change in the way in which nuclear states must organize themselves internally in order to provide for their external security. Because of nuclear weapons' impact on time and geography, security cannot be obtained exclusively through space or distance, but must be achieved technologically. No longer can a state mobilize for war by accumulating men and materiel as war breaks out and organize production and distribution during the war to meet the increased needs of the armed forces. Instead, the state and the military must become directly and permanently involved in the peacetime mobilization of scientific and industrial resources to meet the technological needs of security.[184] Because the centerpiece of national security is the nuclear bomb—a weapon 'used' (in the deterrence sense) constantly during peacetime—the difference between wartime and peacetime becomes largely indistinguishable, at least as far as the state's mobilization of social resources is concerned.

What of the actual interactions and communications between states on questions of security; what have been the impacts of the bomb on the practice of diplomacy? Jervis notes that at the very least, the bomb has introduced an element of caution into great power relations.[185] Greater caution has the effect in theory of reducing the number of crises between nuclear powers. Waltz notes that the bomb makes security alliances unnecessary.[186] Because nuclear deterrence provides a more than adequate level of basic security, alliances to pool power resources and deter aggressors are pointless. During the cold war, states did not exactly shrink from alliances, however. Nuclear states have allied with other nuclear states against a perceived threat from another nuclear power. The East–West confrontation over Central Europe suggests that the threat to be deterred by the alliance was more conventional than nuclear. Evidence from the post-cold-war world suggests that possession of the bomb—or reported possession— seems to give the possessor a certain foreign policy freedom: witness the foreign policy behavior of prewar Iraq or North Korea.

State–Society Relations

International-level effects are only part of the story of the nuclear revolution. Changes at the international level are complemented and

reinforced by changes at the domestic level. The institutional apparatus that produced the atomic bomb during World War II in the
United States was reproduced and further articulated postwar not
only in the United States, but in all other states that wished to remain militarily competitive with the United States. Just as German
science was widely copied during the Imperial era (approximately
1870–1914) so, too, were the achievements and institutions of the
American national security state carefully emulated.[187] The collaboration between state, military, industry, and university on military high-
technology projects, basic science research, and the mobilization of
military technology in the postwar era was a direct outgrowth of the
wartime Manhattan Project and other defense-related research projects.
The institutions created during the war to develop the bomb were the
building blocks on which postwar technology management institutions for national security were constructed.

The most important wartime technology planning organization in
the United States was the National Defense Research Committee, which
in 1942 metamorphosed into the Organization for Scientific Research
and Development (both discussed earlier). The NDRC/OSRD oversaw
several dozen science and technology projects before and during the
war. These projects were housed in hundreds of universities and research labs and employed thousands of scientists. The OSRD nurtured
the two largest and most important science and technology projects of
the war: radar research at what came to be known as the Radlab at
MIT, and the Uranium Project, which, when administration was turned
over to the army in 1942, was renamed the Manhattan Project.

Both projects were extended and expanded after the war in ways
that reshaped national security and state–society–technology relations.
The Radlab developed over 150 different radar and electronic systems
by war's end and emerged as the center of a significant civilian industry in addition to its important role in the national security system.
The Manhattan Project developed the atom bomb during the war.
After the war it metamorphosed into the Atomic Energy Commission
(AEC) and later—during the Carter administration—changed again,
becoming the Department of Energy. The AEC was the primary sup-
porter of atomic energy research and many new developments in nuclear
weapons technology, including the hydrogen bomb, the nuclear-powered
submarine, and the first public-utility nuclear power plant.[188]

The Radlab was important for the products and innovations it
produced, but it was the Manhattan Project that was the organizational model for the postwar American national security state and for

its relations with academy and industry. Thomas Hughes notes, "The Manhattan Project, with its systematic linking of military funding, management, and contract letting, industrial, university, and government research laboratories, and numerous manufacturers, became the model for these massive technological systems. Earlier models for system building, such as Ford's, Insull's, and the TVA's, paled in comparison."[189] The organizational tools developed to create nuclear weapons became the model for the extraction of technology from society during the cold war.[190]

Elsewhere in the industrialized world, the influence of the American model was widespread even if the copies made were not exact. Every industrialized state developed a set of systematized links between universities, industry, and government to generate innovations for use in national security and/or civilian economic arenas. For example, unlike the American military–industrial complex, the British is largely outside the universities: the Royal Radar Establishment, the Atomic Energy Research Establishment, and Aldermaston Laboratory are all large, government-run research labs. The structure, purpose, and institutional origins of the European defense and space industries and their cooperative projects during the cold war are another important set of examples. They show how American institutions were emulated and how competition with the United States has affected the development and evolution of other Western national security states.[191]

In the Soviet Union, the impact of the American example was even more important than in Europe. The Soviets had a long history of borrowing economic and technological techniques from the Americans, whom they considered more pragmatic, less decadent, and closer to the Soviet socialist–technological ideal than their European counterparts. The Depression and World War II and the cold war did much to dampen Soviet enthusiasm for American technology. During the Depression years, the Soviets changed from direct technology transfer to copying from American technical journals and theft. The atomic bomb was a different story and the Soviets pursued it aggressively.[192]

They responded to the American atomic bomb with a successful bomb program of their own—achieving a chain reaction on December 25, 1946, and a nuclear explosion on August 29, 1949. They were aided by German scientists, captured and willing, obtained in the waning days of the European war, and by a fairly successful spy program focused on the bomb programs in the United States and Great

Britain.[193] Their first satellite, *Sputnik*, was a tremendously important success for their national security state not just because it promised the inevitability of the long-range ballistic missile, but because it showed the United States that the Soviet Union was capable of out-doing the Americans. Being a socialist country, the Soviet Union had always had a command, state-administered scientific and technologi-cal development apparatus, but the scale of the postwar projects dwarfed anything attempted before the war, and in each case they were spurred by their new competition with, and the examples provided by, the United States.[194]

What were the effects of this institutional revolution? The most immediate change was the transformation wrought on the natural sciences in the United States. The vast amounts of research funding the various programs and projects provided and the experience of working closely with government, military, and industrial managers for the first time made it so. University-based scientists found that over the course of the war, science had become big science. Bruce Smith notes that the emergence of a science policy in the United States (whether federal or state level) since World War II is a distinc-tive, new feature of government activity. Even during the New Deal, science and technology remained peripheral, and academic scientists retained a disinterested and mistrustful attitude to government fund-ing of scientific research. But the war changed all of that: "The war provided the transforming events from which the modern research system emerged."[195] Since the war, scientific research has for the most part been centered in universities and funded by the federal govern-ment. Scientific research itself has gotten progressively larger in scale and vastly more expensive. The moniker big science refers to the combination of scale, cost, and the quasi-industrial manner in which the enterprise is organized. States who wished to keep up with the pace of scientific research set by the United States had to find similar ways of funding their scientific communities, and most did. The nuclear revolution—and the cyclotrons, linear accelerators, and other building-sized scientific apparatus it brought with it—necessitated a huge and sustained investment in science.

The Manhattan Project also affected the state's relationship with industry. Postwar, states have deepened their ties with industry in pursuit of advanced military hardware and its analogs; government procurement accounts for a large bulk of the production of the aero-space industry, the nuclear industry, and the various space-related industries such as satellites. The American government is in the position of supporting an important segment of the American economy, including some of the economy's most advanced and rapidly growing industries. Other industrialized countries, with much longer traditions of state control and far fewer qualms about government ownership, have de facto control over even larger segments of their economies than the American government.

A third area of social activity affected by the rise of the science-based national security state is the process of technological innovation itself. The development of new technologies under the impact of the science–industry–state collaboration has become routinized and state-directed, and, as Walter McDougall writes, "artificial—that is institutionalized—stimulation of science and technology has become a fundamental source of national power."[196] Gregory McLauchlan describes the same process—but from the perspective of national security—as the shift from geopolitics to technopolitics.[197]

The routinization of technological innovation under the direction of the state is of fundamental importance to the fourth area of social activity affected by the new scientific-industrial state. The institutionalization of relations between state, industry, science, and technological innovation generates feedback with the international system. When these relations are consolidated at the domestic level—with attendant shares of gross domestic product, political influence, and cultural capital (witness the space race)—they ensure that the shift from geopolitics to technology in international security relations continues. The one reinforces the other: a highly technologically dependent international security sphere demands a sophisticated military–industrial complex at the domestic level, which in turn churns out new innovations and new military technologies, guaranteeing that the international security sphere will remain a high-technology race.

This way of looking at nuclear weapons assumes that they are an independent force acting on both the international system and domestic state–science–industry relations. But the use of determinist language obscures a central point of this project—that system transformation by nuclear weapons was not an inevitable by-product of the fact of nuclear fission. Technological development is contingent and path-dependent. The emergence of nuclear weapons was the product of social and political forces, not an act of nature. Growth in science in the United States and decay in Germany were necessary factors in the development of the first bomb in the United States, as were the various pathways of knowledge diffusion—a transnational physics community; copying, borrowing, and stealing by American science departments; and the refugee crisis. The international system—competition between states and transnational processes—laid the foundations for system transformation. But all these factors together cannot account for the bomb. For that, we need the conjuncture of the war. It was a huge historical switch that set nuclear physics off in one direction instead of another. Without the pressure of war, the puzzle of the nuclear explosion would have been delayed—possibly by decades. Without the war, there would not have been the intense commitment of state and scientific resources devoted to the question. The institutional framework made the bomb possible, but a catalyst was needed to complete it. This catalyst fixed the sociotechnical system that was nuclear technology in a particular form, allowing us to speak meaningfully of the impact of the nuclear revolution.

CHAPTER 5

CONCLUSION

In this book, I set out to investigate the relationship between technology and transformation to the international system. Our experience of technology in recent decades is one of overwhelming, rapid change. So the importance of the topic to international politics is obvious. Yet existing theories of international relations treat technology as an afterthought or residual variable. None of them appreciates the social dimensions of technology but instead they view it deterministically and exogenous to politics. To pursue an alternative strategy, I relied on theories of complex sociotechnical systems and the social construction of technology, path-dependent and process-tracing methods, and the concept of interaction capacity from international relations theory. I identified a set of links between technology, the institutions of technology management, and the international system that points to a clear way of examining the relationship between the first and the last. Technology is both a product of the international system and domestic institutions as well as a driver of international system change. For it to be both at once, technology must be treated as an historical, contingent phenomenon (and a political and social one) that—like institutions—matures, hardens, gets "sticky," and develops independent causal efficacy.

The technologies I investigated, by altering the interaction capacity of the international system, had profound effects on world politics. The railways were an important part of Germany's rise to power in the late nineteenth century. They also dramatically increased the military power of states by increasing the size of armies and the speed with which they could be moved. But rail also made preindustrial society and great power status incompatible. The conservative Prussian

Junkers found that if they wished to remain militarily and politically competitive, they would have to give up a society dominated by an agricultural nobility and rooted in a preindustrial mode of production. The Austrian crown discovered that their failure to keep pace with European industrial expansion meant an end to their status as a great power.

Nuclear weapons were the basis of American superpower status in the mid-twentieth century. The weapon's destructive power, reach, and relative cost-effectiveness allowed the United States to convert its economic power and technical capability into a huge security shield extending over its allies in Europe and Asia. The weapon gave a deterrent shield to any country with the resources and desire to acquire it from the United States—most notably the United States's eventual postwar competitor, the Soviet Union. Traditional notions of geography and security were erased by nuclear weapons' reach and power. But they also raised the cost of great power military confrontation to unacceptably high levels. The risk of escalation into nuclear conflict was so great that the superpowers all but rejected direct confrontation and instead carried on their rivalry in a series of conflicts on the periphery of the international system.

But the technologies I investigated were also the products of a complex interaction of systemic level forces, state-level institutions, and previously existing technologies. They did not spring on an unguarded international political system but were developed, moved, and adapted by the pressures of international competition, the tools and institutions of technology development, and the paths of international technology transfer. Whatever effects the technologies may have had on the international system were created by a set of political forces that included that system. The technologies were political.

Thus, Germany's strategic vulnerability fed the desire for unification that in turn facilitated the development of a national railway system. World War II persuaded state, scientific, and military leaders in the United States to fund a huge and largely speculative project to build a superweapon. The economic policies of the eighteenth-century Prussian state were driven by a mercantilist autarkic vision. But the management expertise and technological resources gained by the state agencies that pursued that objective were important factors in Germany's industrialization and railway construction and management. In the early twentieth century, American scientific leaders in concert with the large philanthropies set out to make American science internationally competitive. They were convinced that science would be the driving force behind social and economic development in the new century but worried that the poor organization and lack of emphasis on research in American science would permanently handicap American civilization in global competition. The developments they undertook trained the talent, collected the resources, and built the scientific community necessary (but not sufficient) to build the bomb.

International communities and well-established methods of communication and transfer facilitated the movement of the nascent technologies from one country to another. The English engineers of the 1780s to the 1860s, their foreign contracts, and the years spent abroad as laborers or consultants are the analogs of the physicists in the 1920s and 1930s and their visiting professorships and international conferences. The theft, legal importation, and long observation of railway technology and the emigration of skilled laborers and engineers served the same purpose as the fellowships and study abroad of young American scientists, the journals and conferences of the international physics community and the expulsion, emigration, and permanent placement of refugee physicists in the United States.

The rise of the railway network and the atomic bomb as factors in international politics cannot be explained without reference to the international and domestic political forces that shaped their development, and to the economic and technical factors associated with each technology. The analysis of the relationship between technology and the international system is incomplete if focus is restricted to the effects of technology on the international sphere alone. Instead, as I have shown, the international system is itself a factor in the emergence of the new technologies. The system comes into play in several ways: via the traditional mechanisms of interstate competition and emulation, via various transnational mechanisms including knowledge communities and economic migrants, and via conjunctural historical moments that push the development of technology one way or another.

The explanatory framework that emerges from this analysis of the railways and the atomic bomb is complex. Technological change can induce changes in the nature and distribution of power within the system, but systemic level and state level factors shape technological change. Technology requires an historical approach because technology and its effects are specific to particular technologies. In each case, the process of creating the sociotechnological system transformed the state as well as the system, underlining the historical dimensions of all three—state, system, and technology.

The construction of the German railway network coincided with one kind of state transformation, the building of the atomic bomb with another. The creation and management of a railway network by German state officials, military officers, and private rail line administrators marked a significant departure in the level of public–private planning, peacetime organization for war, and societal penetration by management and planning institutions. The state acquired an expanded set of regulatory and planning capabilities and responsibilities, and the process of war planning and preparation extended much farther into peacetime economic activity than it had previously.

The collaboration between state, military, science, industry, and academy on the atomic bomb project, an enterprise that continued into the cold war, expanded management and planning just as the railway had. Collaborative public–private planning intensified, the organization for war took up more and more peacetime resources, and the penetration of society by management and planning institutions was even greater. Most important, the state took a direct and systematic role in large-scale technology development. This led it into deeper involvement with science and higher education, industrial research and development, and civil administration. State functions and civilian economic and social life were knit even closer together by the cold war; in the developed world the predatory state of the absolutist period has disappeared into a multifunctioned state fully if uncomfortably integrated with society.

The steadily increasing complexity of the environment and increased management activity means that the state in the different eras is actually a slightly different phenomenon; it has changed functions, capabilities, and responsibilities. From an international perspective, states are relatively more concerned with economic competition and the economic components of military strength than they were. They are also, thanks to increased societal penetration and management abilities, able to mobilize more and more of ever-greater societal resources for military competition. Whatever the more specific dimensions of these changes, states in the industrial era are historical creatures. Generalizations about state interests or capabilities that overreach will founder on their changing nature.

The two cases also show how the international system is fundamentally historical in nature. In the period covered, the system has been transformed across four dimensions: its scope, its form, the power and efficacy of force, and the role of geography and space. In the last half of the nineteenth century, industrial economic expansion and technological changes enabled the second great expansion of the European states system. The second wave of colonialism expanded the size and scope of the states system, and the Europeans, thanks to their economic and technological prowess, achieved a level of penetration in Africa and Asia that had before eluded them.

The system also attained institutional homogeneity. The development of nuclear weapons and their aftermath shows how first German educational and scientific institutions were copied in the United States, and then how the entire complex of institutions that organize scientific research and technology for military purposes took on similar form in states of the developed West. Identical technological systems—not just nuclear weapons—seem to require identical research, development, manufacturing, and management institutions.

The railway and nuclear weapons affected the power and efficacy of force and the meaning of geography to security. The railway allowed for an increase in the size of armies, and delivered them faster to fronts farther away, with the troops in better condition, than was previously possible. This increased the power of armies as well as their range. Frontiers that were thought impossible to defend with railways now could be; conquests thought impossible because of distance with railways could be seriously considered.

Railways shrunk space, but nuclear weapons render it meaningless. They deliver massive destructive power anywhere in the world in a matter of hours. Security under nuclear weapons is attainable only through deterrence—the management of technology—not through the management of space and military might (the traditional method of acquiring security). The changing natures of space and force brought about by rail and nuclear weapons are changes to the interaction capacity and therefore the structure of the international system. Changing the nature and efficacy of force changes the currency of international military and political affairs. States face a different set of constraints and incentives to action. Changing the relationship of space to security alters states' relationships with other states; the nature and assessment of threats and determinations of the possible or likely are fundamentally different.

What of diffusion? The transfer of developing sociotechnical systems from one place to another was critical in both cases; each recipient had characteristics that the sender lacked. Does diffusion always play the same role in the relationship between technology and the international system? A new, potentially transformative technology could in principle be created, develop, and mature within one country. Failing that, simultaneous invention (a common phenomenon in the history of technology) could make diffusion irrelevant.[1] Diffusion is, however, a permanent feature of technological development. The movement from inventor's workbench to market, even when within one country's borders, is diffusion. So the real question is, why does country-to-country diffusion play such an important role in the argument here? There are two possible answers.

One possibility is that different levels of economic and technological development form a natural boundary or barrier for further technological development. Either the large size or greater development of a particular national market allows the institutions in that market to be more innovative than those in a smaller market with fewer resources. But given similar levels of development and relatively homogeneous institutions for technology development, the differences would not be great enough to give one national economy much of an advantage. As a corollary, we would expect that as institutions converge on a single set of forms, innovation will either be simultaneous, or diffusion will be so rapid that the sort of pattern that I identified in the case of the railway and the atomic bomb would not develop.

A second answer is more geopolitical. One state might have greater incentive to develop a particular technology based on perceived strategic need or wish. This kind of change would be relatively immune from institutional and economic convergence. So diffusion is likely to continue to be relevant internationally so long as states are either economically, institutionally, or geopolitically different enough to make uneven technology development possible. Were this to change—were strategic and economic need, and levels of institutional and economic development, to become more or less uniform—then country-to-country diffusion would likely cease to exist in any meaningful sense.

On the question of generalizeability, as the argument is historically contingent, is the argument not applicable to other times and cases? I think that it is. Such an analysis starts with the identification of the technology or technologies that are likely to significantly impact interaction capacity in the international system. The next step is to provide an explanation for their emergence, spread, and adaptation. The explanation should be structured around the relevant technology management institutions—both public and private, the attempts at state technological management, and the methods for international technology transfer. The final step is to determine the nature and magnitude of changes to the international system that are likely to result.

The technologies of the "information revolution" are the next likely candidates to remake the international system. Does the framework developed earlier help us understand the impact of the information revolution on international affairs? The argument of this book is that significant technologies are politically malleable in their development and diffusion phases, yet grow increasingly harder to change, and have a greater impact on politics, once mature. There is strong prima facie evidence that digital information technologies are indeed "significant," joining writing, paper, the gun, the printing press, the railroad and telegraph, and nuclear weapons on the list of technologies that have transformed international politics. The volume of scholarship devoted to the information revolution, and the characteristics of digital information technologies themselves, strongly suggest that they are indeed significant.

Yet specification of the likely effects of digital information technologies on the international system is a hazardous business. The new technologies seem to promise a radically decentralized, networked world in which all information transfers—text, voice, video, and even capital—are protected from theft and eavesdropping, and where the information needed to direct military operations can in theory be delivered almost costlessly to soldiers actually viewing the targets and activating the weapons. These changes suggest further alterations in the nature and efficacy of force, and the functions and capabilities of states. But the final form these technologies will take, and the full extent of their spread, is at the moment—even several decades into the 'revolution'—far from certain.

Given the predominant position of the United States in the development of global computer networks, it seems likely that a similar process of diffusion and adaptation will characterize the path the technology takes. The computer and the computer network have their roots in the same science–industry–state nexus that built the atomic bomb and was the technological motor behind the American waging of the cold war. Current political debates between competing industries and between enthusiasts for various versions of the new information technologies will have a profound impact on the mature form of the technology. The medium of transmission abroad, to those countries lagging behind the United States, is likely to be in part the networks themselves, and, eventually, American entrepreneurs driven abroad by a saturated market at home. Finally, competing centers of innovation are likely to arise as well (in many cases already have), just as Germany challenged English industrial prowess and the United States usurped Germany's scientific leadership. The mature form, and the form in which it enters the international system as a transformative tool, will remain uncertain for years to come. This fact only underlines the political nature of technology and helps make the argument of this book all the more emphatically. Without knowing the outcome, it is far clearer with the information revolution to see the impact of politics on the nature and evolution of the technology. Only in retrospect does the mature form of rail and bomb strike us as inevitable. But if computer technology delivers on a fraction of its promises and the international system is remade as a result, then, like the two cases here, the technology-driven transformation will have its explanation in the complex of international politics, domestic institutions, and the politics of technology development.

Does this argument say anything more precise about the information revolution than "just wait"? To begin this tentative exploration, I need to define the information revolution a bit more precisely. By the term I mean a ubiquitous global digital information environment in which all information—text, pictorial, audio, and video—is digital and easily available everywhere to users of all types: citizens, consumers, and private individuals. Information technology in the political sphere affects the character of communications between political authorities and citizens, and structures the nature of political authority itself. States—as products of the modern, bureaucratic project—are specialized, highly effective information processors.[2] So states are likely to be heavily affected by changes in information technology.

The framework used for the rail and bomb cases was a two-step process: focusing first on the development of new technologies, and second on their maturation and political impact. The first step was to identify the emerging sociotechnical system that is/may be dramatically affecting the interaction capacity of the international system. To do this, we needed answers to several questions: In what institutional context is the system developing, who are the important players, what are their interests and objectives, and what is the physically possible (and impossible)—in other words, what are the politics of the emerging system? Next, at what phase in its life cycle is the system? Are great leaps of innovation largely completed and is the system hardening into maturity? Or is there still a great deal of flexibility in the design and (therefore) political meaning of the system?

The second step was to connect the characteristics of the emerging system with likely international political outcomes. How will a change in interaction capacity affect international politics? How significant will the likely change be: will it only produce a temporary shift in the distribution of power, will it alter the nature of security, will it reshape international actors (states), will it empower nonstate actors relative to states, will states be entirely supplanted by some new, fitter organization,[3] or will some combination of all of these result?

The digital information infrastructure is profoundly unfinished, so completing the first step in the same fashion as the bomb and rail is impossible. The explosion of the Internet into the public sphere in the mid-1990s—in the developed world at least—gives the impression of fast, accelerating innovation. Yet in no way is the sociotechnical system complete. Issues of technological immaturity (especially in the area of broadband access, or the so-called last mile), uneven distribution, weak diffusion in the developing world, and political contestation over intellectual property rights, privacy, and security as well as a slowing of the global economy after the 1990s tech boom have left the system in an uncertain and incomplete state.

Yet the digital infrastructure continues to develop. Moore's Law, which predicts a doubling of computer processing speeds every eighteen months, still holds—further driving up computer speeds and driving down prices and processor size. The emergence of a robust market in wireless Internet access—including the promise of regional wireless—suggests that the problem of high-speed ubiquitous access is still receiving the attention of innovators.[4] Developments in embedded systems—the placement of radio tags and/or computer processors in everyday objects (inventory, pets, refrigerator items, small children, etc.)—suggests that a ubiquitous network encompassing almost all spheres of human social activity is closer to reality.[5]

At every step, developments of the system are wrapped up in, actually defined by, political contestation. As Lawrence Lessig has argued, the software that governs the movement of digital information packets over the Internet is code in two senses: it involves software instructions and, by restricting some kinds of activity and encouraging others, the functional equivalent of legal code.[6] The architecture of the Internet is famously open. But it can be, and is being, closed. Security concerns by financial institutions and governments have blocked the emergence of digital cash systems. Consumer concerns over privacy have inhibited the development of digital information systems in medicine.[7] The profusion of spam, or unwanted e-mail—which is estimated at over half the volume of global e-mail—has led to suggestions to rewrite the most basic Internet operating instructions (how e-mail is addressed, routed, and delivered) to cope with the problem.[8] Post-9/11 security worries in the United States have accelerated the placement by the FBI of PCs with so-called Carnivore (now called DCS1000) software installed at the network exchanges of Internet service providers (ISPs). These devices track and record the Internet traffic of targeted individuals.[9] The motion picture and recording industries, worried about protecting their intellectual property rights, have undertaken aggressive global campaigns against piracy—in both the technological and legislative realms of code.[10] Solutions to any of these problems can be crafted as legislation (outlawing spam), as software (rewriting the *sendmail* protocol to make spamming more difficult), or as hardware (changing the design of packet routers to make it easier for authorities to eavesdrop on Internet traffic). In each case, as with the rail and the bomb, the distinction between the technical and the political is blurry. Each of these examples, and many others as well, are sites of technical, economic, social, and finally political contestation. They help illustrate that the political implications of digital information technologies are up for grabs—not just because the rules governing their use are undecided, but because the technologies themselves are being shaped by politics.

As digital information technology alters the interaction capacity of the system, it alters three broad areas of international political life: the nature of security (both for individuals and states), the nature of global political authority, and the character and extent of democracy and citizenship. In all three areas, the political effects of information technologies are likely quite profound—but the effects vary radically. And in all three areas, the amount of difference that political contestation, and the political shaping of technologies, will make is equally significant.

The security of states and individuals is affected by changes in information technology. This occurs in two realms—that of traditional security when states arm themselves to deter or combat other states, and in a more nebulous realm where the ability of states to uphold the state–society security bargain is under threat. Both represent a potentially dramatic alteration of the interaction capacity of the international system. In the first, the "revolution in military affairs"

(RMA) promises to revolutionize traditional war-fighting practices. By applying information technology to military systems and doctrine, the RMA will vastly increase the situational awareness of commanders (improved surveillance, reconnaissance, intelligence), it will increase the ability of military forces to communicate what they know and learn (a globe-spanning closed loop from target acquisition through decision-making through engagement and destruction), and it will increase the precision of force used.[11] But for the future, only the United States will have the resources and expertise to deploy such a system. This has the potential to increase an already vast imbalance in military force between the United States and every other state in the system. The RMA is seen in the United States as the key to its long-term security. For the rest of the world, it is feared as a source of great vulnerability.

In the second security realm, the state–society bargain is weakened by information-powered terrorism and transnational crime. This in turn weakens the trust citizens have in their political system. Cellular and satellite phones, encrypted e-mail, hidden chat rooms, coded web pages, and the miniaturisation of weapons and explosives make it easier and cheaper to be a global terrorist or criminal and harder and harder for states to monitor and/or apprehend them.[12]

Individuals—as citizens and consumers—are made directly less secure by developments in information technology, further blurring the lines between domestic and international security. Fiscal instability affects jobs and savings adversely. Terrorism and crime affects not only states, but individuals. Digital personae—in the form of financial, educational, medical, and citizenship records—are a profound privacy threat and source of insecurity.[13] Individuals are more vulnerable to crime, snooping by private individuals and institutions, and surveillance by governments when digital information technology is widespread.

Countermeasures to all these concerns are possible. If states cannot pursue the RMA with the same intensity as the United States, (relatively) cheap weapons of mass destruction provide one line of deterrence; alliances and regional integration—in economic and security spheres both—another. While the severity of the threat of terrorism and transnational crime is grave, it is not clear that it rises to the level of threatening the existence of nation-states. A continued increase in these threats is only likely to increase demand from citizens for greater and greater protection—as the public response to 9/11 in the United States, or the Israeli response to Palestinian violence, indicates. The key point from the perspective of this project is that information technologies are sufficiently flexible to allow for either potentiality. To defend themselves against privacy intrusions, individuals can arm themselves with technology (anonymizers, encryption), with political activism, or by opting out of digital information systems. If these threats are caused by information technology, the same technology is also available to help counter such threats. Technology can either counter the threat (greater surveillance), or the technology that causes the threat can be altered to make it less so (making Internet anonymity impossible).

The future of the nation-state itself is also thought to be under siege from digital information technologies. The economic functions of states—such as taxation and the money supply—and more traditional security functions are vulnerable. Autonomous, nonterritorial financial zones, such as the faintly comical Sealand[14] off the English coast, combined with the speed and ubiquity of global financial transactions make it harder and harder for states to prevent the repatriation of money offshore to avoid detection (of criminal activity) or taxation, or both.[15] Add to that the possibility of digital cash, and even private currencies,[16] and the future of the nation-state as a fiscal entity seems dire indeed.

Yet the fiscal weakness of the state is probably exaggerated. The phenomenon of a financial "offshore" is a creation of states themselves—either of large and powerful developed states, or smaller states, such as the Cayman Islands, seeking a competitive niche.[17] States are already developing schemes for some form of global tax system through policy harmonization and greater cooperation.[18] The 1990s evangelists for private digital currencies are now glum and confused that their nonstate utopia failed to emerge.[19] The 9/11 attacks, and subsequent crackdowns on money-laundering and other illicit global financial transactions, are examples of how conjunctural moments can push an evolving sociotechnical system one way or the other. The open, anonymous systems that currently exist can be closed, their anonymity stripped, and activities within them carefully tracked. Digital information technology lowers the cost and increases the speed of financial transactions and communications. The same fast processors also empower social actors—such as states—that wish to trace, control, or block those communications.

The growth of digital networks undoubtedly represents a transformation of the interaction capacity of the international system. Such networks enhance commerce and global economic integration by increasing the speed, reliability, and transparency of transactions. They also make possible global, real-time inventory control and other innovations as yet undeveloped. But these developments do not obviously lead politically in one direction or another. The system is incomplete.

Lastly, democratic politics itself will be reshaped by digital information technologies. Depending on the analyst, it is either strengthened by a digital information system or severely weakened.[20] Digital technologies increase the quantity and lower the cost of information about political affairs and make communication between citizens and government much easier. They also lower the cost of political organizing, in terms of money and time, leading to the phenomenon of the "smart-mobs," ubiquitous videotaping of political events and like methods of "surveilling the surveillers," and other techniques of Internet-based political activism.[21] Increased quantity neither necessarily increases the quality of democratic deliberation nor guarantees participation, however. Political leaders need be no more responsive to digital communications and digital organizing than they are to the traditional kind. Authoritarian regimes have found the Internet a remarkably effective tool at restricting access to information when they feel threatened.[22]

Moving beyond traditional democratic politics, the borderless character of the Internet promises, for some, the end of politics in territorial nation-states. Instead, global democracy, crypto-anarchy, and/or the emergence of "temporary autonomous zones"—free enclaves or "islands in the net"[23] will be the politics of the future. Such arguments are premised on the open, ubiquitous, and global character of the Internet. Yet changes to national and international law governing the Internet, to the software that controls navigation, and the hardware that is the actual physical space of the Internet can alter the open, global character. Borderless zones are quickly bordered—whether it be the Recording Industry Association of America bringing legal action against file-swappers in other countries, or France and Germany physically restricting the availability of Holocaust-revisionist materials on the World Wide Web, or Apple Computer Company releasing country-specific versions of the iTunes Music Store to conform with local copyright law and territory-specific licensing deals with music publishers.[24]

The digital information environment is undoubtedly transforming politics. Increased speed, increased ease of organization, and even increased confusion from the multitude of sources of information are among the features of this new world. This is, if the term can properly be applied, an increase in the interaction capacity of political systems. Inasmuch as communications costs in a predigital age placed an inherent barrier to the scale of political units, one could even speculate that digital information technologies make a global polity trivially easy to organize. Yet whether such a polity ever emerges or whether any of the other predictions of the information revolution's effect on democratic politics will come to pass will depend on the way that same politics shapes the developing technology.

All these potential transformations and threats direct our attention to the actors and institutions that will, through their interests and actions, shape the mature character of the information revolution. States, firms, and citizen-consumers are in the midst of a great political tug-of-war over the shape of the mature digital information infrastructure—whether they realize it or not. We cannot read the international political future directly from the technical characteristics of the Internet, or the Automatic Clearing House for financial transactions, or the Revolution in Military Affairs state. The technologies are for the moment much too flexible and too suffused with uncertain politics to be a reliable guide. The situation was the same with the two case studies explored in this book. They, too, began their evolution in conditions of great uncertainty and, pressed on all sides by economic and political pressures, matured into system-transforming technologies. For the current transformation, the same advice applies; we should follow the politics. We need to be alert to conjunctural moments (9/11 may turn out to be one of the most important dates in the evolution of the digital infosphere because of the effect it has had on resistance to intrusive surveillance technologies). We also need to pay attention to innovations that fail as well as those that succeed. Some will fail in part for technical reasons. But the more interesting reasons for success or failure will be social and political. These reasons will give us the best purchase on the future.

NOTES

CHAPTER ONE

1. William H. McNeill (1982), *The Pursuit of Power: Technology, Armed Force, and Society Since A.D. 1000* (Chicago: University of Chicago Press), 117–43.

2. John Gerard Ruggie (1983), "Continuity and Transformation in the World Polity: Toward a Neorealist Synthesis," *World Politics*, 35 (2): 261–85.

3. Kenneth N. Waltz (1979), *Theory of International Politics* (New York: Random House), 117.

4. The classic treatment on technology and growth is: Robert M. Solow (1956), "A Contribution to the Theory of Economic Growth," *Quarterly Journal of Economics*, 70 (1): 65–94. His Nobel address in 1987 and a recent collection of essays revisits the topic: Robert M. Solow (2000), *Growth Theory: An Exposition* (New York: Oxford University Press). Other relevant recent work: Paul M. Romer (1987), "Growth Based on Increasing Returns Due to Specialization," *American Economic Review*, 77 (2): 56–62; Paul M. Romer (1994), "The Origins of Endogenous Growth," *Journal of Economic Perspectives*, 8 (1): 3–22; Luis A. Rivera Batiz and Paul M. Romer (1991), "Economic Integration and Endogenous Growth," *Quarterly Journal of Economics*, 106 (2): 531–55; Philippe Aghion and Peter Howitt (1998), *Endogenous Growth Theory* (Cambridge: MIT Press). See also Joel Mokyr (1990), *The Lever of Riches: Technological Creativity and Economic Progress* (New York: Oxford University Press).

5. Harold A. Innis (1991), *The Bias of Communication* (Toronto: University of Toronto Press); James W. Carey (1992), *Communication as Culture: Essays on Media and Society* (New York: Routledge); Ronald J. Deibert (1997), *Parchment, Printing, and Hypermedia: Communication in World Order Transformation* (New York: Columbia University Press); Ronald J. Deibert (1999),

"Harold Innis and the Empire of Speed," *Review of International Studies*, 25 (2): 273–89.

6. Technology is dealt with explicitly in Marx's writings on historical materialism, in particular the opening passages of "The Communist Manifesto," the *German Ideology*, and the first volume of *Capital*. David McLellan ed. (1977), *Karl Marx: Selected Writings* (New York: Oxford University Press); Karl Marx (1967), *Capital, Volume One* (New York: International Publishers). For an argument that technological change is central to Marx's thinking about historical change, see Jon Elster (1983), *Explaining Technical Change: A Case Study in the Philosophy of Science* (New York: Cambridge University Press), 158–84.

7. On the pike, gun, and ship: McNeill; Geoffrey Parker (1988), *The Military Revolution: Military Innovation and the Rise of the West, 1500–1800* (New York: Cambridge University Press); Carlo Cipolla (1965), *Guns, Sails and Empires: Technological Innovation and the Early Phases of European Expansion, 1400–1700* (New York: Pantheon Books); Lucien Paul, Victor Febvre and Henri Jean Martin (1984), *The Coming of the Book: The Impact of Printing, 1450–1800* (London: Verso); Deibert, *Parchment*. On nationalism and the printing press: Benedict Anderson (1991), *Imagined Communities: Reflections on the Origins and Spread of Nationalism* (London: Verso). On railroads and the steam engine: Robert Gilpin (1981), *War and Change in World Politics* (New York: Cambridge University Press), 56–59; Daniel R. Headrick (1981), *Tools of Empire: Technology and European Imperialism in the Nineteenth Century* (New York: Oxford University Press). On the nuclear revolution: Bernard Brodie ed. (1946), *The Absolute Weapon: Atomic Power and World Order* (New York: Harcourt, Brace and Company); John H. Herz (1956), "Rise and Demise of the Territorial State," *World Politics*, 9 (4): 473–93; Kenneth N. Waltz (1990), "Nuclear Myths and Political Realities," *American Political Science Review*, 84 (3): 731–44; Steve Weber (1990), "Realism, Detente, and Nuclear-Weapons," *International Organization*, 44 (1): 55–92; Robert Jervis (1989), *The Meaning of the Nuclear Revolution: Statecraft and the Prospect of Armageddon* (Ithaca, NY: Cornell University Press).

8. Robert O. Keohane and Joseph S. Nye, Jr. (1998), "Power and Interdependence in the Information Age," *Foreign Affairs*: 81; Susan Strange (1996), *The Retreat of the State: The Diffusion of Power in the World Economy* (New York: Cambridge University Press); Deibert, *Parchment*. The terms are from: Deibert, *Parchment*; James N. Rosenau (1989), "Global Changes and Theoretical Challenges: Toward a Postinternational Politics for the 1990s," in Czempiel and Rosenau eds., *Global Changes and Theoretical Challenges: Approaches to World Politics for the 1990s* (Lexington, MA: Lexington Books), 1–20; and Robert O. Keohane (2001), "Governance in a Partially Globalized World," *American Political Science Review*, 95 (1): 1–13.

9. Works with titles like "Technology and International Politics" have appeared now and then in the international relations literature since World

War II. They tend to fall into three chronological categories: those inspired by the advent of the nuclear age; those inspired by the literature on complex interdependence; and those inspired by the information revolution. William Fielding Ogburn ed. (1949), *Technology and International Relations* (Chicago: University of Chicago Press); Victor Basiuk (1977), *Technology, World Politics, and American Policy* (New York: Columbia University Press); John V. Granger (1979), *Technology and International Relations* (San Francisco: W. H. Freeman); Deibert, *Parchment*. Only the last is a serious effort at integrating international relations theory with technology.

10. Two works that address punctuated equilibrium theory: Gilpin; Stephen D. Krasner (1988), "Sovereignty: An Institutional Perspective," *Comparative Political Studies*, 21 (1): 66–94.

11. For example, in mainstream international relations constructivism, the structure of the system (the collective identity) and individual actor identity constitute each other with no obvious transition from one identity to the next. Alexander Wendt (1999), *Social Theory of International Politics* (New York: Cambridge University Press). I discuss constructivism later.

12. James Mahoney (2000), "Path Dependence in Historical Sociology," *Theory and Society*, 29 (4): 507–48.

13. Hendrik Spruyt (1998), "Historical Sociology and Systems Theory in International Relations," *Review of International Political Economy*, 5 (2): 340–53; John M. Hobson (2000), *The State and International Relations* (New York: Cambridge University Press).

14. Kathleen Thelen and Sven Steinmo (1992), "Historical Institutionalism in Comparative Politics," in Steinmo, Thelen, and Longstreth eds., *Structuring Politics: Historical Institutionalism in Comparative Analysis* (New York: Cambridge University Press); Paul Pierson (2000), "Not Just What, But When: Timing and Sequence in Political Processes," *Studies in American Political Development*, 14 (1): 72–92; Paul Pierson (2000), "Increasing Returns, Path Dependence, and the Study of Politics," *American Political Science Review*, 94 (2): 251–67; Alexander George (1979), "Case Studies and Theory Development: The Method of Structured, Focused Comparison," in Lauren ed., *Diplomacy: New Research and Theories* (New York: The Free Press); Alexander L. George and Andrew Bennett (2004), *Case Studies and Theory Development in the Social Sciences* (Cambridge: MIT Press).

15. Paul A. David (1985), "Clio and the Economics of QWERTY," *American Economic Review*, 75 (2 (Papers and Proceedings)): 332–37; Mahoney.

16. Two studies of unit change are: Hendrik Spruyt (1994), *The Sovereign State and Its Competitors: An Analysis of Systems Change* (Princeton: Princeton University Press) and Deibert, *Parchment*. Economic interdependence is a core factor in international system transformation in these works: Robert Keohane and Joseph S. Nye (1989), *Power and Interdependence* (Glenview, IL: Scott, Foresman); Victor Basiuk (1981), "Technology and the Structure of the International System," in Szyliowicz ed., *Technology and*

International Affairs (New York: Praeger), 219–38; and Stuart J. Kaufman (1997), "The Fragmentation and Consolidation of International Systems," *International Organization*, 51 (2): 173–208. For an argument that the systemic transformation that accompanied the end of the cold war is a shift in the self-conception of the units, not a shift in the balance of power see Rey Koslowski and Friedrich V. Kratochwil (1995), "Understanding Change in International Politics: The Soviet Empire's Demise and the International System," in Lebow and Risse-Kappen eds., *International Relations Theory and the End of the Cold War* (New York: Columbia University Press). Wendt systematizes this argument. Little's contribution to *The Logic of Anarchy* features an investigation of the expansion of the Roman Empire—a shift from subsystem to system dominance. Barry Buzan, Charles A. Jones, and Richard Little (1993), *The Logic of Anarchy: Neorealism to Structural Realism* (New York: Columbia University Press), sec. 2.

17. Waltz, *Theory*, 161.

18. Gilpin, 41–44.

19. My formulation leaves open just how much change to interaction capacity has to take place for systemic change. I develop a test below. The burden of proof weighs more heavily on me because I am introducing a novel way of defining change. But the question can be asked of each definition of system change. How do we know when the character of units has changed? The substantial literature on the medieval to modern transition indicates that this question has not been settled, but the debate suggests how I can answer the question: when observed characteristics of the units change substantially enough that it makes sense to refer to a new entity instead of the old one. I will argue something similar for the technological component of interaction capacity.

20. Renate Mayntz and Thomas Hughes eds. (1988), *The Development of Large Technical Systems* (Boulder: Westview Press).

21. Buzan, Jones, and Little, 66–79; Barry Buzan and Richard Little (2000), *International Systems in World History: Remaking the Study of International Relations* (New York: Oxford University Press).

22. These are the same mechanisms that Waltz argues socialize states into self-help behavior. Waltz, *Theory*, 127–28.

23. I have treated the spread of the Prussian model in greater detail elsewhere. Geoffrey L. Herrera and Thomas G. Mahnken (2003), "Military Diffusion in Nineteenth Century Europe: The Napoleonic and Prussian Military Systems," in Goldman and Eliason eds., *The Diffusion of Military Technology and Ideas* (Stanford: Stanford University Press).

24. Samuel A. Goudsmit (1947), *Alsos* (New York: Schuman); Paul Lawrence Rose (1998), *Heisenberg and the Nazi Atomic Bomb Project: A Study in German Culture* (Berkeley: University of California Press).

25. Alan S. Milward (1977), *War, Economy, and Society, 1939–1945* (Berkeley: University of California Press), 175; Rose.

CHAPTER TWO

1. The institutionalist analog to *Theory of International Politics* is: Robert O. Keohane (1984), *After Hegemony: Cooperation and Discord in the World Political Economy* (Princeton: Princeton University Press). Both works are over twenty years old, but they still inspire well-defined research agendas. Institutionalism has also been called neoliberal institutionalism, but Keohane seems to have dropped the "liberal" in favor of "institutionalism." Robert O. Keohane (2000), "Ideas Part-Way Down," *Review of International Studies*, 26 (1): 126.

2. Alexander Wendt (1999), *Social Theory of International Politics* (New York: Cambridge University Press); Andrew Moravcsik (1997), "Taking Preferences Seriously: A Liberal Theory of International Politics," *International Organization*, 51 (4): 513–53. Moravcsik has three core assumptions: (1) the analytic primacy of individuals and groups; (2) states as pluralist battlegrounds for interest groups, not autonomous entities in themselves; and (3) the international system *is* the configuration of state preferences. Because the individual has analytic primacy, this can hardly be called systemic theory. But this is clearly a response to neorealist thinking. And even here the relevant whole is the international system and the constraints of the system—in the form of the configuration of preferences and capabilities—still impinge significantly on state behavior.

3. Theorists in the 1960s paid more attention to the concept of system, but this work has been largely forgotten. Morton A. Kaplan (1957), *System and Process in International Politics* (New York: Wiley); J. J. Weltman (1973), *Systems Theory in International Relations: A Study in Metaphoric Hypertrophy* (Lexington: Lexington Books).

4. John Gerard Ruggie (1983), "Continuity and Transformation in the World Polity: Toward a Neorealist Synthesis," *World Politics*, 35 (2): 261–85. Ruggie criticized Waltz's systemic theory for lacking a generative logic. This is what led Ruggie to focus on the formation of the modern states system in the Early Modern period. This suggestion has led to some very interesting scholarly production, but it pales in comparison to the mainstream discussion of Waltz's contribution. Ronald J. Deibert (1997), *Parchment, Printing, and Hypermedia: Communication in World Order Transformation* (New York: Columbia University Press).

5. This owes a great deal to: Richard Little (1977), "Three Approaches to the International System: Some Ontological and Epistemological Considerations," *British Journal of International Studies*, 3: 269–85. Jervis discusses feedback in the international system here: Robert Jervis (1997), *System Effects: Complexity in Political and Social Life* (Princeton: Princeton University Press). The concept also plays a large role in new work on path dependency. For a comprehensive review of the literature: Paul Pierson (2000), "Not Just

What, But When: Timing and Sequence in Political Processes," *Studies in American Political Development*, 14 (1): 72–92.

6. The fact of anarchy is not at issue here. I am not implying that the behavioral effects of anarchy are not contested, but that the behavioral implications of anarchy define the international system and justify the existence of the discipline of international relations.

7. Kenneth N. Waltz (1979), *Theory of International Politics* (New York: Random House), 143.

8. There are exceptions to this characterization. Weber has argued within a structural realist framework that nuclear weapons fundamentally changed the nature of the international system, notwithstanding any changes in the distribution of power. Steve Weber (1990), "Realism, Detente, and Nuclear-Weapons," *International Organization*, 44 (1): 55–92. I do not think his argument is successful. His logic leads to a conclusion completely at odds with structural realism. He allows us to imagine a situation in which neither the distribution of power nor the ordering principle of the system has changed, yet nonetheless fundamental system transformation has occurred. This can only happen if something else other than the ordering principle or the distribution of power (nuclear weapons?) is part of the international system. Another example comes from the institutionalist literature. This argument claims that robust international institutions subtly alter the constraints of anarchy. It is not clear to me how much of an exception this is to the neorealist view. Degree of institutionalization is simply part of shifts in the pattern and process of international interactions—not a significant systemic alteration. Institutionalists might claim in response that a profound process of historical learning on the part of states explains greater degrees of institutionalization—in which case there is no going back (short of social catastrophe) because the degree of institutionalization only goes one way (up), and so it is a significant and permanent alteration in the nature of anarchy. It is hard to think of an institutionalist work that argues this, however. The aptly titled *Progress in International Relations* is one possible exception, though the work hardly characterizes institutionalist work as a whole, and the editors identify with the constructivist agenda in any case. Emanuel Adler and Beverly Crawford eds. (1991), *Progress in Postwar International Relations* (New York: Columbia University Press); Emanuel Adler (1997), "Seizing the Middle Ground: Constructivism in World Politics," *European Journal of International Relations*, 3 (3): 319–364.

9. Robert Gilpin (1981), *War and Change in World Politics* (Cambridge: Cambridge University Press); Hendrik Spruyt (1994), *The Sovereign State and Its Competitors: An Analysis of Systems Change* (Princeton: Princeton University Press); Randall L. Schweller (1994), "Bandwagoning for Profit: Bringing the Revisionist State Back In," *International Security*, 19 (1): 72–107; Jack S. Levy (1988), "Domestic Politics and War," *Journal of Interdisciplinary History*, 38 (4): 653–73; William H. McNeill (1982), *The Pursuit of*

Power: Technology, Armed Force, and Society Since A.D. 1000 (Chicago: University of Chicago Press); Carlo Cipolla (1965), *Guns, Sails and Empires: Technological Innovation and the Early Phases of European Expansion, 1400–1700* (New York: Pantheon Books); Geoffrey Parker (1988), *The Military Revolution: Military Innovation and the Rise of the West, 1500–1800* (New York: Cambridge University Press). Spruyt is something of an exception to the neorealist perspective characterized here. He considers change in the nature of the units of the international system—in his case from feudal to modern states—a fundamental transformation. This view is at odds with Waltz. But he also locates the source of the change in an exogenous shock—the expansion of trade—not in the international system itself. Spruyt, 6.

10. Randall L. Schweller (1998), *Deadly Imbalances: Tripolarity and Hitler's Strategy of World Conquest* (New York: Columbia University Press).

11. The literature on the revolution in military affairs, or RMA, can be seen in this same light. The application of information technology to warfighting will either (depending on the analyst in question) extend American dominance or end it prematurely. This is a vast, confusing, and at times confused literature. Owens and Arquilla and Ronfeldt are examples of enthusiasts; Biddle is skeptical; Knox and Murray offer an excellent historical overview. William A. Owens (1995), "The Emerging System of Systems," *U.S. Naval Institute Proceedings*, 121 (5): 35–39; John Arquilla and David F. Ronfeldt eds. (2001), *Networks and Netwars: The Future of Terror, Crime and Militancy* (Santa Monica: Rand); Stephen Biddle (1996), "Victory Misunderstood: What the Gulf War Tells Us about the Future of Conflict," *International Security*, 21 (2): 139–79; MacGregor Knox and Williamson Murray eds. (2001), *The Dynamics of Military Revolution, 1300–2050* (New York: Cambridge University Press).

12. John Gerard Ruggie (1986), "Continuity and Transformation in the World Polity: Towards a Neorealist Synthesis," in Robert O. Keohane, ed., *Neorealism and Its Critics* (New York: Columbia University Press), 152.

13. Barry Buzan, Charles A. Jones, and Richard Little (1993), *The Logic of Anarchy: Neorealism to Structural Realism* (New York: Columbia University Press), 39, 42.

14. Spruyt.

15. Ibid., 17.

16. Robert Gilpin (1996), "Economic Evolution of National Systems," *International Studies Quarterly*, 40 (3): 411–31; Jennifer Sterling-Folker (2001), "Evolutionary Tendencies in Realist and Liberal IR Theory," in William R. Thompson ed., *Evolutionary Interpretations of World Politics* (London: Routledge), 62–109.

17. Stuart J. Kaufman (1997), "The Fragmentation and Consolidation of International Systems," *International Organization*, 51 (2): 173–208.

18. Norman Angell (1912), *The Great Illusion* (New York: Arno).

19. Joseph S. Nye (2004), *Soft Power: The Means to Success in World Politics* (New York: Public Affairs). Keohane and Nye have written the most

important work on interdependence in recent decades. Robert Keohane and Joseph S. Nye (1989), *Power and Interdependence* (Glenview, IL: Scott, Foresman). Morse is an interesting work contemporary with that of Keohane and Nye. Edward Morse (1976), *Modernization and the Transformation of International Relations* (New York: Free Press). More recently, Zacher and a Keohane and Milner edited volume linked interdependence with changes in the interrelations of states, anarchy, and power. Mark W. Zacher (1992), "The Decaying Pillars of the Westphalian Temple: Implications for International Order and Governance," in James N. Rosenau and Otto Ernst Czempiel eds., *Governance without Government: Order and Change in World Politics* (New York: Cambridge University Press), 58–101; Robert O. Keohane and Helen V. Milner eds. (1996), *Internationalization and Domestic Politics* (New York: Cambridge University Press).

20. This argument anticipates a point I make later: there are compelling empirical reasons for considering technology as a part of the international political system.

21. Keohane and Nye, *Power and Interdependence*, 40.

22. Ernest B. Haas (1964), *Beyond the Nation State: Functionalism and International Organization* (Stanford: Stanford University Press); Stanley Hoffman (1966), "Obstinate or Obsolete: The Future of the Nation-State and the Case of Western Europe," *Daedalus*, 95 (3): 862–915; Raymond Vernon (1971), *Sovereignty at Bay: The Multinational Spread of U.S. Enterprises* (New York: Basic Books); Richard Rosecrance (1986), *The Rise of the Trading State: Commerce and Conquest in the Modern World* (New York: Basic Books); Margaret E. Keck and Kathryn Sikkink (1998), *Activists Beyond Borders: Advocacy Networks in International Politics* (Ithaca, NY: Cornell University Press).

23. An example of the weaker form is the more radical variants of regime theory. See, for example, Donald J. Puchala and Raymond F. Hopkins (1983), "International Regimes: Lessons from Inductive Analysis," in Stephen Krasner ed., *International Regimes* (Ithaca, NY: Cornell University Press), 61–92. Regime theory's more realist variants share the basic conceptualization of the system as delineated by Waltz and so would fall outside the company of critics of the Waltzian system. Another example is the epistemic community literature spearheaded by Haas. Peter M. Haas (1992), "Introduction: Epistemic Communities and International Policy Coordination," *International Organization*, 46 (1): 1–35. In this approach, transnational groups of experts can prove to be causally important and distinct from any state interest. They can fulfill this role only in particular circumstances when policy options are highly uncertain, however. Nevertheless, the implicit argument is that the international system includes transnational groups of experts as causally significant 'variables.' There are examples of a more institutional nature in Hoffman. Here, international institutions play important causal roles in international outcomes. Examples of the aggressive variety of political critics

include the most radical statements of the integration literature, such as Haas. Haas, *Beyond the Nation State*. Keck and Sikkink shift the focus of transformation from international organizations to nongovernmental organizations. They argue that the emergence of networks of global activists is undermining state authority both internationally and domestically. Rosenau's work from the 1990s and on has argued an even more radical line. States now share authority across the whole range of issue areas—from security to production to the global environment—with organizations, firms, social movements, and individuals. James N. Rosenau (1997), *Along the Domestic-Foreign Frontier: Exploring Governance in a Turbulent World* (New York: Cambridge University Press); James N. Rosenau and J. P. Singh eds. (2002), *Information Technologies and Global Politics: The Changing Scope of Power and Governance* (Albany: State University of New York Press). The result, for Rosenau, is more than just shared authority but total system transformation. While I think the logic of their arguments places them within the liberal camp, both Keck and Sikkink and Rosenau claim to be outside the liberal theoretical tradition and have openly embraced a constructivist viewpoint.

24. Joseph M. Grieco (1988), "Anarchy and the Limits of Cooperation: A Realist Critique of the Newest Liberal Institutionalism," *International Organization*, 42 (3): 485–507.

25. Keohane, *After Hegemony*.

26. Karl W. Deutsch (1954), *Political Community at the International Level: Problems of Definition and Measurement* (Garden City, NY: Doubleday); Emanuel Adler and Michael N. Barnett eds. (1998), *Security Communities* (New York: Cambridge University Press).

27. Most of the contributors to the Adler and Barnett volume would wish to see themselves characterized as constructivists rather than liberals. Adler and Barnett, eds., *Security Communities*. While I do not want to disagree with anyone's characterization of their own work, the logic of the shift from ally to community member strikes me as quintessentially liberal, even if the mechanisms (collective identity change) are seen as constructivist. Recent debate about the possibility of 'liberal' and 'realist' constructivism might with time clear up these confusions. J. Samuel Barkin (2003), "Realist Constructivism," *International Studies Review*, 5 (3): 325–42; Patrick Thaddeus Jackson (2004), "Bridging the Gap: Toward a Realist-Constructivist Dialogue," *International Studies Review*, 6 (2): 337.

28. Robert O. Keohane (1999), "The Demand for International Regimes," in Charles Lipson and Benjamin J. Cohen eds., *Theory and Structure in International Political Economy* (Cambridge: MIT Press), 147–78.

29. Robert Axelrod (1984), *The Evolution of Cooperation* (New York: Basic Books); Keohane, *After Hegemony*.

30. Robert O. Keohane, Andrew Moravcsik, and Anne-Marie Slaughter (2000), "Legalized Dispute Resolution: Interstate and Transnational," *International Organization*, 54 (3): 457–88.

31. Andrew Kydd (2000), "Trust, Reassurance, and Cooperation," *International Organization*, 54 (2): 325–58.

32. Emanuel Adler, Beverly Crawford, and Jack Donnelly (1991), "Defining and Conceptualizing Progress in International Relations," in Emanuel Adler and Beverly Crawford eds., *Progress in Postwar International Relations* (New York: Columbia University Press), 28.

33. Sterling-Folker, 83.

34. By orthodox constructivism, I mean that body of literature generated and inspired by Wendt. Orthodox and heterodox constructivism share a conception of the social world as socially constructed. They differ principally over ontological and epistemological issues—the extent to which social actors are ideas or discourse 'all the way down' and the extent to which science in the positivist sense is possible. Wendt, 39–40; Friedrich Kratochwil (2000), "Constructing a New Orthodoxy? Wendt's 'Social Theory of International Politics' and the Constructivist Challenge," *Millennium: Journal of International Studies*, 29 (1): 73–101.

35. Wendt; Nicholas Onuf (1998), "Constructivism: A User's Manual," in Vendulka Kubálková, Nicholas Onuf, and Paul Kowert eds., *International Relations in a Constructed World* (Armonk, NY: M. E. Sharpe), 58–78. This is an important point. As will be made clearer in the section on technology, while I share with constructivism an appreciation for the social construction of actors' identities and interests, I do not find the mainstream's particular application of constructivist ideas to international relations particularly useful. As I will argue, there is more to international politics than relations between states, however defined, and so there should be more to our systemic theorizing.

36. Wendt.

37. Ibid., 314, 317, 343–62.

38. Thomas J. Biersteker and Cynthia Weber, eds. (1996), *State Sovereignty as Social Construct* (Cambridge: Cambridge University Press); Dana P. Eyre and Mark C. Suchman (1996), "Status, Norms and the Proliferation of Conventional Weapons: An Institutional Theory Approach," in Peter J. Katzenstein ed., *The Culture of National Security: Norms and Identity in World Politics* (New York: Columbia University Press), 79–113; Adler and Barnett eds. *Security Communities*.

39. Waltz, 79. Wendt, 194. Buzan and Little, by contrast, expand the conception of international relations to include five "sectors"—security, economic, political, cultural or social, and environmental. Barry Buzan and Richard Little (2000), *International Systems in World History: Remaking the Study of International Relations* (New York: Oxford University Press), 72. At the very least, Wendt's narrowing of the subject matter of international politics is contested.

40. Wendt, 344.

41. Ibid., 364.

42. Buzan, Jones, and Little, *The Logic of Anarchy*; Buzan and Little, *International Systems in World History*; Spruyt; John Gerard Ruggie (1993), "Territoriality and Beyond: Problematizing Modernity in International Relations," *International Organization*, 47 (1): 139–74.

43. Kaufman; Keohane and Nye, *Power and Interdependence*; Wendt. For example, technology is implicated in the emergence of the modern state, the national state, and transnational advocacy networks. McNeill; Benedict Anderson (1991), *Imagined Communities: Reflections on the Origins and Spread of Nationalism* (London: Verso); Keck and Sikkink. Linking the two is intriguing, but for analytic coherence I will not take up the task in any rigorous fashion here.

44. A technology might also be both—as is the railroad, discussed in detail later.

45. There is great potential for confusion here. International relations constructivism and technological constructivism are two well-developed literatures that share a common name, but differ in important respects. International relations constructivism studies the construction and evolution of social identities in international relations and how those identities shape actor behavior. Technological constructivism focuses on the social forces that shape the evolution of technologies; it tends not to focus on the social effects of those technologies. To avoid confusion, I will refer to technological constructivism from here on as either the social construction of technology or social constructionism

46. Three separate flavors of technological determinism can be distinguished: nomological, normative, and one based on unintended consequences. Bruce Bimber (1994), "Three Faces of Technological Determinism," in Merritt Roe Smith and Leo Marx eds., *Does Technology Drive History?: The Dilemma of Technological Determinism* (Cambridge: MIT Press), 79–100. Only the first, which argues that the laws of nature impose an inevitable logic on social order and that technology itself has independent agency, is determinist in the sense used here. Normative determinist arguments claim that societies can place such great meaning in technology and technological change that it is as if technology has independent agency. The unintended consequences position argues that decisions and choices that lead to the introduction of certain technologies can also lead to uncertain and uncontrollable outcomes. Since my argument will make use of the latter two forms of determinism, it is worthwhile to make this distinction clearly.

47. Merritt Roe Smith and Leo Marx, eds. (1994), *Does Technology Drive History?: The Dilemma of Technological Determinism* (Cambridge: MIT Press); Robert L. Heilbroner (1994), "Do Machines Make History?," in Smith and Marx eds., *Does Technology Drive History?: The Dilemma of Technological Determinism* (Cambridge: MIT Press), 53–65; Robert L. Heilbroner (1994), "Technological Determinism Revisited," in Smith and Marx, eds., *Does Technology Drive History?: The Dilemma of Technological Determinism* (Cambridge: MIT Press), 67–78.

48. Heilbroner, "Do Machines Make History?," 59.

49. In his retrospective essay, Heilbroner only allows that the first essay deserves clarification on one point: the "force field" that connects technological developments with social outcomes is economic man or, more precisely, profit-seeking behavior. Heilbroner, "Technological Determinism Revisited," 71–72. In the original essay he argued that technological determinism as he understood it could only be a product of capitalist, industrial societies—societies in which the profit motive is a pervasive component of the social structure. This can be construed as a nondeterminist argument, but only by stretching the definition beyond all utility. It could be claimed, for example, that as Heilbroner is only a determinist within the framework of a capitalist system, he is not truly a determinist. This erases all distinctions between the nature of Heilbroner's claims about the role of technology in society and other, less "determinist" ones.

50. Waltz; Keohane, *After Hegemony.*

51. Waltz, 127–28.

52. Waltz is theoretically incoherent on the question of nuclear weapons. At times the theory treats them as an force affecting the distribution of power (as in the passage quoted). At other times, the theory treats nuclear weapons in their particularity—as having unique effects on the international system as a consequence of their special characteristics. Weber has tried to square this circle by claiming that nuclear weapons have changed the structure of the international system and this can be captured by neorealism. The argument is not fully convincing. Deudney details the inconsistencies in neorealism's treatment of nuclear weapons. Daniel Deudney (1993), "Dividing Realism: Structural Realism versus Security Materialism on Nuclear Security and Proliferation," *Security Studies*, 2 (3/4): 7–36.

53. Keohane, *After Hegemony*, 85–109.

54. Deudney "Dividing Realism;" Daniel Deudney (1995), "Nuclear Weapons and the Waning of the Real-State," *Daedalus*, 124 (2): 209–31; Daniel Deudney (2000), "Geopolitics as Theory: Historical Security Materialism," *European Journal of International Relations*, 6 (1): 77–108.

55. John H. Herz (1956), "Rise and Demise of the Territorial State," *World Politics*, 9 (4): 473–93; Daniel Deudney (2004), "Publius Before Kant: Federal-Republican Security and Democratic Peace," *European Journal of International Relations*, 10 (3): 323.

56. Deudney "Dividing Realism," 21. Deudney would likely object to the determinist label. In a recent essay, he qualifies his earlier position: "Together the forces of destruction and the modes of protection constitute the base or infrastructure . . . which determines the superstructure of political, social and cultural relations . . . but not every aspect of a particular superstructure can be reduced to, or fully explained by, the constraints and opportunities posed by the base of material destructive conditions." Deudney "Geopolitics as Theory," 90. What isn't fully explained, he elaborates, are

time lags in the adjustment of political forms and practices to the underlying structural reality. This qualification perhaps adjusts the accuracy of the relationship between base and superstructure, but does not modify the essential determinism of Deudney's position—that technological and geographical conditions determine the nature of political relations. There is no theoretical space for the political shaping of technology.

57. James Rosenau (1990), *Turbulence in World Politics: A Theory of Change and Continuity* (Princeton: Princeton University Press).

58. Ibid., 16–17.

59. George F. Gilder (2000), *Telecosm: How Infinite Bandwidth Will Revolutionize Our World* (New York: Free Press); Nicholas Negroponte (1995), *Being Digital* (New York: Knopf).

60. Negroponte, 229.

61. George Gilder (1994), "Life After Television, Updated," *Forbes ASAP* (February 28).

62. Wiebe E. Bijker, Thomas P. Hughes, and Trevor J. Pinch eds. (1987), *Social Construction of Technological Systems: New Directions in the Sociology and History of Technology* (Cambridge: MIT Press); Donald A. MacKenzie and Judy Wajcman, eds. (1999), *The Social Shaping of Technology* (Milton Keynes: Open University Press).

63. Wendt.

64. Donald A. MacKenzie (1990), *Inventing Accuracy: A Historical Sociology of Nuclear Missile Guidance* (Cambridge: MIT Press).

65. Ronald Kline and Trevor Pinch (1996), "Users as Agents of Technological Change: The Social Construction of the Automobile in the Rural United States," *Technology and Culture*, 37: 766.

66. Ibid., 767.

67. Daniel R. Headrick (1981), *Tools of Empire: Technology and European Imperialism in the Nineteenth Century* (New York: Oxford University Press); Langdon Winner (1980), "Do Artifacts Have Politics?," *Daedalus*, 109 (1): 121–36.

68. Headrick, 10–11.

69. Ibid., 58–79.

70. MacKenzie, *Inventing Accuracy*.

71. Winner.

72. The historical accuracy of Winner's claim has been disputed. The example is drawn from Caro's mean-spirited biography of Moses. Robert A. Caro (1974), *The Power Broker: Robert Moses and the Fall of New York* (New York: Vintage), 951–52. Joerges argues Winner has compounded Caro's error. Bernward Joerges (1999), "Do Politics Have Artefacts?," *Social Studies of Science*, 29 (3): 418–19. The bridges were too low to allow for the passage of buses, but this was standard practice on parkways around the country, and there were other routes that racial minorities and the poor could use to reach Long Island beaches and suburbs.

73. Winner, 128–33; Alfred D. Chandler (1977), *The Visible Hand: The Managerial Revolution in American Business* (Cambridge: Belknap Press).

74. Kenneth N. Waltz (1983), "Toward Nuclear Peace," in Robert J. Art and Kenneth N. Waltz, eds., *The Use of Force: Military Power and International Politics* (Lanham, MD: University Press of America), 573–602. Sagan in this light makes a social constructivist argument. Scott D. Sagan (1994), "The Perils of Proliferation: Organization Theory, Deterrence Theory, and the Spread of Nuclear Weapons," *International Security*, 18 (4): 66–107. He argues that the effects of nuclear weapons depend on the social and political organizations in which they are embedded. In one social/political setting nuclear weapons are stable deterrent weapons, in another exactly the opposite—same 'technology,' two different effects.

75. Harvey Brooks (1980), "Technology, Evolution, and Purpose," *Daedalus*, 109 (1): 66.

76. Exceptions here would be "technologies" that exist in the form of information or ideas. This is too complex a definition and fraught with too many dangers to be analytically useful here. While I will argue that technologies can be carried as ideas stored in the brains of humans—for example, the atom bomb was diffused from Europe to the United States in the form of refugee scientists—the technologies in question still have a physical form. Organizational forms and innovations are also technologies, though here I am rapidly approaching the edge of the distinction between technology and institutions. As with their more physical counterparts, organizations have a physical manifestation, even if it is the arrangement of things and humans in space and time. To speak of democracy or on-time production as technologies, however, impedes clearly distinguishing technology from everything else and the distinction becomes meaningless. Of course, democracy and on-time production—as ideas with practical consequences—have technologies associated with them: for example, voting booths and elected legislatures, or networked storage and delivery complexes. But neither the idea of democracy nor on-time production can be usefully thought of as technology.

77. This discussion owes much to a rich theoretical tradition in the literature on the history of technology. MacKenzie, *Inventing Accuracy*; David F. Noble (1984), *Forces of Production: A Social History of Industrial Automation* (New York: Knopf); Michael Adas (1989), *Machines as the Measure of Man: Science, Technology, and Ideologies of Western Dominance* (Ithaca, NY: Cornell University Press).

78. Thomas P. Hughes (1980), "The Order of the Technological World," *History of Technology*, 5: 1–16; Thomas P. Hughes (1987), "The Evolution of Large Technological Systems," in Wiebe Bijker, Thomas P. Hughes, and Trevor Pinch, eds., *Social Construction of Technological Systems: New Directions in the Sociology and History of Technology* (Cambridge: MIT Press), 51–82; Renate Mayntz and Thomas Hughes, eds. (1988), *The Devel-*

opment of Large Technical Systems (Boulder: Westview Press); Thomas P. Hughes (1994), "Technological Momentum," in Smith and Marx, eds., *Does Technology Drive History?: The Dilemma of Technological Determinism* (Cambridge: MIT Press), 101–13.

79. Everett M. Rogers (1983), *Diffusion of Innovations* (New York: Free Press).

80. Hughes, "Technological Momentum," Keohane, *After Hegemony*, 100–3.

81. Reuse in novel ways is also possible—a point that underlines the flexibility of artifacts. Rail beds throughout much of the United States have fallen into neglect and disuse. Victims of declining relative competitiveness and a changing regulatory climate that encouraged the use of trucks for overland transport over rail, many of the country's rail beds have been converted to recreation and wilderness trails (http://www.railtrails.org/).

82. For example, energy analysts have speculated that hydrogen-powered fuel cells could provide an almost inexhaustible, inexpensive, and nearly pollution-free energy source for, among other things, automobiles. Paul Hawken, Amory B. Lovins, and L. Hunter Lovins (1999), *Natural Capitalism: Creating the Next Industrial Revolution* (Boston: Little Brown). One of the principal and enduring obstacles—even if the technical hurdles can be cleared—is the existing sociotechnical system of the petroleum-fueled automobile including a network of refineries, tanker-trucks, and gas stations around the world; the political interest actors in these industries have in maintaining the system; and the cost of re-outfitting or replacing the network of gas stations with hydrogen ones. It looks hard, if not impossible, to get there from here. And if all these obstacles are overcome and fuel-cell automobiles do replace internal-combustion ones, it will not be because fuel-cell cars are technically feasible, but because political, economic, and social actors and forces align to make them feasible for human society.

83. Hugh G. J. Aitken (1976), *Syntony and Spark: The Origins of Radio* (New York: Wiley).

84. "Significance" is a troubling word. Its use in a social scientific context carries with it the implication of selection bias. If only those cases that are deemed "significant" are chosen, the findings are immediately suspect and "significant" is merely a stand-in for "cases that fit the theory." Yet, as I have argued above, we cannot avoid assessing significance when studying technology and international relations. There is every reason to expect that nuclear weapons will be of greater significance to international politics than ballpoint pens—even though both are clearly in the broader class "technology." I will say more on this point.

85. Barry Buzan and Eric Herring (1998), *The Arms Dynamic in World Politics* (Boulder: Lynne Reinner); D. Eleanor Westney (1986), "The Military," in Marius B. Jansen and Gilbert Rozman, eds., *Japan in Transition, from Tokugawa to Meiji* (Princeton: Princeton University Press), 168–94; Lynn

White (1968), "The Act of Invention," in *Machina Ex Deo: Essays in the Dynamism of Western Culture* (Cambridge: MIT Press), 107–31.

86. Neorealism has made more of diffusion and emulation than neoliberalism. Waltz gave it prominent, if brief, attention when he argued that as states compete with each other in the manner and material of security provision, they will come to resemble each other on that dimension. Waltz, *Theory*, 127–28. Others have applied the argument to actual case studies. Joao Resende-Santos (1996), "Anarchy and the Emulation of Military Systems: Military Organization and Technology in South America, 1870–1914," in Benjamin Frankel, ed., *Realism: Restatements and Renewal* (London: F. Cass), 193–260. For neoliberalism, it could be argued that the diffusion of innovations and ideas is crucial to the spread of cooperation and the strengthening of the normative support for institutions. The literature on learning and epistemic communities can be seen in this light. Judith Goldstein and Robert O. Keohane, eds. (1993), *Ideas and Foreign Policy: Beliefs, Institutions, and Political Change* (Ithaca, NY: Cornell University Press); Haas "Introduction"; Peter M. Haas (1992), *Knowledge, Power, and International Policy Coordination* (Cambridge: MIT Press).

87. Deborah Avant (2000), "From Mercenaries to Citizen Armies: Explaining Change in the Practice of War," *International Organization*, 54 (1): 41–72; Eyre and Suchman; Emily Goldman and Leslie Eliason, eds. (2003), *Diffusion of Military Technology and Ideas* (Stanford: Stanford University Press).

88. Deudney, "Geopolitics as Theory."

89. Emile Durkheim (1933), *The Division of Labor in Society* (New York: Free Press).

90. Harold A. Innis (1991), *The Bias of Communication* (Toronto: University of Toronto Press); Deibert.

91. Buzan, Jones, and Little, *The Logic of Anarchy*; Buzan and Little, *International Systems in World History*.

92. Peter Gourevitch (1978), "The Second Image Reversed: The International Sources of Domestic Politics," *International Organization*, 32 (4): 881–912.

93. I am stating the causal relationship this simply solely for the purpose of making a point about method and research design. Causality runs both ways—from international system to technological change and back again. Ronald Rogowski (1995), "The Role of Theory and Anomaly in Social-Scientific Inference," *American Political Science Review*, 89 (2): 467–70; Timothy J. McKeown (1999), "Case Studies and the Statistical Worldview: Review of King, Keohane, and Verba's Designing Social Inquiry: Scientific Inferences in Qualitative Research," *International Organization*, 53 (1): 161–90.

94. David Collier and James Mahoney (1996), "Insights and Pitfalls: Selection Bias in Qualitative Research," *World Politics*, 49 (1): 56–91; Rogowski.

95. Gary King, Robert O. Keohane, and Sidney Verba (1994), *Designing Social Inquiry: Scientific Inference in Qualitative Research* (Princeton: Princeton University Press); Alexander George (1979), "Case Studies and Theory Development: The Method of Structured, Focused Comparison," in Gordon Lauren, ed., *Diplomacy: New Research and Theories* (New York: Free Press), 43–68; Alexander L. George and Andrew Bennett (2004), *Case Studies and Theory Development in the Social Sciences* (Cambridge: MIT Press).

96. Buzan and Little, *International Systems in World History*, 386–406; James Mahoney (2000), "Path Dependence in Historical Sociology," *Theory and Society*, 29 (4): 507–48; Theda Skocpol (1979), *States and Social Revolutions: A Comparative Analysis of France, Russia, and China* (New York: Cambridge University Press).

97. Buzan and Little, *International Systems in World History*.

98. Deibert; Richard N. Rosecrance (1999), *The Rise of the Virtual State: Wealth and Power in the Coming Century* (New York: Basic Books); Michael J. Mazarr, ed. (2002), *Information Technology and World Politics* (New York: Palgrave Macmillan); Rosenau and Singh, eds., *Information Technologies and Global Politics*. I have addressed this issue elsewhere and do so in the conclusion. Geoffrey L. Herrera (2002), "The Politics of Bandwidth: International Political Implications of a Digital Information Infrastructure," *Review of International Studies*, 28 (1): 93–122.

99. Winner.

CHAPTER THREE

1. David Landes (1969), *The Unbound Prometheus: Technological Change and Industrial Development in Western Europe from 1750 to the Present* (New York: Cambridge University Press), 41.

2. 'States' here is shorthand for the variety of governance structures that existed in what after 1871 became Germany: states, kingdoms, grand duchies, duchies, principalities, and free cities.

3. English law forbade workers under contract to an employer from taking employment aboard with foreign firms or states. Passed in the 1780s, these laws persisted well into the nineteenth century. Arthur Redford (1934), *Manchester Merchants and Foreign Trade, 1794–1858* (Manchester: Manchester University Press).

4. Jay Luvaas (1959), *The Military Legacy of the Civil War: The European Inheritance* (Chicago: University of Chicago Press), 122.

5. Steven E. Miller, ed. (1985), *Military Strategy and the Origins of the First World War* (Princeton: Princeton University Press).

6. Landes, 84–85.

7. Ibid., 78.

8. Ibid., 91.

9. Ibid., 95.

10. L. T. C. Rolt (1958), *Thomas Telford* (London: Longman), 153.

11. Gary Hawke and Jim Higgins (1983), "Britain," in Patrick O'Brien, ed., *Railways and the Economic Development of Western Europe, 1830–1914* (New York: St. Martin's), 177–81.

12. Rolt, 153.

13. Landes, 102–3.

14. Maurice W. Kirby (1993), *The Origins of Railway Enterprise: The Stockton and Darlington Railway, 1821–1863* (Cambridge: Cambridge University Press), 2–3; *Mechanics Magazine* (1829), "Comparative Statement of the Performances of the Engines which competed for the Premium offered by the Directors of the Liverpool and Manchester Railway," 325 (October 31).

15. The opening of the Liverpool & Manchester railroad, finally completed in 1830, provided a major link between England's busiest western port and its greatest manufacturing center. Support emerged because poor service on the two major canals between the cities meant goods that traveled three weeks from America to Liverpool took six to make the trip inland to Manchester. Frank Dobbin (1994), *Forging Industrial Policy: The United States, Britain, and France in the Railway Age* (New York: Cambridge University Press), 168–70.

16. *Mechanics Magazine*; Jack Simmons (1978), *The Railway in England and Wales, 1830–1914. Vol. 1: The System and its Workings* (Leicester: Leicester University Press), 18. To speculate, if stationary steam-engine-powered railroads had prevailed over the steam locomotive, the interaction between the railroad and international politics would most likely have been very different. A stationary system with a network of pulleys and cables would not be as robust or flexible during wartime. The resulting system would likely have been far more "pacific."

17. Rolt, 162–66.

18. Ibid., 154–55.

19. Ibid., 159.

20. Kirby, 180.

21. B. R. Mitchell (1975), *European Historical Statistics, 1750–1970* (New York: Columbia University Press), 582.

22. Hawke and Higgins, 188–95.

23. Kirby, 18.

24. Hawke and Higgins, 182.

25. Simmons, 40, 42–43.

26. Landes, 61.

27. R. A. Buchanan (1985), "Institutional Proliferation in the British Engineering Profession, 1847–1914," *Economic History Review*, 2nd ser. 38 (1): 43.

28. Samuel Smiles (1864), *Industrial Biography* (Boston: Ticknor and Fields), 245–88.

29. W. H. G. Armytage (1961), *A Social History of Engineering* (Cambridge: MIT Press), 27–28.

30. Smiles, 284–85.

31. Guy Stanton Ford (1938), "The Lost Year in Stein's Life," in *On and Off the Campus* (Minneapolis: University of Minnesota Press), 161–203.

32. T. H. Marshall (1925), *James Watt* (London: Leonard Parsons Ltd.), 153.

33. The over 500 short biographical sketches confirm this picture. John Marshall (1978), *A Biographical Dictionary of Railway Engineers* (Newton Abbot: David & Charles).

34. Despite the similarities of the basic technologies of the industrial revolution—the steam engine, the iron forge, mechanized cloth production, and so on—implementation by engineers and workers was idiosyncratic. Interchangeable parts and common design were slow in coming. It was not until the latter part of the nineteenth century that the value of uniformity in machine work, the most important example, was recognized. A. E. Musson (1963), "Sir Joseph Whitworth: Toolmaker and Manufacturer," *Chartered Mechanical Engineer*, 10 (4): 188–93.

35. Buchanan.

36. Robert H. Parsons (1947), *A History of the Institution of Mechanical Engineers, 1847–1947* (London: Institution of Mechanical Engineers), 9.

37. Ibid., 12.

38. Buchanan, 43.

39. Ibid., 46.

40. Smiles, 328.

41. Musson, 193.

42. The third mechanism, the patent system, functioned much as the various institutions' papers and meetings. Christine MacLeod (1988), *Inventing the Industrial Revolution: The English Patent System, 1660–1800* (New York: Cambridge University Press).

43. M. W. Kirby (1988), "Product Proliferation in the British Locomotive Building Industry, 1850–1914: An Engineer's Paradise?," *Business History*, 30 (3): 287–305.

44. Hawke and Higgins, 183.

45. Dobbin, 171, 179, 188, 190–91.

46. Hawke and Higgins, 182.

47. Dobbin, 168–72.

48. Eric Dorn Brose (1993), *The Politics of Technological Change in Prussia: Out of the Shadow of Antiquity, 1809–1848* (Princeton: Princeton University Press), 220, 213.

49. Alexander Gerschenkron (1962), "Economic Backwardness in Historical Perspective," in Alexander Gerschenkron, ed., *Economic Backwardness in Historical Perspective* (Cambridge: Harvard University Press), 5–30.

50. For example, Friedrich List. More on List follows.

51. F. Crouzet (1974), "Western Europe and Great Britain: 'Catching Up' in the First Half of the Nineteenth Century," in A. J. Youngson, ed., *Economic Development in the Long Run* (London: George Allen and Unwin), 111.

52. Ford, 187.

53. William O. Henderson (1977), "Friedrich List: Railway Pioneer," in W. H. Chaloner and Barrie M. Ratcliffe, eds., *Trade and Transport: Essays in Economic History in Honour of T. S. Willan* (Manchester: Manchester University Press), 136.

54. Clive Trebilcock (1981), *The Industrialization of the Continental Powers, 1780–1914* (London: Longman), 22.

55. Landes, 127.

56. Trebilcock, 29–32.

57. Sidney Pollard (1973), "Industrialization and the European Economy," *Economic History Review*, 2nd ser. 26 (4): 640.

58. Frank B. Tipton (1974), "The National Consensus in German Economic History," *Central European History*, 7 (3): 199.

59. Landes, 144–45.

60. Trebilcock, 33–34.

61. Rondo Cameron (1985), "A New View of European Industrialization," *Economic History Review*, 38 2nd ser. (1): 8.

62. Richard H. Tilly (1966), "The Political Economy of Public Finance and the Industrialization of Prussia, 1815–1866," *Journal of Economic History*, 26 (3): 484; Karl W. Hardach (1972), "Some Remarks on German Economic Historiography and Its Understanding of the Industrial Revolution in Germany," *Journal of European Economic History*, 1: 70; Rainer Fremdling (1983), "Germany," in Patrick O'Brien, ed., *Railways and the Economic Development of Western Europe, 1830–1914* (New York: St. Martin's), 121.

63. Tipton, 197.

64. Pollard, 645.

65. Landes, 174.

66. Ibid., 183.

67. Fritz Redlich (1944), "The Leaders of the German Steam-Engine Industry during the First One-Hundred Years," *Journal of Economic History*, 4 (2): 122, 130, 134–35; William O. Henderson (1965), *Britain and Industrial Europe, 1750–1870* (Leicester: Leicester University Press), 147.

68. Alan S. Milward and S. B. Saul (1973), *The Economic Development of Continental Europe, 1780–1870* (Totowa, NJ: Rowman and Littlefield), 405, 407.

69. Fremdling, 128.

70. Roy E. H. Mellor (1979), *German Railways: A Study in the Historical Geography of Transport* (Aberdeen: Department of Geography, University of Aberdeen), 3; Milward and Saul, 367–70.

71. William O. Henderson (1958), *The State and the Industrial Revolution in Prussia, 1740–1870* (Liverpool: Liverpool University Press), 154; Dennis E. Showalter (1975), *Railroads and Rifles: Soldiers, Technology, and the Unification of Germany* (Hamden, CT: Archon Books), 20–21.

72. Milward and Saul, 374–76; Hardach, 80.

73. Tipton, 200–1.

74. Landes, 157–58.

75. Ibid., 135.

76. Henderson, *State*, xvi.

77. Landes, 135–36; Trebilcock, 28.

78. Trebilcock, 25; Landes, 135–36.

79. Henderson, *State*, xiii; Trebilcock, 27.

80. Trebilcock, 26; Henderson, *State*, xix; Landes, 136.

81. Landes, 157–58; Tilly, 484.

82. Milward and Saul, 208.

83. Hardach, 57.

84. Henderson, *Britain*, 164.

85. Hardach, 86; Henderson, *Britain*, 165.

86. Hardach, 84–86.

87. Michael J. T. Lewis (1970), *Early Wooden Railways* (London: Routledge), 332.

88. Trebilcock, 27–28; Landes, 91; Lewis, 331.

89. Witt Bowden (1965), *Industrial Society in England towards the End of the Eighteenth Century* (London: Frank Cass), 129–30; Landes, 148; A. E. Musson (1972), "The 'Manchester School' and the Export of British Machinery," *Business History*, 14 (1): 17–50.

90. Landes, 149–50; Lewis, 331; Trebilcock, 28.

91. Hardach, 84–86.

92. Henderson, *Britain*, 148. The behavior of the English workmen abroad was so poor that in 1824 an English journal (the *Quarterly Review*) published a report that described the men as "in general, persons of extremely bad character, continually drunk, constantly quarrelling and occasioning most serious complaints. . . . Two men, employed from Chaillot in setting up a steam engine, drank 18 bottles of wine in three hours." Henderson, *Britain*, fn., 148.

93. Carl von Oeynhausen and Heinrich von Dechen (1953), "Report on the Railways in England in 1826–27," *Transactions of the Newcomen Society*, 29: 1–12.

94. Henderson, *Britain*, 158.

95. Werner Sombart and Joseph Schumpeter are among an older generation of historians who view the railroad as critical to German industrialization. Hardach, 53, 57. For more recent support, see Landes, 153; Milward and Saul, 378; Robert Lee (1991), "The Paradigm of German Industrialization: Some Recent Issues and Debates in the Modern Historiography of

German Industrial Development," in W. R. Lee, ed., *German Industry and German Industrialization: Essays in German Economic and Business History in the Nineteenth and Twentieth Centuries* (London: Routledge), 15; Fremdling, 136; Henderson, *Britain*, 158; Tilly: 484; Knut Borchardt (1976), "The Industrial Revolution in Germany, 1700–1914," in Carlo M. Cipolla, ed., *The Fontana Economic History of Europe: The Emergence of Industrial Societies Part One, vol. 4, pt. 1* (New York: Collins/Fontana Books), 107; and Hardach, 80–83, 89–90.

96. Milward and Saul, 370.

97. Hajo Holborn (1986), "The Prusso-German School: Moltke and the Rise of the General Staff," in Peter Paret, ed., *Makers of Modern Strategy: From Machiavelli to the Nuclear Age* (Princeton: Princeton University Press), 281–95; Arden Bucholz (2001), *Moltke and the German Wars, 1864–1871* (Houndmills, Basingstoke, Hampshire: Palgrave).

98. R. A. Buchanan (1986), "The Diaspora of British Engineering," *Technology and Culture*, 27 (3): 508–9.

99. Andrew C. O'Dell and Peter S. Richards (1956), *Railways and Geography* (London: Hutchinson University Library), 34.

100. Henderson, *State*, 152–55.

101. Brose, 213, 212.

102. Henderson "List: Railway Pioneer;" Edward Mead Earle (1986), "Adam Smith, Alexander Hamilton, Friedrich List: The Economic Foundations of Military Power," in Peter Paret, ed., *Makers of Modern Strategy: From Machiavelli to the Nuclear Age* (Princeton: Princeton University Press), 254–55; Henderson, *State*, 154; Milward and Saul, 379.

103. Edwin A. Pratt (1916), *The Rise of Rail Power in War and Conquest, 1833–1914* (London: J. B. Lippincott), 3; Brose, 212.

104. Brose, 217; Mitchell, 581–82.

105. Henderson, *Britain*, 158; Borchardt, 82–83; G. Wolfgang Heinze and Heinrich H. Kill (1988), "The Development of the German Railroad System," in Renate Mayntz and Thomas Hughes, eds., *The Development of Large Technical Systems* (Boulder: Westview Press), 116; Rainer Fremdling (1975), *Eisenbahnen und deutsches Wirtschaftswachstum 1840–1879* (Dortmund: Gesellschaft für Westfälische Wirtschaftsgeschichte E.V.), 195.

106. They were "hothouse plants easily upset by any change in the micro-climate artificially maintained for them by the state." Trebilcock, 26.

107. Redlich, 144.

108. Ibid., 130.

109. Trebilcock, 60.

110. Marshall, *Biographical Dictionary*, 74, 232; Henderson, *Britain*, 158.

111. Milward and Saul, 378.

112. Henderson, *Britain*, 158–59; Fremdling, *Eisenbahnen*, 76.

113. Milward and Saul, 208; Henderson, *Britain*, 159.

114. Marshall, *Biographical Dictionary*, 37–38; Henderson, *Britain*, 7.

115. Olinthus J. Vignoles (1889), *Life of Charles Blacker Vignoles: A Reminiscence of Early Railway History* (London: Longman), 293.

116. Henderson, *Britain*, 159.

117. Biographical information from: Marshall, *Biographical Dictionary*. Vignoles, 225; Hawkshaw and Walker, 228; Ballard, 20–21; Buck, 44; and Kitson, 134–35.

118. "[T]he English driver on the footplate of a locomotive was as familiar a figure on the Continent as the marine engineer on a river steamboat." Henderson, *Britain*, 7.

119. Arthur Helps (1872), *Life and Labours of Mr. Brassey* (Boston: Roberts Brothers).

120. Milward and Saul, 379, 380; Tilly: 484.

121. Tipton, 200–1; Milward and Saul, 383.

122. Henderson, *State*, 154–68.

123. Mitchell, 581, 583.

124. Milward and Saul, 381.

125. Brose, 217–28.

126. A. G. Kenwood and A. L. Lougheed (1982), *Technological Diffusion and Industrialization before 1914* (New York: St. Martin's), 196; Jan C. Bongaerts (1985), "Financing Railways in the German States 1840–1860: A Preliminary View," *Journal of European Economic History*, 14 (2): 332.

127. Henderson, *State*, 152.

128. Brose, 213–22.

129. Ibid., 223–28; Henderson, *State*, 164.

130. Henderson, *State*, 161, 163–64.

131. Brose, 234; Henderson, *State*, 167.

132. Henderson, *State*, 163–64; Detlev F. Vagts (1979), "Railroads, Private Enterprise and Public Policy: Germany and the United States 1870–1920," in Norbert Horn and Jürgen Kocka, eds., *Recht und Entwicklung der Grossunternehmen im 19. and freuhen 20. Jahrhundert* (Göttingen: Vendenhoeck & Ruprecht), 612; Bongaerts: 342; Colleen A. Dunlavy (1990), "Organizing Railroad Interests: The Creation of National Railroad Associations in the United States and Prussia," *Business and Economic History*, 19 2nd ser.: 135–36; Henderson, *State*, 166. The southern states refused to join. Milward and Saul, 382.

133. Brose, 237.

134. Ibid., 231; Henderson, *State*, 167–68.

135. During his tenure, the Commerce Ministry approved exactly one private concession, but even there the state built and ran the line for the shareholders. Henderson, *State*, 172.

136. Ibid., 170–83.

137. Kirby, "Product Proliferation," 292.

138. Henderson, *State*, 158. Quote from Earle, 248.

139. Quoted in Showalter, 21. An 1833 editorial in the Leipzig *Sachsenzeitung* also argued that railroads would bring peace. Showalter, 22.

140. Showalter, 22–24; Martin Van Creveld (1977), *Supplying War: Logistics from Wallenstein to Patton* (New York: Cambridge University Press), 82.

141. Showalter, 19; Van Creveld, 82–83.

142. Showalter, 25.

143. Ibid., 27; Brose, 224–28 (quote on p. 227).

144. Brose, 233.

145. Bucholz, 40; Helmuth von Moltke (1843), "Considerations in the Choice of Railway Routes," in W. Streckery, ed., *Essays, Speeches, & Memoirs of Field-Marshal Count Helmuth von Moltke* (New York: Harper & Brothers), 225, 262.

146. Brose, 233–34.

147. Showalter, 33; Brose, 231.

148. Dennis E. Showalter (1990), "Weapons and Ideas in the Prussian Army from Frederick the Great to Moltke the Elder," in John A. Lynn, ed., *Tools of War: Instruments, Ideas, and Institutions of Warfare, 1445–1871* (Urbana: University of Illinois Press), 200; Showalter, *Railroads and Rifles*, 37.

149. Showalter, *Railroads and Rifles*, 36–37; Van Creveld, 83.

150. Showalter, *Railroads and Rifles*, 36–38; Showalter "Weapons and Ideas," 201–2.

151. Showalter, *Railroads and Rifles*, 38–40.

152. Bucholz, 30.

153. Alfred Vagts (1959), *A History of Militarism: Civilian and Military* (New York: Free Press), 202; Van Creveld, 112; Geoffrey Wawro (1996), *The Austro-Prussian War: Austria's War with Prussia and Italy in 1866* (New York: Cambridge University Press), 54–55, 60; Michael Howard (1961), *The Franco-Prussian War: The German Invasion of France, 1870–1871* (New York: Macmillan), 62, 78. In theory, the Austrian army consisted of 850,000 soldiers, a figure that "unfortunately, existed only on paper." Gordon A. Craig (1964), *The Battle of Königgrätz: Prussia's Victory over Austria, 1866* (New York: Lippincott), 6.

154. Holborn, 287; George Quester (1977), *Offense and Defense in the International System* (New York: Wiley), 78; Craig, 32–36.

155. Van Creveld, 96.

156. Gordon A. Craig (1964), *The Politics of the Prussian Army, 1640–1945* (New York: Oxford University Press); Allan Mitchell (1984), *Victors and Vanquished: The German Influence on Army and Church in France after 1870* (Chapel Hill: University of North Carolina Press); Bruce Menning (1992), *Bayonets Before Bullets: The Imperial Russian Army, 1861–1914* (Bloomington: Indiana University Press).

157. Howard, 448.

158. Earle, 255.

159. Brose, 225; Van Creveld, 86.

160. Van Creveld, 82; Wawro, 15; William Carr (1991), *A History of Germany, 1815–1990* (New York: Edward Arnold), 61–64.

161. Van Creveld, 82; Wawro, 11–13; Showalter, *Railroads and Rifles*, 42–43.

162. Pratt, 103, 122; Showalter, *Railroads and Rifles*, 46.

163. Agatha Ramm (1967), *Germany 1789–1919: A Political History* (London: Methuen), 290–91.

164. Carr, 88, quote from p. 97.

165. Ibid., 99–101. The casualty figures from the battle are stunning and show clearly why it was such a decisive defeat for the Austrians. The Prussians lost 400 officers to the Austrians 1,300; 8,800 men to the Austrian 41,500; and 900 horses to 6,000. The greatest disparity—in horses—indicates that Austrian tactics were anachronistic. Craig, *Battle of Königgrätz*, 166.

166. Craig, *Battle of Königgrätz*, 170; William Carr (1991), *The Origins of the Wars of German Unification* (London: Longman), 138.

167. The first important industrial war in the world was the American Civil War. Had the Europeans, especially the Austrians, paid closer attention to that conflict, they might have avoided some of their larger blunders. Luvaas details the European interpretations and misunderstandings of the Civil War.

168. Craig, *Battle of Königgrätz*, 175. Figures from p. x.

169. Showalter, *Railroads and Rifles*, 52–53; J. F. C. Fuller (1981), *The Conduct of War* (Westport, CT: Greenwood Press), 118.

170. Craig, *Battle of Königgrätz*, 28–29; Showalter, *Railroads and Rifles*, 55–56; Wawro, 52–56.

171. Austria moved first on April 21. There was no Prussian response of any kind until May 3, and full mobilization was not ordered until May 12. Craig, *Battle of Königgrätz*, 30.

172. There was a fair amount of resistance to the strategy among the high command. Many, still unconvinced of the benefits of separation, thought Moltke's adjustment far too risky. Ibid., 33.

173. Ibid., 32–33; Showalter, *Railroads and Rifles*, 63; Wawro, 274.

174. Pratt, 104; Van Creveld, 84; Showalter, *Railroads and Rifles*, 66–67.

175. Showalter, *Railroads and Rifles*, 59; Craig, *Battle of Königgrätz*, 37.

176. Showalter, *Railroads and Rifles*, 68.

177. Ibid., 59.

178. Henderson, *State*, 167, 174; Van Creveld, 83.

179. Van Creveld, 84.

180. Ibid., 86.

181. Showalter, *Railroads and Rifles*, 223.

182. Howard, 23.

183. Showalter, *Railroads and Rifles*, 221; Wawro, 284.

184. Howard, 41, 43; Fremdling, *Eisenbahnen*, 48–49; Pratt, 105–6.

185. Showalter, *Railroads and Rifles*, 222; Pratt, 106–7.

186. Pratt, 106–7; Showalter, *Railroads and Rifles*, 222.

187. Howard, 57, 59.

188. Pratt, 287; Howard, 43–44.

189. German General Staff (1918), "The Railroad Concentration for the Franco-Prussian War," *The Military Historian and Economist*, 3 (Spec. Supp.): 33.

190. Howard, 60.

191. Allan Mitchell (2000), *The Great Train Race: Railways and the Franco-German Rivalry, 1815–1914* (New York: Berghahn Books), 81.

192. Geoffrey Wawro (2003), *The Franco-Prussian War: The German Conquest of France in 1870–1871* (New York: Cambridge University Press), 48–49; quote from Howard, 37.

193. Howard, 39. See Adriance for a detailed study of French efforts at military reform between 1866 and 1870. Thomas J. Adriance (1987), *The Last Gaiter Button: A Study of the Mobilization and Concentration of the French Army in the War of 1870* (New York: Greenwood Press).

194. Wawro, *Franco-Prussian War*, 67; Howard, 45, 68–70.

195. Howard, 68.

196. Ibid., 78.

197. Ibid., 82.

198. Wawro writes, "If Spicheren and Wissembourg cracked the door into France, Froeschwiller knocked it off its hinges." Wawro, *Franco-Prussian War*, 137. See also Howard, 84–85, 120.

199. Howard, 71; Showalter, *Railroads and Rifles*, 222; Van Creveld, 105.

200. Howard, 433.

201. German General Staff, 2.

202. Craig, *Battle of Königgrätz*, 177; Howard, 77.

203. Geoffrey L. Herrera and Thomas G. Mahnken (2003), "Military Diffusion in Nineteenth Century Europe: The Napoleonic and Prussian Military Systems," in Emily O. Goldman and Leslie C. Eliason, eds., *The Diffusion of Military Technology and Ideas* (Stanford: Stanford University Press), 205–42.

204. Van Creveld, 109–11; Heinze and Kill, 125.

205. Larry H. Addington (1971), *The Blitzkrieg Era and the German General Staff, 1865–1941* (New Brunswick, NJ: Rutgers University Press), 9.

206. Pratt, 115–17.

207. Ibid., 282, 287, 288; Mitchell, *European Historical Statistics*, 583.

208. Pratt, 278.

209. Heinze and Kill, 127.

210. Dennis E. Showalter (1991), "Total War for Limited Objectives: An Interpretation of German Grand Strategy," in Paul Kennedy, ed., *Grand Strategies in War and Peace* (New Haven: Yale University Press), 108; Holborn, 291; Addington, 12.

211. Van Creveld, 114.

212. Addington, 14–17; Vagts, *History*, 217; Van Creveld, 111–13.

213. Van Creveld, 117–20; Addington, 17.

214. Addington, 14–17, 22–24.

215. Van Creveld, 122, 128–29, 134.

216. Daniel R. Headrick (1988), *The Tentacles of Progress: Technology Transfer in the Age of Imperialism* (New York: Oxford University Press), 3.

217. A more comprehensive treatment, which would include more of Latin America and Australia has already been done. Daniel R. Headrick (1981), *Tools of Empire: Technology and European Imperialism in the Nineteenth Century* (New York: Oxford University Press); Headrick, *Tentacles of Progress*; William Roger Louis, ed. (1976), *Imperialism: The Robinson and Gallagher Controversy* (New York: New Viewpoints).

218. Ronald E. Robinson (1991), "Introduction: Railway Imperialism," in Clarence B. Davis, Kenneth E. Wilburn, and Ronald E. Robinson, eds., *Railway Imperialism* (Westport, CT: Greenwood), 2; Headrick, *Tentacles of Progress*, 51.

219. Headrick, *Tentacles of Progress*, 50.

220. Robinson, 1–3; Headrick, *Tentacles of Progress*, 87.

221. Headrick, *Tentacles of Progress*, 53, 62; Daniel Thorner (1950), *Investment in Empire: British Railway and Steam Shipping Enterprise in India 1825–1849* (Philadelphia: University of Pennsylvania Press), 4.

222. Thorner, 1; Headrick, *Tools of Empire*, 180–83.

223. Thorner, 48.

224. Ibid., 5.

225. Ibid., 54–60; Headrick, *Tentacles of Progress*, 59–60.

226. Headrick, *Tools of Empire*, 181, 187; Headrick, *Tentacles of Progress*, 62, 64, 72.

227. Robinson, 2; Headrick, *Tentacles of Progress*, 65, 72.

228. Headrick, *Tentacles of Progress*, 60, 56, 89.

229. Ibid., 66–68, 87–88.

230. Clarence B. Davis (1991), "Railway Imperialism in China, 1895–1939," in Clarence B. Davis, Kenneth E. Wilburn, and Ronald E. Robinson, eds., *Railway Imperialism* (Westport, CT: Greenwood), 155.

231. Ibid., 158, 159, 155.

232. E-tu Zen Sun (1955), "The Pattern of Railway Development in China," *Journal of Asian Studies*, 14 (2): 180, 188–87, 182, 186; Davis, 158, 170.

233. Sun, 182; Robinson, 2.

234. Headrick, *Tools of Empire*, 192.

235. Ibid., 192–94, 200–1; Robinson, 2; Headrick, *Tentacles of Progress*, 50.

236. Headrick, *Tools of Empire*, 194; Pratt, 296–98.

237. Pratt, 303, 304–5, 306–9.

238. See Van Creveld for a general discussion of the evolution of the modern state. Martin Van Creveld (1999), *The Rise and Decline of the State*

(New York: Cambridge University Press). For the nineteenth century, two studies of the American political economy inspire this point: Chandler's history of the industrial-era business enterprise and Dunlavy's study of the intersection between state and business organization. Alfred D. Chandler (1977), *The Visible Hand: The Managerial Revolution in American Business* (Cambridge, MA: Belknap Press); Colleen A. Dunlavy (1993), *Politics and Industrialization: Early Railroads in the United States and Prussia* (Princeton: Princeton University Press).

CHAPTER FOUR

1. John S. Brubacher and Willis Rudy (1976), *Higher Education in Transition: A History of American Colleges & Universities, 1636–1976* (New York: Harper & Row), 175; Charles F. Thwing (1928), *The American and the German University: One Hundred Years of History* (New York: Macmillan), 10; Charles Weiner (1969), "A New Site for the Seminar: The Refugees and American Physics in the 1930s," in Donald H. Fleming and Bernard Bailyn, eds., *The Intellectual Migration: Europe and American, 1930–1960* (Cambridge: Harvard University Press), 196.

2. Laura Fermi (1971), *Illustrious Immigrants* (Chicago: University of Chicago Press), 175.

3. Stanley Goldberg (1992), "Inventing a Climate of Opinion: Vannevar Bush and the Decision to Build the Bomb," *Isis*, 83: 429–52.

4. Gregory McLauchlan (1989), "World War, the Advent of Nuclear Weapons, and Global Expansion of the National Security State," in Robert K. Schaeffer, ed., *War in the World-System* (New York: Greenwood Press), 91.

5. James Phinney Baxter (1946), *Scientists Against Time* (Cambridge: MIT Press), 423.

6. Robert Jervis (1989), *The Meaning of the Nuclear Revolution: Statecraft and the Prospect of Armageddon* (Ithaca, NY: Cornell University Press); John H. Herz (1956), "Rise and Demise of the Territorial State," *World Politics*, 9 (4): 473–93; Daniel Deudney (1995), "Nuclear Weapons and the Waning of the Real-State," *Daedalus*, 124 (2): 209–31.

7. Physicists were not an epistemic community in the sense defined in the literature. Peter M. Haas (1992), "Introduction: Epistemic Communities and International Policy Coordination," *International Organization*, 46 (1): 1–35; Clair Gough and Simon Shackley (2001), "The Respectable Politics of Climate Change: The Epistemic Communities and NGOs," *International Affairs*, 77 (2): 329–46. While nuclear physicists shared a common view of science, they were not attached to a global public policy problem.

8. Given the time frame, it is inaccurate to refer to Germany as the political unit here. German-speaking world is somewhat more satisfactory because it incorporates a sense of the educational and scientific hegemony of

Prussia-Germany in Central Europe. The German universities and technical institutes drew the finest scientific talent from their Central European hinterlands. A fair number of the important 'German' atomic scientists were not in fact German (Leo Szilard, Hungarian by birth and early education, is one example), but all received their advanced training in Germany and/or taught and did their research there.

9. The scientific foundations of the bomb were not all the work of German scientists. For example, three giants of atomic physics—Ernest Rutherford, Niels Bohr, and Enrico Fermi—were not German but English, Danish, and Italian, respectively. Nevertheless, the contribution of German scientists overshadows those of any other national origin.

10. Historians of the sciences typically divide accounts of the developments of science into externalist and internalist versions. An externalist account holds that institutional, political, economic, social, and/or cultural environments determine the development of science. An internalist account claims that science develops as a series of intellectual problems and solutions more or less free from outside influences. Critics of internalist accounts argue that the causal connections between the world of science and political and economic reality, however "indirect, circuitous, even convoluted," are of equal if not greater importance. David Cahan (1988), "Pride and Prejudice in the History of Physics: The German Speaking World, 1740–1945," *Historical Studies in the Physical and Biological Sciences*, 19: 180. The version of nuclear physics' development here will be largely an externalist one. The project is concerned ultimately with political phenomena, so an environmental or externalist account is most appropriate, even though it is impossible to have one without the other.

11. Alexander Gerschenkron (1962), "Economic Backwardness in Historical Perspective," in Alexander Gerschenkron, ed., *Economic Backwardness in Historical Perspective* (Cambridge: Harvard University Press), 5–30; David Landes (1969), *The Unbound Prometheus: Technological Change and Industrial Development in Western Europe from 1750 to the Present* (New York: Cambridge University Press), 4; David Cahan (1989), *An Institute for an Empire: The Physikalisch-Technische Reichsanstalt, 1871–1918* (New York: Cambridge University Press), 15.

12. The connections between science and the second Industrial Revolution are neatly illustrated in the following example. Between 1924 and 1934, Albert Einstein and his partner Leo Szilard applied for twenty-nine patents in Germany—all of them related to home refrigeration. Einstein and Szilard were also distinguished theoretical physicists and the two collaborated on the famous 1939 letter from Einstein to President Roosevelt warning the latter of the possibility of the atomic bomb. Rhodes is an excellent source for this story. Richard Rhodes (1986), *The Making of the Atomic Bomb* (New York: Touchstone), 20–21.

13. Alan Beyerchen (1987), "On the Stimulation of Excellence in Wilhelmian Science," in Joachim Remak and Jack Dukes, eds., *Another Germany: A Reconsideration of the Imperial Era* (Boulder: Westview Press), 139; Pamela Spence Richards (1990), "The Movement of Scientific Knowledge from and to Germany Under National Socialism," *Minerva*, 28 (4): 401; A. Baracca, S. Ciliberto, R. Livi, A. Lorini, M. Pettini, S. Ruffo, and A. Russo (1980), "Research Programme on Science and Society: Germany and the United-States, 1870–1940," *Radical Science Journal*, 10: 121.

14. Joseph Ben-David (1984), *The Scientist's Role in Society: A Comparative Study* (Chicago: University of Chicago Press), 108; R. Steven Turner (1980), "The Prussian Universities and the Concept of Research," *Internationales Archiv fur Sozialgeschichte der Deutschen Literatur*, 5: 68; Lenore O'Boyle (1983), "Learning for Its Own Sake—The German University as 19th-Century Model," *Comparative Studies in Society and History*, 25 (1): 12.

15. Turner, 83.

16. Konrad Jarausch (1987), "The Universities: An American View," in Joachim Remak and Jack Dukes, eds., *Another Germany: A Reconsideration of the Imperial Era* (Boulder: Westview Press), 184–90; Turner: 77.

17. Baracca, Ciliberto, Livi, Lorini, Pettini, Ruffo and Russo, 122; Beyerchen, 141, 147.

18. Ben-David, 134. Germany used science for diplomatic purposes quite consciously. After World War I, the state manipulated the ideology of scientific internationalism to protect Germany's declining scientific reputation in the hopes of boosting Germany's deflated international prestige. For example, Germany tied Eastern European states (especially the Soviet Union) into bilateral scientific agreements in which foreign scientists would receive training in Germany, but would be restricted from reading non-German scientific journals or meeting with non-German scientists. Paul Forman (1973), "Scientific Internationalism and the Weimar Physicsts: The Ideology and Its Manipulation in Germany after World War I," *Isis*, 64: 165. The activity extended into the National Socialist era as well. Richards, 401–3.

19. Charles E. McClelland (1980), *State, Society, and University in Germany, 1700–1914* (New York: Cambridge University Press), 308, 240, 258; Cahan, *An Institute for an Empire*, 20; O'Boyle, 7.

20. Fritz K. Ringer (1967), "Higher Education in Germany in the Nineteenth Century," *Journal of Contemporary History*, 2 (3): 125.

21. Long-standing *Länder* policy mandated the free transfer of credits and free movement of professors between institutions. The individual universities were forced by dual competitive pressures—from below by potentially dissatisfied students and from above by potentially dissatisfied research stars—to support excellence in research and instruction. State policy successfully counteracted the natural tendency on the part of the corporate university to insulate itself from market pressures. Ben-David 123–24.

22. Ringer, 125; McClelland, 297.

23. Ringer, 219.

24. Cahan, *An Institute for an Empire*, 2.

25. Ben-David, 120. This situation contrasts markedly with the United States where the university president's power was virtually unchecked. Jarausch, 188.

26. Ben-David, 127; Lewis Pyenson and Douglas Skopp (1977), "Educating Physicists in Germany 'circa' 1900," *Social Studies of Science*, 7 (3): 360.

27. David Cahan (1985), "The Institutional Revolution in German Physics, 1865–1914," *Historical Studies in the Physical and Biological Sciences*, 16 (1): 3, 17; McClelland, 280, quote from p. 279.

28. Cahan, *An Institute for an Empire*, 29–34.

29. Frank R. Pfetsch (1970), "Scientific Organization and Science Policy in Imperial Germany, 1871–1914: The Foundation of the Imperial Institute for Physics and Technology," *Minerva*, 8 (4): 567–72; Cahan, *An Institute for an Empire*, 49–51, 1.

30. Ringer, 130; Cahan, "Institutional Revolution," 16; McClelland, 236; Beyerchen, 152–53.

31. Cahan, "Institutional Revolution."

32. Jeffrey Allan Johnson (1990), *The Kaiser's Chemists: Science and Modernization in Imperial Germany* (Chapel Hill: University of North Carolina Press), 11.

33. Ibid., 17–18.

34. Forman, 161.

35. Kristie Macrakis (1989), "The Rockefeller Foundation and German Physics under National Socialism," *Minerva*, 27 (1): 36, 37. The generation of theoretical physicists trained at Göttingen during the 1920s include Paul Debye (who would head the Planck Physics Institute after the Nazi takeover before emigrating to the United States and Cornell University in 1940), Eugene Wigner (later a Manhattan Project physicist), Wolfgang Pauli (in 1940 emigrated to the United States and the Institute for Advanced Studies), Werner Heisenberg (the head of the German atomic bomb project), Hans Bethe (later an MIT Radlab physicist and director of theoretical physics for the Manhattan Project), Paul Epstein (left the University of Leiden for Caltech in 1921 and became the first theoretical physicist lured from Germany to the United States), and Robert Oppenheimer. Klaus Fischer (1993), *Changing Landscapes of Nuclear Physics: A Scientometric Study on the Social and Cognitive Position of German-Speaking Emigrants Within the Nuclear Physics Community 1921–1947* (Berlin: Springer-Verlag), 235.

36. Macrakis, 56.

37. Paul Forman (1974), "The Financial Support and Political Alignment of Physicists in Weimar Germany," *Minerva*, 12 (1): 53.

38. Ibid., 39–42, 44–51.

39. Ibid., 41, 61.

40. Max Planck retained her as a researcher at his Institute for Theoretical Physics in Berlin as long as he could after the 1933 law was passed.

41. Otto R. Frisch (1939), "Physical Evidence for the Division of Heavy Nuclei under Neutron Bombardment," *Nature*, 143: 276; Lise Meitner and Otto R. Frisch (1939), "Disintegration of Uranium by Neutrons: A New Type of Nuclear Reaction," *Nature*, 143: 239; Rhodes, 264–65.

42. Paul Forman, John L. Heilbron, and Spencer Weart (1975), "Physics *circa* 1900: Personnel, Funding, and Productivity of the Academic Establishments," *Historical Studies in the Physical and Biological Sciences*, 5: 1–185. This is a broad aggregate including secondary school physicists, positions in 'mathematics and physics,' and eighteen subspecies of physicists including astrophysics, electrochemistry, photography and optics, physical chemistry, and others.

43. Ibid., 34–35, 117.

44. Henry A. Boorse, Lloyd Motz, and Jefferson Hane Weaver (1989), *The Atomic Scientists: A Biographical History* (New York: Wiley). The X ray is a convenient place to start as it signals both the "beginnings of modern physics" according to Boorse and the maturation of German physics during the Empire.

45. Forman, Heilbron, and Weart, "Physics *circa* 1900," 31, 177.

46. Due to the fluidity of national boundaries in Central Europe in the late nineteenth and early twentieth centuries, 'German scientists' refers to those trained and employed within the German sphere of cultural influence. In practice, that usually meant a Ph.D. from a German university, and a post at a German university or institute. But, for example, Erwin Schrödinger was Viennese by birth, and Leo Szilard, John von Neumann, Eugene Wigner, and Edward Teller were Hungarian. All had their scientific careers in Germany (for Schrödinger also in Switzerland) before emigration to the United States (or Great Britain, in the case of Schrödinger).

47. Alan D. Beyerchen (1977), *Scientists under Hitler: Politics and the Physics Community in the Third Reich* (New Haven: Yale University Press), 6–8.

48. Forman, Heilbron and Weart, "Physics *circa* 1900," 34.

49. There were some exceptions. One is Paul Dirac who was born in England to Swiss and English parents. In 1926, Dirac made an important contribution to quantum mechanics and quantum theory with his general version of Heisenberg's mechanics. However, despite his ostensible career in physics, Dirac's Ph.D. was in mathematics and his academic position was in Cambridge's math department. Rutherford's Cavendish lab—the center of British physics—showed little interest in quantum physics. Alan Wilson was graduate student in mathematics at Cambridge in the 1920s and early 1930s with an interest in the new quantum theory coming out of Germany. In the early 1920s, he writes, separation of subjects into college- and university-based groups "meant that no mathematician was allowed to attend any lec-

tures on physics . . . and even the phrase 'theoretical physics' was never used, it being considered a minor part of 'applied mathematics.' " Wilson reports that the situation had 'improved' by the early 1930s when semiregular meetings were held to discuss developments in quantum theory and he gave a series of lectures on quantum mechanics. But even by the late 1930s, the regular colloquia held by Wilson and his colleagues were unable to find meeting space in the Cavendish. Alan Wilson (1984), "Theoretical Physics at Cambridge in the Late 1920s and Early 1930s," in John Hendry, ed., *Cambridge Physics in the Thirties* (Bristol: Adam Hilger Ltd.), 174–75. In the United States, positions in theoretical physics were being created in the late 1920s and early 1930s at places such as Caltech and the University of California at Berkeley.

50. McClelland, 259, 242.

51. Ibid., 299.

52. In 1930, Max von Laue—who had been chosen by Planck to head the Planck Institute for Physics—visited the United States to observe the laboratories at Schenectedy, Baltimore, Pasadena, Chicago, and Cambridge. Von Laue came away very impressed with American physics, especially the large experimental machines. He lamented the lack of funds for experimental work in Germany. Macrakis, 38–39. Paul Epstein was wooed away from Leiden to Caltech in 1921; George Uhlenbeck and Samuel Goudsmit from Leiden and Otto LaPorte went from Munich to Michigan in 1926; Gerhard Dieke from Leiden to Berkeley in 1925; Fritz Zwicky from Zurich to Caltech in 1925; and John von Neumann and Eugene Wigner went from Berlin to Princeton in 1929. Stanley Cobden (1971), "The Scientific Establishment and the Transmission of Quantum Mechanics to the United States, 1919–1932," *American Historical Review*, 76 (2): 452.

53. Charles Weiner writes, "The social environment for science and the organization of the scientific community in the United States in the 1930s suggest that the conditions for a 'brain drain' already existed at that time, and that large numbers of European scientists would have emigrated to the Unites States even without the stimulus of the political upheavals of Nazism. . . . they [would] have come because of the greater opportunities for professional development and self-expression in their work, better pay, and the better facilities available." Weiner, 226 fn. 71.

54. The debate began immediately after the war. Samuel Goudsmit was a Dutch physicist who emigrated to the United States in 1926. He participated in the Manhattan Project and toward the end of the war was sent as part of an army intelligence unit to Europe to evaluate the German bomb program. Over many weeks, Goudsmit interviewed ten German atomic scientists, including Heisenberg, whom the Allies were holding in Farm Hall, a farmhouse near Cambridge. He condemned Heisenberg and the other German atomic scientists for crucial scientific errors and their complicity in the horrors of Nazism. Samuel A. Goudsmit (1947), *Alsos* (New York: Schuman).

Heisenberg denied the collaboration charge and claimed that he had purposefully downplayed the ease of building an atomic bomb in reports to his Nazi overseers to prevent Hitler from obtaining the weapon. Thomas Powers, with the use of recently released audiotapes of the Farm Hall interrogations, argues that a combination of lack of resources and pessimistic reports from Heisenberg convinced the Nazi authorities not to pursue the bomb. Thomas Powers (1993), *Heisenberg's War: The Secret History of the German Bomb* (New York: Knopf). Paul Rose has updated Goudsmit's charge with a deeper analysis of Heisenberg's writings and attempts—until his death in 1976—to exonerate himself. Paul Lawrence Rose (1998), *Heisenberg and the Nazi Atomic Bomb Project: A Study in German Culture* (Berkeley: University of California Press).

55. A small group of physicists led by the Nobel Prize winners Philip Lenard and Johannes Stark founded a fascist physics movement even before the Nazis came to power. *Deutsche Physik,* as they called it, sought to rid German physics of Jews; theoretical and quantum physics; and the mechanistic, rational, anti-German worldview they implied. *Deutsche Physik* advocates were very influential in shaping early Nazi policy toward physics. For example, by accusing Heisenberg of advocating a Jewish science (and of possibly being Jewish himself), they managed in 1936 to block his appointment to the Munich chair in theoretical physics made vacant by the retirement of Arnold Sommerfeld. However, *Deutsche Physik* influence over Nazi science policy was short-lived. Once the war began, the German high command quickly learned that modern physics could supply weapons and *Deutsche Physik* could not. Mark Walker (1989), "National Socialism and German Physics," *Journal of Contemporary History,* 24 (1): 65, 68, 80, 69–70; Richards, 423.

56. Beyerchen, *Scientists under Hitler,* 47; Stanley Goldberg and Thomas Powers (1992), "Declassified Files Reopen the 'Nazi Bomb' Debate," *Bulletin of the Atomic Scientists,* 48 (7): 36.

57. David Irving (1967), *The German Atomic Bomb* (New York: Simon and Schuster).

58. Mark Walker (1991), "Legends Surrounding the German Atomic Bomb," in Mark Walker and Teresa Meade, eds., *Science, Medicine, and Cultural Imperialism* (New York: St. Martin's), 181–82. Albert Speer was charged with making the decision on the bomb's funding. In his memoirs he reports hearing from the scientists in the spring of 1942 that the bomb was possible, but "I had been given the impression that the atom bomb could no longer have any bearing on the course of the war . . . we could not count on anything for three or four years." Quoted in Rhodes, 404–5. This is evidence to Powers that the German scientists, specifically Heisenberg, persuaded Speer that the bomb could not be built in time to affect the war's outcome. American scientists, however, were no more convinced of the possibility of bringing the theory of a fission-induced explosion to reality than their German counterpart. But American scientists, managers, and government officials were in

agreement that the threat of a possible German bomb was great enough that even the remotest chance for success justified the effort.

59. Baxter, 248.

60. The most politically powerful German scientist in the first three decades of the twentieth century was a theoretical physicist—Max Planck. In addition to being one of the most prominent faculty members at the University of Berlin (Germany's most important university), he held a large number of administrative posts and directorships (including the directorship of the KWG—the most important source for scientific research support into the early 1920s), and was the most influential spokesman for science on issues of science policy. Only Denmark with Niels Bohr had a theoretical physicist of comparable political stature. In the United States, Great Britain, France, and Italy—as it had been for more than a century—the experimentalists dominated the professional associations and monopolized contacts with the political system.

61. Paul Hanle (1982), *Bringing Aerodynamics to America* (Cambridge: MIT Press), 110–11.

62. William E. Leuchtenburg (1964), "The New Deal and the Analogue of War," in John Braeman, Robert H. Bremner, and Everett Walters, eds., *Change and Continuity in Twentieth Century America* (Columbus: Ohio State University Press), 81–143.

63. Brubacher and Rudy, 191–92, 195–96.

64. Howard S. Miller (1970), *Dollars for Research: Science and Its Patrons in Nineteenth-Century America* (Seattle: University of Washington Press), viii–ix.

65. Bruce L. R. Smith (1990), *American Science Policy Since World War II* (Washington, DC: Brookings Institution), 21.

66. Charles W. Eliot (president of Harvard from 1869 to 1909), Daniel C. Gilman (president of the Johns Hopkins University from its founding in 1875 to 1889), Andrew D. White (president of Cornell University from its founding in 1868 to 1885), James B. Angell (president of the University of Michigan from 1871 to 1909), Timothy Dwight (president of Yale from 1886 to 1899), William Watts Folwell (president of the University of Minnesota from its founding in 1869 to 1884), G. Stanley Hall (president of Clark University from its founding in 1888 to 1920), Nicholas Murray Butler (president of Columbia from 1902 to 1945), Charles Kendall Adams (president of Cornell University from 1885 to 1892 and president of the University of Wisconsin from 1892 to 1901), and Frederick A. P. Barnard (president of Columbia from 1864 to 1889). Brubacher and Rudy, 178.

67. Clark Kerr (1963), *The Uses of the University* (Cambridge: Harvard University Press), 15; Jürgen Herbst (1965), *The German Historical School in American Scholarship: A Study in the Transfer of Culture* (Ithaca, NY: Cornell University Press), 3–5; Brubacher and Rudy, 174. Another historian of American higher education, Lawrence Vesey, argues that we should be cautious

in attributing too much to the German example. He argues that the American university-builders fundamentally misunderstood the German ideal of *Wissenschaft*. They—perhaps intentionally—mistook the ideal's emphasis on unified contemplation of human existence and turned it simply into a exhortation for pure science. Laurence R. Veysey (1965), *The Emergence of the American University* (Chicago: University of Chicago Press). Yet misinterpreting *Wissenschaft* hardly invalidates the importance of the German model. The method of organization and the influence of the emphasis on pure research are substantial enough. Jarausch, 197–98. And even if the Americans misunderstood *Wissenschaft*, they admired it. A Carnegie Commission report from the period cites the ideal as one of the secrets of German academic success. Jarausch, 187–88.

68. Brubacher and Rudy, 175–76; Herbst, 2; Jarausch, 187.

69. For the 1870s, Thwing records "considerably more than a thousand" students in Germany.

70. Herbst, 15, 11, 12; Jarausch, 199. American applicants were also required by English law to join the Anglican Church, a requirement that was not abolished until 1871.

71. Herbst, 5; Jarausch, 181–82.

72. Dorothy Ross (1991), *The Origins of American Social Science* (New York: Cambridge University Press); Edward Shils (1978), "The Order of Learning in the United States from 1865 to 1920: The Ascendancy of the Universities," *Minerva*, 16 (2): 166, 159–65.

73. Shils, 172; Brubacher and Rudy, 183–84; Roger L. Geiger (1986), *To Advance Knowledge: The Growth of American Research Universities, 1900–1940* (New York: Oxford University Press), v.

74. Ben-David, 141–66.

75. Geiger, 233.

76. Spencer R. Weart (1979), "The Physics Business in America, 1919–1940: A Statistical Reconnaissance," in Nathan Reingold, ed., *The Sciences in the American Context: New Perspectives* (Washington, DC: Smithsonian Institution), 333; Cobden, 442–43.

77. John Heilbron (1982), "Fin-de-Siècle Physics," in Carl Gustaf Bernhard, Elisabeth Crawford, and Per Sorbom, eds., *Science, Technology and Society in the Time of Alfred Nobel* (Oxford: Pergamon), 63.

78. Weart, 302, 304.

79. Silvan S. Schweber (1986), "The Empiricist Temper Regnant: Theoretical Physics in the United States 1920–1950," *Historical Studies in the Physical and Biological Sciences*, 17 (1): 70; Daniel J. Kevles (1978), *The Physicists: The History of a Scientific Community in Modern America* (New York: Knopf), 169; Geiger, 236; quote from Cobden: 446.

80. Cobden, 444.

81. Ibid., 450.

82. Kevles, 168.

83. Cobden, 451; Schweber, 57; Kevles, 168; Paul Forman (1971), "Weimar Culture, Causality, and Quantum Theory, 1918–1927: Adaptation by German Physicists and Mathematicians to a Hostile Intellectual Environment," *Historical Studies in the Physical and Biological Sciences*, 3: 1–116; Gerald Holton (1981), "The Formation of the American Physics Community in the 1920s and the Coming of Albert Einstein," *Minerva*, 19 (4): 576.

84. Katherine Sopka (1981), *Quantum Physics in America, 1920–1935* (New York: Arno Press), A.1–A.10.

85. Ibid., A.26; Holton, 578–79; Paul K. Hoch (1983), "The Reception of Central European Refugee Physicists of the 1930s—USSR, UK, USA," *Annals of Science*, 40 (3): 232; Cobden, 452.

86. Sopka, A.11–A.28, 3.40–3.42; Cobden, 453. Caltech students with such fellowships include: Carl Eckart, William Houston, Roy J. Kennedy, Boris Podolsky, and Howard Robertson.

87. Robert E. Kohler (1991), *Partners in Science: Foundations and Natural Scientists, 1900–1945* (Chicago: University of Chicago Press), 402–3; quote from Stanley Cobden (1976), "Foundation Officials and Fellowships: Innovation in the Patronage of Science," *Minerva*, 14 (2): 225.

88. Howard Plotkin (1978), "Edward C. Pickering and the Endowment of Scientific Research in America, 1877–1918," *Isis*, 69 (246): 54–57; Robert E. Kohler (1978), "A Policy for the Advancement of Science: The Rockefeller Foundation, 1924–29," *Minerva*, 16 (4): 481; Nathan Reingold (1977), "The Case of the Disappearing Laboratory," *American Quarterly*, 29 (1): 79–101.

89. Kohler, *Partners in Science*, 84–87.

90. Paul K. Hoch (1988), "The Crystallization of a Strategic Alliance: The American Physics Elite and the Military in the 1940s," in Everett Mendelsohn, Merritt Roe Smith, and Peter Weingart, eds., *Science, Technology, and the Military* (Dordrecht: Kluwer Academic Publishers), 91; Gerald Holton (1983), "The Migration of Physicists to the United States," in Jarrel C. Jackman and Carla M. Borden, eds., *The Muses Flee Hitler: Cultural Transfer and Adaptation, 1930–1945* (Washington, DC: Smithsonian Institution), 176.

91. Cobden, "Foundation Officials," 231; Hoch, "Crystallization," 91; Raymond B. Fosdick (1952), *The Story of the Rockefeller Foundation* (New York: Harper), 153–54; Kohler, *Partners in Science*, 207–13.

92. Kohler, *Partners in Science*, 204–5; Fosdick, 150.

93. Cobden, "Foundation Officials," 238.

94. Kohler, *Partners in Science*, 102–3; Fosdick, 146; Sopka, 3.40–3.42.

95. Cobden, "Foundation Officials," 231; Sopka, 3.40–3.42.

96. Kohler, *Partners in Science*, 205–6.

97. Schweber, 75, quote from p. 74.

98. Fosdick, 171.

99. Ibid., 172, 171; Weart, 313.

100. Schweber, 62–63.

101. Rhodes, 146, 447; Cobden, "Scientific Establishment," 459. Quote from Hans Bethe (1968), "J. Robert Oppenheimer," *Biographical Memoirs of Fellows of the Royal Society*, 14: 396.

102. Kevles, 282.

103. Christophe Lecuyer (1992), "The Making of a Science Based Technological University: Karl Compton, James Killian, and the Reform of MIT, 1930–1957," *Historical Studies in the Physical and Biological Sciences*, 23 (1): 153, 160.

104. Weiner, 193–95.

105. John C. Slater (1967), "Quantum Physics in America between the Wars," *Physics Today*, 21 (1): 43.

106. John H. Van Vleck (1964), "American Physics Comes of Age," *Physics Today*, 17 (June): 21–26.

107. Weart, 299.

108. Ibid.; Kevles, 200, 202.

109. Hugh G. J. Aitken (1976), *Syntony and Spark: The Origins of Radio* (New York: Wiley), 19.

110. Weiner, 224; Roger H. Stuewer (1984), "Nuclear Physicists in a New World: The Émigrés of the 1930s in America," *Berichte zur Wissenschaftsgeschichte*, 7 (1): 32–33; Kevles, 283–84.

111. Smith, 1; Joel Genuth (1987), "Groping Towards Science Policy In The United States in the 1930s," *Minerva*, 25 (3): 238–68.

112. Robert Cuff (1981), "American Mobilization for War 1917–45: Political Culture vs. Bureaucratic Administration," in N. F. Dreisziger, ed., *Mobilization for Total War: The Canadian, American and British Experience 1914–1918, 1939–1945* (Waterloo, Ontario: Wilfrid Laurier University Press), 75–76; James E. Hewes (1975), *From Root to McNamara: Army Departmental Organization and Administration, 1900–1963* (Washington, DC: Center of Military History, U.S. Army), 29–31; David M. Kennedy (1980), *Over Here: The First World War and American Society* (New York: Oxford University Press), 123.

113. Kennedy, 140–41.

114. Daniel J. Kevles (1968), "George Ellery Hale, the First World War, and the Advancement of Science in America," *Isis*, 59: 427, 431.

115. Ibid., 436.

116. Genuth; Larry Owens (1990), "MIT and the Federal 'Angel': Academic R&D and Federal-Private Cooperation before World War II," *Isis*, 81: 190; Carroll W. Pursell (1965), "The Anatomy of a Failure: The Science Advisory Board, 1933–35," *Proceedings of the American Philosophical Society*, 109 (6): 342–51.

117. Robert H. Millikan (1919), "The New Opportunity in Science," *Science*, 50 (Setember 26): 297.

118. For a brief and informative survey of the early engineering accomplishments of the NACA, see Roger E. Bilstein (1989), *Orders of Magnitude: A History of the NACA and NASA, 1915–1990* (Washington, DC: National Aeronautics and Space Administration Office of Management Scientific and Technical Information Division), 1–30.

119. Ibid., 3.

120. Ibid., 7, 5, 17. The transfer of aeronautics expertise from Germany to the United States paralleled that of physics. German engineers had virtually invented aeronautical theory while the subdiscipline was almost nonexistent in Britain and the United States. Anti-Semitism and a dwindling number of positions relative to aspirants plagued aeronautical engineering in Germany. Once the discipline had established itself in the United States—and the shortfall in theory had been recognized—the employment opportunities, wonderful equipment, and level of compensation made American universities irresistible. Hanle shows how all these factors played a role in von Kármán's decision to come to Caltech in 1922.

121. Alex Roland (1985), *Model Research: the NACA, 1915–1958* (Washington, DC: Scientific and Technical Information Branch, NASA), 33; Norriss S. Hetherington (1990), "The National Advisory Committee for Aeronautics: A Forerunner of Federal Governmental Support for Scientific Research," *Minerva*, 28 (1): 77. Despite the success of the cowling, NACA was not a favorite within government and in the aviation industry. A 1937 Brookings report commissioned by the Senate was but one of several studies and public calls for the abolition of the committee. Through much of the 1930s, the magazine *Aero Digest* was a staunch opponent of NACA; in editorial after editorial the committee was denounced for its failure to conduct research of any significance despite the most remarkable facilities in the world. The cowling itself was a source of some controversy, though NACA—despite constant use of the innovation as justification for more funding in budget arguments before Congress—was careful never to claim either scientific or industrial credit (in the form of a patent) for the device. Roland, 131, 142–49, 113.

122. Kevles, *Physicists*, 298.

123. Thomas K. McKraw (1971), *TVA and the Power Fight, 1933–1939* (Philadelphia: J. B. Lippincott), 24–30. Roosevelt is another example of a prominent policy-maker who first encountered public management and planning during World War I. He was Assistant Secretary to the Navy during the war and was responsible for procuring armor plate for warships.

124. On the directors, see ibid., 37–41; on A. Morgan: Thomas P. Hughes (1989), *American Genesis: A Century of Invention and Technological Enthusiasm* (New York: Penguin), 364–76; on Lilienthal: Hughes, 371–72.

125. The public relations campaign included picture essays in national magazines, articles by the commissioners, pamphlets, tours of the site, exhibits, and films. The famous plaque at the base of all TVA dams reads, Built

for the People of the United States, and in this spirit—as a demonstration project for the New Deal itself—the campaign was an enormous success. Nearly four and one-half million tourists visited the project before 1940 and approximately one-million viewed the Authority's film of the dam's construction. McKraw, 146.

126. Ibid., 144; Hughes, 373.

127. C. Herman Pritchett (1943), *The Tennessee Valley Authority: A Study in Public Administration* (Chapel Hill: University of North Carolina Press), 321–22. The OSRD was not without its political enemies. Carroll Pursell (1979), "Science Agencies in World War II: The OSRD and Its Challenges," in Nathan Reingold, ed., *The Sciences in the American Context: New Perspectives* (Washington, DC: Smithsonian Institution), 359–378.

128. McKraw, 141.

129. For example, Arthur Compton's account of his involvement in the decision to build the bomb presumes a large government role. Arthur H. Compton (1956), *Atomic Quest: A Personal Narrative* (New York: Oxford University Press), 6–7.

130. Centralized, but in the American style—still more flexible and less authoritarian than the research and development styles of the other great powers. Matthew Evangelista (1988), *Innovation and the Arms Race: How the United States and the Soviet Union Develop New Military Technologies* (Ithaca, NY: Cornell University Press); Aaron L. Friedberg (2000), *In the Shadow of the Garrison State: America's Anti-Statism and Its Cold War Grand Strategy* (Princeton: Princeton University Press), especially pp. 296–339.

131. Kevles, *Physicists*, 326; Richard G. Hewlett (1976), "Beginnings of Development in Nuclear Technology," *Technology and Culture*, 17 (3): 471.

132. David A. Hounshell and John Kenly Smith (1988), *Science and Corporate Strategy: Du Pont R & D, 1902–1980* (New York: Cambridge University Press), 187.

133. Alfred D. Chandler (1962), *Strategy and Structure: Chapters in the History of the Industrial Enterprise* (Cambridge: MIT Press); Alfred D. Chandler (1977), *The Visible Hand: The Managerial Revolution in American Business* (Cambridge, MA: Belknap Press); Louis Galambos (1983), "Technology, Political Economy, and Professionalization: Central Theme of the Organizational Synthesis," *Business History Review*, 57: 472–77.

134. Ernest Dale (1957), "Du Pont: Pioneer in Systematic Management," *Administrative Science Quarterly*, 2 (1): 26–29; Chandler, *Strategy and Structure*, 54, 79–84.

135. Chandler, *Strategy and Structure*, 85–113.

136. David A. Hounshell (1992), "Du Pont and the Management of Large-Scale Research and Development," in Peter Galison and Bruce Hevley, eds., *Big Science: The Growth of Large Scale Research* (Stanford, CA: Stanford University Press, 238–39, 243–44.

137. Ibid., 246; Hughes, 389.

138. Hughes, 401.

139. Ben-David, 158.

140. Kevles, *Physicists*, 222–35.

141. Norman Bentwich (1953), *The Rescue and Achievement of Refugee Scholars: The Story of Displaced Scholars and Scientists, 1933–1952* (The Hague: M. Nijhoff), 2; Fermi, 42; Klaus Fischer (1988), "The Operationalism of Scientific Emigration Loss 1933–1945: A Methodological Study on the Measurement of a Qualitative Phenomenon," *Historical Social Research*, 48: 99–121.

142. Stephen Duggan and Betty Drury (1948), *The Rescue of Science and Learning* (New York: Macmillan).

143. For England, see Beveridge's introductory note in Bentwich, ix–xiv. For the United States, see Robin E. Rider (1984), "Alarm and Opportunity: Emigration of Mathematicians and Physicists to Britain and the United States, 1933–1945," *Historical Studies in the Physical and Biological Sciences*, 15 (1): 144.

144. See Bentwich; William Henry Beveridge (1959), *A Defence of Free Learning* (New York: Oxford University Press); Duggan and Drury.

145. The only case of heavy state involvement was in Turkey, where the *Notgemeinschaft deutscher Wissenschaftler im Ausland* (Emergency Society of German Scholars Abroad) arranged with President Ataturk to place nearly one hundred exiled scholars in the new University of Istanbul. A partial exception to this is the British Society for the Protection of Science and Learning (SPSL) that in 1940, after seven years of operation, began to receive a small stipend from the government to supplement their private fund-raising efforts. Rider, 142.

146. Norman Bentwich (1936), *The Refugees from Germany, April 1933 to December 1935* (London: George Allen and Unwin), 193–94.

147. Rider, 135–38, 142–43; Weiner, 210–11; Hoch, "Reception," 222–24.

148. Hoch, "Reception," 229.

149. Ibid., 223; Rider, 155.

150. Weiner, 214; Duggan and Drury, 66. That sixteen included, however, the Nobel laureate James Franck, Lothar Nordheim, Felix Bloch, Arthur von Hippel, and Richard Courant. Rider, 110; Duggan and Drury, 193, 204–8.

151. That figure includes scientists such as Albert Einstein, who joined the Institute for Advanced Studies in 1933, but had avoided spending much time in Germany since 1930. It also includes a number of non-Germans, such as Enrico Fermi and Emilio Ségré. Hoch, "Reception"; Fischer, *Changing Landscapes*; Rider.

152. The number of successful 'rescues' is probably an undercount since those not included were left off because I could not find evidence of their emigration to the United States or Great Britain. Rider, 156; Weiner, 215, 229–33.

153. Rider, 144–45.

154. Why this is so is beyond the scope of this inquiry.

155. Edward Y. Hartshorne (1937), *The German Universities and National Socialism* (London: Allen & Unwin), 98; Rider, 110; Schweber, 79; Weiner, 190; Hoch, "Reception," 223; Beyerchen, *Scientists under Hitler*, 47.

156. Beyerchen, *Scientists under Hitler*, 47; Fischer, "Operationalism," 107; Beyerchen, *Scientists under Hitler*, 44; Rider, 156–57.

157. Fischer, "Operationalism;" Fischer, *Changing Landscapes*.

158. Fischer, "Operationalism," 117–19, 114, 110.

159. Quoted in Rider, 111.

160. They include: J. McKeen Cattell (1961), *American Men of Science*, 10 ed. (New York: Science Press); J. McKeen Cattell (1965), *American Men of Science*, 11th ed. (New York: Science Press); Fischer, "Operationalism;" Fischer, *Changing Landscapes*; Hoch, "Reception"; Thomas S. Kuhn, John L. Heilbron, Paul Forman, and Lini Allen (1967), *Sources for History of Quantum Physics* (Philadelphia: American Philosophical Society); Rhodes; Rider; Stuewer; Weiner.

161. Schweber, 77.

162. Rhodes, 460.

163. Hoch, "Reception," 236; Kevles, *Physicists*, 282–83; Schweber, 82–83; Stuewer, 37; Weiner, 224–25.

164. Nuel Pharr Davis (1968), *Lawrence and Oppenheimer* (New York: Simon and Schuster), 50; Hans A. Bethe and Robert F. Bacher (1936), "Nuclear Physics: A. Stationary States of Nuclei," *Reviews of Modern Physics*, 8: 82–229; Hans A. Bethe (1937), "Nuclear Physics: B. Nuclear Dynamics, Theoretical," *Reviews of Modern Physics*, 9: 69–244; Hans A. Bethe and M. Stanley Livingston (1937), "Nuclear Physics: C. Nuclear Dynamics, Experimental," *Reviews of Modern Physics*, 9: 245–390; Stuewer, 32–33.

165. Roger L. Geiger (1993), *Research and Relevant Knowledge: American Research Universities Since World War II* (New York: Oxford University Press), 3; Vannevar Bush (1949), *Modern Arms and Free Men: A Discussion of the Role of Science in Preserving Democracy* (New York: Simon and Schuster); A. Hunter Dupree (1972), "The Great Instauration of 1940: The Organization of Scientific Research for War," in Erik H. Erikson and Gerald J. Holton, eds., *The Twentieth-Century Sciences: Studies in the Biography of Ideas* (New York: Norton), 447.

166. Dupree, 445; Daniel S. Greenberg (1971), *The Politics of Pure Science* (New York: New American Library), 71; Greenberg, 74–75.

167. Dupree, 456; Goldberg, "Inventing," 432, 435–36, 445. Quote is from Rhodes, 360.

168. Goldberg, "Inventing," 438–49; Baxter, 428.

169. For enriched uranium production: centrifuge separation, gaseous diffusion, thermal diffusion, electromagnetic separation; and for plutonium production: graphite and heavy water piles of uranium 238. Centrifuge sepa-

ration was dropped in the spring of 1943 and heavy water piles soon there-after. Baxter, 436.

170. Hughes, 414.

171. Richard G. Hewlett and Oscar E. Anderson (1962), *The New World, 1939/1946: A History of the United States Atomic Energy Commission, Volume 1* (University Park: Pennsylvania State University Press), 162–67.

172. Rhodes, 540, 610–14, 465; Hewlett and Anderson, *New World*, 244, 246.

173. Hewlett and Anderson, *New World*, 311; Rhodes, 548.

174. Rhodes, 539.

175. Ibid., 577–78, 667, 704, 738; Hewlett and Anderson, *New World*, 317–18.

176. Stuewer, 35.

177. Wigner was director of theoretical studies at Chicago's Metallur-gical Lab. Fermi was director of research at the Met Lab and was an assistant director at Los Alamos as well as director of 'F Division' in charge of ther-monuclear research.

178. Seymour Melman (1970), *Pentagon Capitalism: The Political Economy of War* (New York: McGraw-Hill); Robert Gilpin (1968), *France in the Age of the Scientific State* (Princeton: Princeton University Press); Jügren Schamndt and James Everett Katz (1986), "The Scientific State: A Theory with Hypotheses," *Science, Technology and Human Values*, 11 (1): 40–52; Gregory McLauchlan (1992), "The Advent of Nuclear Weapons and the Formation of the Scientific-Military-Industrial Complex in World War II," in Gregg B. Walker, David A. Bella, and Steven J. Sprecher, eds., *The Military-Industrial Complex: Eisenhower's Warning Three Decades Later* (New York: Peter Lang), 101–27; Greenberg.

179. Bernard Brodie (1946), "War in the Atomic Age," in Bernard Brodie, ed., *The Absolute Weapon: Atomic Power and World Order* (New York: Harcourt Brace), 26.

180. Ibid., 44; Jervis, 74–106; Robert Jervis (1980), "Why Nuclear Superiority Doesn't Matter," *Political Science Quarterly*, 94 (4): 617–33.

181. Thomas C. Schelling (1966), *Arms and Influence* (New Haven: Yale University Press), 20.

182. John Lewis Gaddis (1987), "Learning to Live with Transparency: The Emergence of a Reconnaissance Satellite Regime," in *The Long Peace: Inquiries into the History of the Cold War* (New York: Oxford University Press), 195–214; Robert Jervis (1988), "The Political Effects of Nuclear-Weapons: A Comment," *International Security*, 13 (2): 83; McLauchlan, "Advent," 116; Kenneth N. Waltz (1979), *Theory of International Politics* (New York: Random House), 188.

183. United States Strategic Bombing Survey (1945), *Over-All Report (European War)* (Washington, DC: U.S. GPO); McLauchlan, "Advent," 117.

184. McLauchlan, "Advent," 106.

185. Jervis, "Political Effects," 80; Jervis, *Meaning,* 35.

186. Waltz, 182.

187. Schamndt and Katz, 46–47.

188. Geiger, *To Advance Knowledge,* 10; Hughes, 421–42.

189. Hughes, 442.

190. Friedberg, 296–339.

191. Hoch, "Crystallization," 99; Walter A. McDougall (1985), "Space-Age Europe: Gaullism, Euro-Gaullism, and the American-Dilemma," *Technology and Culture,* 26 (2): 179–203; Edward A. Kolodziej (1987), *Making and Marketing Arms: The French Experience and Its Implications* (Princeton: Princeton University Press); Andrew Moravcsik (1990), "The European Armaments Industry at the Crossroads," *Survival,* 32 (1): 81.

192. Kendall E. Bailes (1981), "The American Connection: Ideology and the Transfer of American Technology to the Soviet Union, 1917–1941," *Comparative Studies in Society and History,* 23 (3): 424–31, 443, 445; Hans Rogger (1981), "Amerikanizm and the Economic Development of Russia," *Comparative Studies in Society and History,* 23 (3): 382–420.

193. The most famous spy case of the immediate postwar period concerned Klaus Fuchs, a German émigré who had settled in Birmingham, England, to work with Rudolph Peirls, another refugee who was instrumental in the British bomb project. Fuchs was brought to Los Alamos in 1943 along with the cream of the British program—Otto Frisch and Peirls included—an experience on which he based a long report passed on to the Soviets in 1945. The information passed by Fuchs and another spy—a British physicist working at a Montreal atomic laboratory, Alan Nunn May—is generally thought to have been quite valuable. Alwyn McKay (1984), *The Making of the Atomic Age* (New York: Oxford University Press), 94, 123; Powers, 472.

194. Walter A. McDougall (1982), "Technocracy and Statecraft in the Space Age: Toward the History of a Saltation," *American Historical Review,* 87 (4): 1016–17; Kendall E. Bailes (1978), *Technology and Society Under Lenin and Stalin* (Princeton: Princeton University Press); Evangelista.

195. Smith, 1–3; quote from p. 34.

196. McDougall, "Technocracy," 1025. The institutionalization of technological development is Pearton's central theme. Maurice Pearton (1982), *The Knowledgeable State: Diplomacy, War and Technology Since 1830* (London: Burnett Books Limited).

197. McLauchlan, "Advent," 116.

CHAPTER FIVE

1. William F. Ogburn and Dorothy Thomas (1922), "Are Inventions Inevitable? A Note on Social Evolution," *Political Science Quarterly,* 37 (1): 83–98.

2. Max Weber (1946), "Bureaucracy," in H. H. Gerth and C. Wright Mills, eds., *From Max Weber: Essays in Sociology* (New York: Oxford University Press), 196–244; Max Weber (1976), *The Protestant Ethic and the Spirit of Capitalism* (New York: Scribner's).

3. Hendrik Spruyt (1994), *The Sovereign State and Its Competitors: An Analysis of Systems Change* (Princeton: Princeton University Press).

4. Currently thirty-two states have municipalities with functioning public wireless systems and twelve have functioning fiber-to-home systems. C-NET News.com (2005), "Municipal Broadband Nationwide." The city of Philadelphia has recently announced plans to use public funds to install a city-wide wireless Internet network—making it one of the most ambitious plans to date. Jim Hu (2005), "Philadelphia Reveals Wi-Fi Plan," CNET News.com (April 7).

5. See, for example, this scheme to embed radio-frequency devices in Euro notes: Janis Mara (2003), "Euro Scheme Makes Money Talk," *Wired News* (July 9).

6. Lawrence Lessig (1999), *Code: And Other Laws of Cyberspace* (New York: Basic Books).

7. Peter Wayner (2005), "Cybercash on Vacation," *Technology Review*, 108.3 (March): 18–19; Steve Crocker (1999), "The Siren Song of Internet Micropayments," *iMP Magazine* (April 22); Tatsuo Tanaka (1996), "Possible Economic Consequences of Digital Cash," *First Monday*, 1.2 (August).

8. Mark Glassman (2003), "Fortifying the In Box as Spammers Lay Siege," *New York Times* (July 31).

9. Kevin Hogan (2001), "Will Spyware Work?," *Technology Review* (December).

10. Orrin Hatch, United States senator from Utah and music recording artist, has proposed that intellectual property rights holders should have the legal right to disable the computers of suspected pirates. Steven Levy (2003), "Pirates of the Internet," *Newsweek* (August 4).

11. See for example: William A. Owens and Edward Offley (2001), *Lifting the Fog of War* (Baltimore: Johns Hopkins University Press).

12. Walter Laqueur (1996), "Postmodern Terrorism," *Foreign Affairs*, 75 (5): 24–36; Bruce Hoffman (1997), "Responding to Terrorism Across the Technological Spectrum," in John Arquilla and David F. Ronfeldt, eds., *In Athena's Camp: Preparing for Conflict in the Information Age* (Santa Monica: Rand), 339–67; Phil Williams (1997), "Transnational Criminal Organisations and International Security," in John Arquilla and David F. Ronfeldt, eds., *In Athena's Camp: Preparing for Conflict in the Information Age* (Santa Monica: Rand), 315–37; Audrey Kurth Cronin (2002), "Behind the Curve: Globalization and International Terrorism," *International Security*, 27 (3): 30–58.

13. See the essays in Philip Agre and Marc Rotenberg, eds. (1997), *Technology and Privacy: The New Landscape* (Cambridge: MIT Press).

14. John Markoff (2000), "Rebel Outpost on Fringes of Cyberspace," *New York Times* (June 4). See also the official website of the Principality of Sealand (http://www.sealandgov.com/).

15. Ronen Palan (1998), "Trying to Have Your Cake and Eating It: How and Why the State System Has Created Offshore," *International Studies Quarterly*, 42 (4): 625–44.

16. Stephen J. Kobrin (1997), "Electronic Cash and the End of National Markets," *Foreign Policy*, 107: 65–77.

17. Palan.

18. Roland Paris (2003), "The Globalization of Taxation? Electronic Commerce and the Transformation of the State," *International Security* 47 (2): 153–82.

19. Wayner.

20. Pool called information technologies technologies of freedom. Ithiel de Sola Pool (1983), *Technologies of Freedom* (Cambridge: Belknap Press). Barney argues that network technology is "involved in the collapse of politics" and has little democratic potentiality. Darin Barney (2000), *Prometheus Wired: The Hope for Democracy in the Age of Network Technology* (Chicago: University of Chicago Press), 237. Rondfeldt argues that the Internet will radically transform politics by shortening the communications path between leaders and citizens and flattening traditional government bureaucracies—though he admits to a potential "dark" side. David Ronfeldt (1992), "Cyberocracy Is Coming," *Information Society*, 8 (4): 243–96.

21. William Finnegan (2000), "After Seattle," *The New Yorker*, 76.8 (April 17): 40–51; Howard Rheingold (2002), *Smart Mobs: The Next Social Revolution* (Cambridge, MA: Perseus Publishing); George Packer (2003), "Smart-Mobbing the War," *New York Times Magazine* (March 9); David Brin (1998), *The Transparent Society: Will Technology Force Us to Choose Between Privacy and Freedom?* (Reading: Addison-Wesley); Jim Dwyer (2005), "Videos Challenge Accounts of Convention Unrest," *New York Times* (April 12).

22. Shanthi Kalathil and Taylor C. Boas (2003), *Open Networks, Closed Regimes: The Impact of the Internet on Authoritarian Rule* (Washington, DC: Carnegie Endowment for International Peace).

23. Hakim Bey (2001), "The Temporary Autonomous Zone," in Peter Ludlow, ed., *Crypto Anarchy, Cyberstates, and Pirate Utopias* (Cambridge: MIT Press), 402.

24. Lisa Guernsey (2001), "Welcome to the World Wide Web: Passport, Please?," *New York Times* (March 15).

INDEX

SUNY SERIES IN GLOBAL POLITICS
James N. Rosenau, Editor

Hierarchy Amidst Anarchy: Transaction Costs and Institutional Choice—Katja Weber

Counter-Hegemony and Foreign Policy: The Dialectics of Marginalized and Global Forces in Jamaica—Randolph B. Persaud

Global Limits: Immanuel Kant, International Relations, and Critique of World Politics—Mark F. N. Franke

Money and Power in Europe: The Political Economy of European Monetary Cooperation—Matthias Kaelberer

Why Movements Matter: The West German Peace Movement and U.S. Arms Control Policy—Steve Breyman

Agency and Ethics: The Politics of Military Intervention—Anthony F. Lang, Jr.

Life After the Soviet Union: The Newly Independent Republics of the Transcaucasus and Central Asia—Nozar Alaolmolki

Information Technologies and Global Politics: The Changing Scope of Power and Governance—James N. Rosenau and J. P. Singh (eds.)

Theories of International Cooperation and the Primacy of Anarchy: Explaining U.S. International Monetary Policy-Making After Bretton Woods—Jennifer Sterling-Folker

Technology, Democracy, and Development: International Conflict and Cooperation in the Information Age—Juliann Emmons Allison (ed.)

Systems of Violence: The Political Economy of War and Peace in Colombia—Nazih Richani

The Arab-Israeli Conflict Transformed: Fifty Years of Interstate and Ethnic Crises—Hemda Ben-Yehuda and Shmuel Sandler

Debating the Global Financial Architecture—Leslie Elliot Armijo

Political Space: Frontiers of Change and Governance in a Globalizing World—Yale Ferguson and R. J. Barry Jones (eds.)

Crisis Theory and World Order: Heideggerian Reflections—Norman K. Swazo

Political Identity and Social Change: The Remaking of the South African Social Order—Jamie Frueh

Social Construction and the Logic of Money: Financial Predominance and International Economic Leadership—J. Samuel Barkin

What Moves Man: The Realist Theory of International Relations and Its Judgment of Human Nature — Annette Freyberg-Inan

Democratizing Global Politics: Discourse Norms, International Regimes, and Political Community—Rodger A. Payne and Nayef H. Samhat

Landmines and Human Security: International Politics and War's Hidden Legacy—Richard A. Matthew, Bryan McDonald, and Kenneth R. Rutherford (eds.)